DESIGN
otherwise

Transforming
Design
Education
in the
Arab Region

DANAH
ABDULLA

BLOOMSBURY VISUAL ARTS
LONDON · NEW YORK · OXFORD · NEW DELHI · SYDNEY

BLOOMSBURY VISUAL ARTS
Bloomsbury Publishing Plc

50 Bedford Square
London
WC1B 3DP
UK

1385 Broadway
New York
NY 10018
USA

29 Earlsfort Terrace
Dublin 2
Ireland

BLOOMSBURY, BLOOMSBURY VISUAL ARTS

and the Diana logo are trademarks of Bloomsbury Publishing Plc

First published in Great Britain 2025

Copyright © Danah Abdulla 2025

Danah Abdulla has asserted her right under the Copyright, Designs and Patents Act, 1988, to be identified as Author of this work.

For legal purposes the Acknowledgements on p. 12 constitute an extension of this copyright page.

Cover design: eyen design, Amman - Jordan
www.eyen.design

All rights reserved. No part of this publication may be reproduced or transmitted in any form or by any means, electronic or mechanical, including photocopying, recording, or any information storage or retrieval system, without prior permission in writing from the publishers.

Bloomsbury Publishing Plc does not have any control over, or responsibility for, any third-party websites referred to or in this book. All internet addresses given in this book were correct at the time of going to press. The author and publisher regret any inconvenience caused if addresses have changed or sites have ceased to exist, but can accept no responsibility for any such changes.

A catalogue record for this book is available from the British Library.

A catalog record for this book is available from the Library of Congress.

ISBN: HB: 978-1-3502-9578-0
PB: 978-1-3502-9577-3
ePDF: 978-1-3502-9580-3
eBook: 978-1-3502-9579-7

Typeset by eyen design, Amman - Jordan
Printed and bound in India

To find out more about our authors and books

visit www.bloomsbury.com and sign up for our newsletters.

For Essam Abu Awad, for the Arab
world, and for Palestine, always
and forever.

CONTENTS

Acronyms   10
Arabic chat alphabet (Arabizi)   11
Acknowledgements   12
About the book design   15

Introduction   16

CHAPTER 1:
DESIGN EDUCATION   36

CHAPTER 2:
POWER AND BUREAUCRACY   56

CHAPTER 3:
REGIONAL AND LOCAL DESIGN CULTURES   86

CHAPTER 4:
CRITICAL [DESIGN] PEDAGOGY   116

CHAPTER 5:
SHIFTING PERCEPTIONS ON DESIGN   154

CHAPTER 6:
TOWARDS DESIGN OTHERWISE:
AN ACTIONABLE ROADMAP   176

References   190
Index   202

EXTENDED TABLE OF CONTENTS

ACRONYMS	10
ARABIC CHAT ALPHABET (ARABIZI)	11
ACKNOWLEDGEMENTS	12
ABOUT THE BOOK DESIGN	15

INTRODUCTION	16

CHAPTER 1:
DESIGN EDUCATION   36

38 —Higher education and the landscape of design education

40 —The Westernised university

    41 –The Arabic language

44 —Jordan

    45 –Design education in Jordan

47 —A myriad of graduates and limited jobs

    51 –Clients and the design industry

    52 –Education, employment and women

CHAPTER 2:
POWER AND BUREAUCRACY 56

58 —Curriculum as product transmission

60 —The teacher as authority figure

63 —More than oil and gas in value: brain drain

67 —Challenging the culture of conformity

69 —Chains of bureaucracy
- **69** –Box-ticking exercises
- **71** –Faculty recruitment
- **72** –Faculty promotion
- **74** –A middle-class area of studies
- **75** –With great wealth comes great responsibility?
- **77** –'Design is easy'
- **78** –The diploma disease
- **79** –Admission requirements, choice and values

81 —Abolish grades, embrace failure

82 —Resources

CHAPTER 3:
REGIONAL AND LOCAL DESIGN CULTURES 86

88 —Fetishized consciousness

88 —Design culture(s)
- **89** –Global ambitions: the growing influence of GCC capital
- **93** –Another side of the coin

95 —Elitism and design

96 —Meaningful engagement or parachuting in?
- **97** –Design weeks
- **99** –Community engagement
- **104** –NGOisation and international expertise

109—Milieu
- **113** –The city that always sleeps

CHAPTER 4:
CRITICAL [DESIGN] PEDAGOGY 116

118—Teaching philosophies

122—Decolonising education in the Arab context: alternative curriculum models
123 –Curriculum as process
124 –Curriculum as praxis
125 –Student centred pedagogy
126 –Arabisation
129 –Global bilingual outlook

130—Milieu is everything
131 –On the sly

134—Equipping future designers
134 –Writing as practice
136 –Histories
138 –Where is our history?
142 –Design research and thinking
144 –Eroding specialisations
146 –Typography
150 –Experimentation to break the phobia
152 –Business and communication skills

CHAPTER 5:
SHIFTING PERCEPTIONS ON DESIGN 154

156—Design's role in society
157 –Possibilities: community service
158 –Possibilities: outreach
160 –Possibilities: open studios, workshops and libraries
163 –Possibilities: design advocates

165—Establishing new forms of practice: who is design for?
166 –Possibilities: dialogue
167 –Placements, internships and educators with ties to industry
169 –Local and regional connections
170 –Possibilities: defining design
172 –Possibilities: generalist and graduate studies
173 –Possibilities: design vocabularies

CHAPTER 6:
TOWARDS DESIGN OTHERWISE:
AN ACTIONABLE ROADMAP 176

178—Student-centred pedagogy: process and praxis

179—Valuing and representing design

180—Toppling inefficient bureaucracies

181—Resisting neopatriarchy, redefining design: curricular elements

182 –The Arab story of design and design advocacy
183 –Tackling brain drain
184 –Connections
184 –Admissions and recruitment
185 –Encouraging research
186 –Onwards

186—What is design and design education for?

REFERENCES 190
INDEX 202

ACRONYMS

ADW — Amman Design Week

BDW — Beirut Design Week

D3 — Dubai Design District

DDD — Design Days Dubai

DIDI — Dubai Institute of Design and Innovation

DDW — Dubai Design Week

GAM — Greater Amman Municipality

GCC — Gulf Cooperation Council

MENA — Middle East and North Africa

MoHESR — Ministry of Higher Education and Scientific Research (Jordan)

UAE — United Arab Emirates

USD — United States Dollar

ARABIC CHAT ALPHABET (ARABIZI)

7 = ح (Haa)

3 = ع ('Ayn)

9 = ص (Saad)

5 = خ (Khaa)

6 = ط (Taa)

8 = ق (Qaaf)

2 = ء & أ (Alef & Hamza)

ACKNOW-LEDGEMENTS

Writing a book is never the work of one person, it is a collective effort. There are always too many people to thank and, for the sake of brevity, I will acknowledge those who participated in helping make this book a reality.

My biggest thanks to all the students, designers and educators who took part in the interviews, focus groups and charrettes, your insights helped form the ideas presented in this work. I cannot forget the generosity shown to me during the research from Dima Hanna, Rana Beiruti and Abeer Seikaly who lent me spaces for events, and Noura Al-Khasawneh who opened her 'rolodex' to me. My sincere thanks to my grandparents Fatima and Hilmi and my uncle Salim for housing me, feeding me and driving me while in Jordan, and for their curiosity about my research.

Expanding the scope of the book would not have been possible without the help of the UAL research office, who awarded me a short sabbatical to provide respite from head-of-department duties to complete the book.

Thank you to Rebecca, Hattie, Louise and Leafy and the Bloomsbury team for their help and support during the process. Next, I want to thank Haya Alfadhel and Aya Al Thani for their help with transcription and translation.

A massive thank you to eyen design – Omar Al'Zobi and Yousef Abedrabbo, for designing this book and their belief in my work. I am indebted to Vera Sachetti and Nina Paim, friends in design, friends in life, for constantly encouraging me to write, to share my ideas and providing me with platforms to do so.

Many ideas that shaped my thinking were because of the Decolonisation Design crew. These scholars have provided me with a sense of community during the loneliest of times and their brilliance encourages me to better myself every day. Thank you to Tristan Schultz, Matt Kiem, Luiza Prado de O. Martins, Pedro Vieira de Oliveira, Ece Canlı and Mahmoud Keshavarz.

My deepest gratitude to my PhD supervisor and friend Professor Kay Stables, for her patience and attention to detail and professionalism. The learnings I gathered from her provide me with inspiration every time I enter the classroom.

To my parents, who instilled in me and my siblings the importance of education.

To Jan, for tolerating the ups and downs that come with book writing. Thank you for being the greatest husband in the galaxy!

Finally, thank you to Dr Essam Abu Awad, who passed away in 2021. Essam dedicated his life to bettering design in the Arab region and supporting young academics. He provided me with so much support and insight. Rest in power.

ABOUT THE BOOK DESIGN

Inspired by early artefacts of education in Jordanian culture; the design drew inspiration from the pattern found in state-produced notebooks named 'daftar tabiaa' (English: 'nature notebook'). While pulling elements from the seamless modernist patterns found in these notebooks covers, the modules lent themselves to another reference found in Levantine and Arab architecture; the breeze blocks. This duality presented the theme of building blocks in relation to education and new blocks have been developed and incorporated into the design.

More importantly; the cover artwork features a geometric Arabic typographic composition as an homage to Arab modernist visual communication; it reads the two words 'design' and 'education'; in an alternating pattern, it carries both the meaning of 'design education' and 'learning design'.

The entirety of this book has been designed by eyen. Established in 2016 by co-founders Omar Al-Zo'bi and Yousef Abedrabbo in Amman, eyen is a Jordanian collective that aims to congregate a great network of agile working designers, artists, practitioners and creative thinkers from multiple disciplines from Jordan, the region and more. eyen (stylised transliteration for "eye, spring, letter ein" in Arabic) primarily functions in graphic design, art and design education, contemporary practice and public programming. eyen has extensive experience in branding and visual identities, spatial narratives, Arabic typography, publication and editorial design and publishing.

INTRODUCTION

"That we accept the world as it is does not in any sense weaken our desire to change it into what we believe it should be – it is necessary to begin where the world is if we are going to change it to what we think it should be." (Alinsky, 1989, p. xix)

On 25 January 2011, I sat glued to the screen of my laptop watching the 'Day of Revolt' in Cairo unravel. I was over 9,000 kilometres away in Toronto, but I wanted – more than anything – to be there. Less than a year before, I was in Egypt with a group of activists for the Gaza Freedom March, being chased around the pyramids by guards and police for climbing the pyramid and holding a sign that said, 'Open the Border' (in reference to the Gaza border). The image was captured by a journalist and published on the front page of a local newspaper, my head, black sunglasses and curly locks peering above the banner (Figure 1). Being in Cairo during that time, and spending days in Tahrir Square, made me feel the influence the city has on the Arab region. While Egypt's hegemony over the Arab world was waning, Arabs believed that if change was to happen it had to start in Egypt.[1] Watching the protests on Al Jazeera on a 15-inch MacBook Pro screen was one of the first times I felt excited and hopeful about change in the Arab region. In 2023, the euphoria around the 18 days of the 2011 events are nothing but a distant memory, but the trip and subsequent events that followed changed my life forever. After returning to Toronto, I became increasingly restless, daydreaming about using the power of cultural production in the Arab region to enact change.

That summer, I travelled to the Basque Country, Lebanon and Palestine. I spent one month volunteering at An-Najah University in Nablus and had my first experience teaching university students. Through conversations with students, I quickly realised they seldom conducted group work, took part in discussions or prepared presentations, and many expressed frustration with the dismissive attitudes from professors, the excessive attention to rote learning and how disconnected the courses were from reality. For Palestinian students, the Israeli Occupation was

---

1 Egypt has the largest population in the Arab region, and for the larger part of the twentieth century it was the political, economic, educational and cultural centre of the Arab region. Its film, television and music industry shaped Arab culture, where the Egyptian dialect became synonymous with Arabic proper. Despite Egypt's decline over the last twenty years, for Arabs worldwide it signified the centre of policies and change, reignited by the 25 January 2011 revolutions. However, the coup in July 2013 where the Egyptian army chief General Abdel-Fatah Sisi removed the democratically elected president extinguished this hope.

Figure 1
Image of newspaper clipping showing the author protesting to open the Gaza borders at the Pyramids of Giza, Egypt. Scan courtesy of Danah Abdulla

a part of daily life, and it affected their education. But the Occupation was not in the textbook, and it had no place in the curriculum.

I spoke to the faculty from the graphic design department at An-Najah who described feeling completely helpless when it came to the education system. What I realised was that design and design education served two purposes: that it was a degree with uncompetitive admission requirements, created to absorb students who performed poorly in the high school matriculation exam but could afford the tuition fees; and that design was limited to a service-provider role. The experience encouraged me to better understand higher education and design education. Despite how much our lives are tied and shaped by design, it was regarded with little importance – trivialised and perceived as irrelevant to anything other than absorbing students and servicing the commercial sector. Worse, people knew the education system was broken but felt helpless to change it. For me, design is a discipline that goes beyond the mere application of technique and aesthetics. It is, as John Heskett (2002, p. 4) puts it:

one of the basic characteristics of what it is to be human and an essential determinant of the quality of human life. It affects everyone in every detail of every aspect of what they do throughout each day.

I do not define design as a problem-solving, solution-oriented field, but as an opening of possibilities through negotiations with the given (Dilnot, 2005). Education is imperative to change. It is through education that we move from being passive recipients to active participants (Freire, 2000), that we challenge the status quo and move towards undoing paralysing systems.

Frustrated by my experience at An-Najah, I began working on a project whose aim was to challenge the status quo by providing an open space for political, social and cultural expression for Arab cultural producers globally, as well as for those based in the region. Launched as a newsletter in November 2010, one month before the actions of a young street vendor named Mohamed Bouazizi led to mass demonstrations in Tunisia, and subsequently across different cities, *Kalimat Magazine* emerged from the new sense of hope that spread across the Arab world through the uprisings, which saw the development of grassroots initiatives dedicated to alternative and critical forms of creative education, relevant to the local contexts and committed to engaging the public with their work.

Kalimat developed from my design practice into a research project about visual communication as a medium to highlight cultural production in marginalised communities. It evolved into PhD research on design education and design culture(s) in the Arab region. This book forms part of a research journey started in 2012 where I worked with a range of designers, students and educators to investigate the potential of these actors to contribute to the development of a pedagogy for design education that is relevant to the context and locality.

Using Amman, Jordan as a case study, I draw on examples from Beirut, Cairo and Dubai to provide a roadmap into contextually-based design education in the Arab region. The work reported on here is drawn from extensive field research conducted in Jordan in 2015–2016 with designers, design educators and design students, using a mixture of semi-structured interviews, focus groups and design charrette workshops to collect data. Additional data was collected to ensure material is up to date, extending the work to Beirut, Dubai and Cairo. This was collected in the form of semi-structured interviews with educators and designers across Amman, Beirut, Cairo and Dubai in 2022–2023. I preserve the anonymity of participants by changing names but keep the correct location. I express my deepest appreciation to everyone who has spoken with me to make this work possible.

Readers might wonder why I have limited the scope to four countries. The book is not a survey of design education, and it is impossible to represent the entire Arab region in one book on design education, nor is this the goal. I have drawn on cities that reflect some of the issues and questions faced by designers, students and educators region wide, while not assuming that there are not issues unique to other places such as Palestine, Iraq, Syria, Tunisia, Morocco, Yemen or Sudan, to name a few. The choice to focus on four locations is to allow a richer and more thorough analysis rather than a generalised overview. The countries chosen for the study have universities following a similar system (including satellite campuses of American universities or chartered American universities), and largely – with some exceptions – teach design in English. Moreover, Jordan, Lebanon, Egypt and the United Arab Emirates (UAE) have the largest quantity and variety of design programmes and their design cultures are or have become more influential in the last decade.

Political situations across countries in the Arab region are, at times, vastly different, including an ongoing civil war in Syria which has led to a broken higher education system through curriculum stagnation, the disappearance of research, increased government control and militarisation and diminished quality. The civil war has caused damaging effects to cultural and intellectual life in Syria, and the contemporary challenges faced by the country are different from those covered in the book. Palestine is under Israeli occupation, and the situation and context are unique, where there are extensive hurdles and challenges placed on universities by Israel. For example, Palestinian institutions are frequently the targets of military assault and demolition – including, most recently, when Israel destroyed all universities in Gaza through constant bombardment, killing Professor Sufian Tayeh, the president of the Islamic University of Gaza and an accomplished scientist and researcher, alongside his entire family. In addition, Palestine is composed of a complex system of barriers, checkpoints, the Apartheid Wall and permits that hinder the freedom of movement of Palestinians, and arrests and closures are frequent. Therefore, Palestine would require a whole study on its own.

Definitions

Before setting the context, it is important to define some of the terms used in the book. An effective definition of 'curriculum' considers that it is 'an ongoing social activity shaped by various contextual influences within and beyond the classroom and accomplished interactively' (Cornbleth, 1988, p. 89). It is about the interactions of educators, students, knowledge, and the milieu, and cannot be removed from its context. As a social process, a curriculum is not a tangible product or syllabus, nor about the subjects taught, transmitted or delivered, but an examination of the effects of the chosen knowledge and subjects on its recipients (Kelly, 2009). A curriculum examines the values reflected in knowledge and learning and 'explicitly recognizes critical philosophical, social, and political questions about what is taught, how, and to whom' (Cornbleth, 1988, p.89). Therefore, it should be attentive to its setting and context, open to critical scrutiny and translatable into effective practice.

The term 'Arab region' is a cultural construct that refers to the Arab-speaking countries stretching from the Atlantic Coast in North Africa to the Persian Gulf in Asia, and terminates in the east at Iran and Turkey in the north (Dawisha, 2003). While the term excludes Israel, it includes the Palestinian-Arab population residing within Israeli borders who were given citizenship (though of second class) after the creation of the state of Israel, often referred to as 'Palestinians of '48'. The countries clustered under the term Arab region should not be viewed as homogenous. The region itself is diverse, though despite some significant and complex differences it possesses similarities including language, majority religion, pan-Arab political and economic organisations, political systems, history and the experience of regional politics (Herrera, 2006). Finally, the term 'milieu' is defined as places, people, environments and institutions that individuals encounter that shape daily life and inform their worldview. These conditions influence the environment in which someone lives and acts in the world.

The Arab region is composed of 22 states sharing a common language and similar cultural values, where family is the social unit around which lives are centred. In a space where loyalty and generosity are of vital importance, Arab society emphasises the group over the individual. Most Arab states are overtly centralised, controlling resources and provision of public services. Local governments are allocated limited resources and have restricted roles in decision-making. Its economies, resources, infrastructure, health status and geographies are heterogenous. Economies are a mix of rentier and semi-rentier, relying on external rents, leading to unproductive and uncompetitive domestic sectors. In the case of the Gulf Cooperation Council (GCC) countries, government revenues are made from oil exports to foreign countries, and the state can afford not to impose high taxes on its citizens.

Semi-rentier states like Lebanon rely heavily on rents and finance from international donors and remittances. Jordan and Egypt utilise strategic rent based on their geopolitical importance, allowing US military bases to operate there, for example. Moreover, Jordan, Egypt and Lebanon are large providers of external labour forces for companies in the GCC. For over 30 years, the Arab world had the highest rates of youth unemployment in the world – teetering between 23–27 per cent and contributing to a wasting of youthful energy and potential – what Nader Kabbani (2019) terms 'waithood'.

The Arab region suffers from stereotypical portrayals in the media as a space of armed conflict and crisis on the one hand, and futuristic Blade Runner-esque skyscrapers in the desert on the other. As Booker and Darkish (2019, p. 2) write:

Radical Islamist imams in the Middle East are at this moment furiously conjuring up fatwas against the evils of America and American culture. [...] These Arabs live in a harsh and morally rigid world starkly opposed to the seductive gleam of Western consumer culture. On the other hand, their world is also starkly opposed to the world in which the majority of people in most Arab countries live their daily lives.

While several conflicts, crises and inequality plague the region[2], these portrayals deny the existence of a thriving cultural scene and grassroots initiatives led by the large youth population.

Beirut

No city in the Arab region can be categorised as homogeneous because there are many Ammans, as there are many Beiruts, Dubais and many Cairos. I will briefly touch on Cairo, Beirut and Dubai, and provide a more extensive overview of Amman.

Since 2019, Lebanon has been mired in one of the world's largest economic and financial crises, exacerbated by the COVID-19 pandemic and the Port of Beirut explosion on 4 August 2020. The currency has crashed and devastated the banking sector, turning the country into a cash-based society with three operating currencies. Its most reliable export is human capital. Lebanon has a plural and delicate political system, and its public sector is significantly smaller than the rest of the region, meaning the state is not the de facto employer and has minimum intervention in private enterprise. Historically, its education system was the responsibility of religious communities and foreign groups, encompassing more private universities than its neighbours. Lebanon

---

2 Conflicts in Iraq, Libya, Sudan, Syrian Arab Republic, Yemen and illegal occupation in Palestine means over 58 percent of the world's refugees originate from the region.

is considered one of the more open Arab countries, with the freest press in the region, and a centre of commerce and culture. It has a strong crafts tradition, where ceramics, wood products and textiles are some of its leading industries. But Beirut is a deeply divided city. Whereas Amman's division is largely class based, Beirut's areas represent the deep social divisions in the city due to past conflicts between religious and political groups and the city's rapid expansion.

Cairo

Egypt's capital for over 1,000 years, Cairo is the Arab region's most populous city. The city is of political and cultural importance, historically the centre of music, film and literature regionally. Egypt is called *umm al-dunya* (mother of the world), symbolising its great civilisation and importance to the Arab region and globally. It led the Arab region as a centre of culture, education and reference for policies for much of the twentieth century. However, Egypt's Arab leadership has waned in the last twenty years.

Unlike Beirut, Dubai and Amman, its inhabitants are largely homogenous with few minority groups. Egypt's political system is authoritarian, dominated by a president, the ruling party and the *mukhabarat* (secret service). The economy is highly centralised and dominated by the public sector despite the country having a free market. The impact of the COVID-19 pandemic, the Ukraine–Russia war and the devaluation of the Egyptian pound is likely to increase the poverty rate, with over 27.7 per cent of the population already poor.

Egypt has a crafts tradition dating back thousands of years,[3] and its large manufacturing sector includes chemicals, pharmaceuticals, food, textiles and garments, building materials, paper and derivatives of hydrocarbons.

Dubai

Dubai is one of seven emirates that make up the UAE, a port city that in the last 30 years has become one of the world's fastest growing cities, attempting to set itself up as a financial centre for the Middle East and South Asia region. Its role in regional affairs, alongside many GCC countries, has grown over the last twenty years through financial and military aid. The UAE is a federal presidential elective constitutional monarchy, composed of the tribal rulers of the seven emirates who have absolute authority. Within this 'tribal autocracy' Dubai has signif-

---

3 For an overview of Egypt's crafts traditions, see El-Batraoui (2016).

icant autonomy. Whereas the capital of the UAE Abu Dhabi's wealth is from oil, Dubai is a commercial and financial centre, housing many multinational corporations, and diversifying income streams to avoid dependence on oil. Dubai's demographic make-up is made of diverse nationalities and ethnic groups, where citizens make up only 11 per cent of the population.

The education system is a mix of private and public; public universities teach mostly in Arabic and are open to local Emiratis only. Many private American, British and Australian universities operate there, including satellite campuses of prominent universities. Dubai responds to global trends and tourism and attracts business investment and large-scale events. It invested heavily in establishing a vibrant arts and culture scene to become a destination for the region and beyond. This has been the work of the Dubai Culture and Arts Authority, established in 2008, under the leadership of Her Highness Sheikha Latifa bint Mohammed bin Rashid Al Maktoum, whose goal is 'to enhance Dubai's position as a global center for art and culture, an incubator for creativity, and a thriving hub for talent' (Dubai Culture, 2023).

In focus: Amman, Jordan

Established in 1921 by the British and Amir Abdallah – a member of the Hashemite branch of the Quraysh tribe (who claim descent from the Prophet Muhammad [peace and blessings be upon him] from the Hijaz region in Saudi Arabia – 'Transjordan' is a relatively new country. The boundary lines created by the secret Sykes–Picot Agreement in 1916 – where the French and the British divided remnants of the Ottoman Empire in the Levant/Fertile Crescent between them – created 'Transjordan' (Hinchcliffe and Milton-Edwards, 2009). This has led the country to be 'perceived throughout the Arab world as an artificial and inconsequential creation by the British to pacify Emir 'Abdallah' (Dawisha, 2003, p.88). In 1946, Amir Abdallah crowned himself King and Transjordan became an independent kingdom, renamed the Hashemite Kingdom of Jordan in 1948. Now ruled by King Abdullah II, who ascended the throne in 1999 after the death of his father, Jordan is a relatively small middle-income country of 11 million people. Categorised as a constitutional monarchy where the King holds legislative and executive power, the King exerts his authority through the army and the *mukhabarat*, and power is the privilege of the very few.

Waves of migrations

Jordan's relative stability made it no stranger to waves of migrations which have shaped its population (Nortcliff et al., 2009). The make-up of Amman's inhabitants reflects the region's turbulent history, categorising it as a refuge city. Its population began taking shape in 1878, with the settlement of Circassian immigrants from the Caucasus. The waves that followed came from the Levant, the Arabian Peninsula, Kurdistan, Central Asia, Armenia, and Palestine. The largest population influxes came in 1948, when the creation of the state of Israel made over 750,000 Palestinians refugees. The year 1948 became known as the *Nakba* (catastrophe), as hundreds of villages and towns 'and a whole country and its people disappeared from international maps and dictionaries' (Masalha, 2012, p. 3). Jordan (East Bank) absorbed the West Bank and formerly annexed it in April 1950. The loss of the West Bank to Israeli occupation in the 1967 Six Day War exiled 250,000 Palestinians to the East Bank. The events in 1967, referred to as *Al-Naksah* (the setback), saw the rise of the Palestine Liberation Organisation (PLO) and its guerrilla movements. Clashes between PLO fighters and the Jordanian army in 1970 drove guerrillas, political sympathisers and many members of the bourgeoisie to Beirut, but the outbreak of the Lebanese civil war in 1975 brought the bourgeoisie back and new refugees from Lebanon. The oil boom of the 1970s and 1980s saw migrations out of Jordan to the Gulf countries, and Jordan's economy improved because of remittances, foreign aid and land speculation, which skyrocketed and edged the economy towards collapse by the end of the 1980s (Massad, 2001). This period placed Jordan as one of the region's leading labour export countries. However, it also left the country with labour shortage. Thus, Jordan became a labour importing and exporting country as more Arabs and non-Arabs came seeking work opportunities. The first Gulf War saw over 300,000 citizens (mostly Jordanian Palestinians) move back and over two million 'transit migrants' settle in Jordan (from Egypt, Sri Lanka, Indonesia and the Philippines), and Bosnians fleeing the Yugoslav wars. The United Nations (UN) sanctions in Iraq meant that a great number of Iraqis also began to settle, a number that increased following the 2003 American invasion of Iraq, and since March 2011 Jordan has received over 715,000 refugees due to the war in Syria.[4]

Originally intended as a transit stop for many of these communities, for most Amman ended up being their final destination. As Jordanian anthropologist Seteney Shami describes, the subsequent

---

4 This number reflects registered refugees. Other figures place this number closer to 1.2 million Syrian refugees.

generations of communities that have settled 'continue to look in two directions at once: toward home/homeland and toward a preferred temporary destination of a "second home" (2007, p. 215). This could explain why most of Amman's inhabitants have difficulty in identifying themselves as *Ammani* (from Amman) and see it as a temporary 'welcome mat.' Shami (2007) claims that the inhabitants of the city all have complaints about Amman. These complaints – Amman is dull, austere, it lacks charm, it lacks cosmopolitanism, it lacks artistic and literary movement, it lacks student and campus life, it lacks authenticity, it lacks ethnic neighbourhoods – represent how '[e]ach segment of urban society appears to be complaining about its own failure to realize itself' (ibid., p. 208). Although each 'segment' has its own explanation for this 'malaise' they do collectively agree on one explanation: 'Amman is not a city' (ibid.). In Chapter 3, I will demonstrate how design is attempting to break away from this idea.

The economy, history, social composition and spatial density of Amman are factors that explain the malaise, and other factors include the establishment of the country by a deterritorialised royalty, which led to inconclusive nation-building projects, an ambiguous discourse on national identity, and fast and arbitrary solutions to urban planning (Innab, 2016). Furthermore, Amman is not a global financial centre nor a major tourist destination; it lives in the shadow of historical neighbouring cities such as Damascus, Cairo, Fez and Beirut. Amman is not traditional, nor modern, nor global – it is 'decentered, fragmented, privatized' (Shami, 2007, p. 211), a city 'that portrays itself as in a state of permanent temporariness, a metropolis on the cusp of emerging' (Innab, 2016, p. 119).

Economy

By the end of the 1980s, Jordan was drowning in debt and trapped in the conditions of World Bank and International Monetary Fund (IMF) loan packages. Its economy collapsed, forcing it to implement an IMF rescue package by aggressively adopting neoliberal reforms: lifting trade restrictions, privatising state-owned enterprises and deregulating labour markets (Hanieh, 2013). Even after 'political liberalisation' to instigate 'democratic reforms', Jordan remains a liberalised autocracy with a limited opposition that is constantly hounded by the *mukhabarat* (Hinchcliffe and Milton-Edwards, 2009). Political liberalisation was therefore used 'to defuse popular dissatisfaction while the economic crisis played itself out' (Yom, 2009, p. 154). Despite a decade of liberalisation, a peace treaty with Israel in 1994 (where millions in debt was forgiven and rescheduled) and promised prosperity, Jordan's dependence on foreign aid expanded, and authoritarian tendencies deepened as electoral tampering established compliant parliaments (Alissa, 2007; Hourani, 2014). Privatisation and the deregulation of the labour market have impacted employment security and wages, leading to more temporary contracts and increased precariousness of work, changing the ways people meet their basic needs (Hanieh, 2013).

The early 2000s saw the economy at the top of the agenda for King Abdullah II, who inherited 7.8 billion US dollars (USD) in debt and a country mired in poverty and unemployment. For a one billion USD write down of debts, Abdullah implemented free-trade pacts, established Qualifying Industrial Zones, Special Economic Zones, privatised state-owned enterprises, invested heavily in tourism and a competitive programme to attract foreign investment (Hanieh, 2013). Reforms continue to increase divisions between the residents of East and West Amman, further fragmenting the landscape and the people.

A divided city, a divided public

Amal and Nour are two girls from West Amman driving through downtown (located in the East). Lost, scared and feeling out of place amongst what they call *nawaris* (low-class people), they attempt to get back to 'Amman'. Amal tells Nour, 'Look! A Mercedes G class, I'm sure they are going to "Amman"! We should follow them. I'm sure they will lead us home.'

The scene described is from the short film *#Hashtag* (2014) by Jordanian filmmaker Muhammad El-Khairy. It is slightly exaggerated by the director for comedic effect, but it illustrates a very real disconnect between citizens from the same city. Both Amal and Nour want to get back to 'Amman', when they are clearly *in* Amman. The Amman they speak of is West Amman, home to the city's wealthier residents, luxurious villas surrounded by agricultural lands and lower density. East Amman, on the other hand, is home to the city's working class, informal settlements and refugee camps. The area of residence is the main determinant of class in Amman, which is also measured through income, education, occupation, behaviours, honour, attitudes, lifestyles and religious affiliation. Remittances from the 1970s oil boom in the GCC states contributed to Amman's East/West dichotomy and the city's altering landscape: increased density in the East, and land speculation, increased land prices and a construction boom in the West. The wealth from abroad pushed the city further and further west, altering people's social networks as Amman became more scattered and car ownership

Figure 2
A view of Amman from Jabal Al Lweibdeh in East Amman, photo by Danah Abdulla

turned into a necessity (Shami, 2007), leaving 'uneven patterns of growth, abandonment, and sprawl...[and] gaps in the urban fabric due to the city's multimodal nature' (Innab, 2016, p. 132). The adoption of neoliberal reforms in 1989 and the return of migrant workers in the early 1990s developed a new visual landscape in West Amman, one influenced by GCC capital (both from remittances and aid), transforming lifestyles, consumption and the configuration of public space (Shami, 2007).

Adam Hanieh (2013) argues that assessments of neoliberalism often overlook the influence of GCC capital on the political economy of the region. Gulf capital has dramatically altered the landscape in Arab cities in the last fifteen years, visible through Amman's attempts to lure international investment and tourism, and to promote a modern international image. The influence of GCC capital is noticeable in several neoliberal urban restructuring projects across Amman, including high-end business towers, shopping malls, urban islands and gated communities with slogans celebrating excessive consumption (Daher, 2013). These development projects celebrate a consumerist society, displace populations, businesses and transportation hubs, and further enforce the socio-economic and spatial polarisation that exists between

---

5 The most reflective of this is the Al-Abdali Regeneration Project, encompassing over 1.7 million square metres of offices, apartments, retail, hotels and entertainment. The project's aim is to re-centre Amman's downtown, while preserving some 'heritage' such as the *souk* (market) and gentrifying the rest of the area for tourist consumption.

East and West Amman, and between these elite gated communities from the rest of the city, pushing the city further West.[5]

The distinction between East and West helps contextualise the milieu of students and the environment in which citizen-led alternative and grassroots projects emerge, as the city is always being altered beyond recognition, further dividing Ammanis from each other. Citizens are countering divisive neoliberal urban policies through neighbourhood associations committed to improving urban quality, alternative spaces for artists and activists, cultural bodies and organisations, art galleries, centres and foundations, and film production centres. Moreover, many of these initiatives revived historic buildings in East Amman (Daher, 2009). Architect Rami Daher argues that these projects are enabling people to feel more connected to Amman by creating joint solutions between all residents through genuine collaboration. These citizen actions and responses signal a break of sorts from the malaise described by Shami (2007), and demonstrate how grassroots organising helps shape the design culture of not just Amman but also Beirut and Cairo.

Contextualising design

Limited to fields such as graphic and interior design, design education in the Arab region possesses only a handful of universities offering multimedia design, industrial/product design and fashion design, despite the fashion industry being valued in the billions.[6] Design practice has largely been within the commercial art realm and was historically the domain of artists, architects and printers practicing as designers and working in advertising, printing and the interior design market.[7] These elements sealed the reputation of design across the region as merely servicing the market. Design education has helped reinforce this reputation by focusing on specialised, technical skill training at the undergraduate level to produce 'industry-ready' graduates, leaving students with little room to develop critical skills, to engage in critical practice, or to venture beyond their specialisation. Furthermore, uncompetitive admission requirements means design attracts poorly performing students looking to obtain the necessary university qualifications to join the workforce.

Since the 1990s, higher education across the region has become extensively privatised. The market-driven privatisation of higher education has replaced principles such as ethics, community responsibility and citizenship-building with 'individual interest and economic rationality',

---

6 According to the Business of Fashion 2023 report, the GCC luxury market alone is expected to be valued at nearly $11 billion USD. The market has increased by over 23 per cent from pre-pandemic levels due to citizens being unable to travel to Europe. Brands are now localising content and opening stores in the GCC to accommodate. See State of Fashion (2023) and Maki and Schneider (2023).

7 The interior design market was valued at 7.1 billion USD in 2014 across the Middle East and North Africa (MENA) region, see Dubai Design and Fashion Council and Monitor Deloitte (2016).

raising broader questions about the role of educational institutions 'in the production of an educated citizenry capable – developmentally, technically, and ethically – of serving local, regional, and global needs' (Herrera, 2006, p. 418).

Globally, design and design education are undergoing transformations due, in part, to the blurring boundaries of design disciplines. Increasingly, governments and organisations are using design to fuel the 'knowledge economy'. With the design industry in the Arab region valued at billions of dollars, the only government capitalising on its power, however, is the United Arab Emirates (UAE).

Understanding power and society: neopatriarchy

To understand how power, education, culture and social relations operate in Jordan and the Arab region at large, I draw on the term neopatriarchy, coined by the late Palestinian academic and intellectual Hisham Sharabi. Neopatriarchy refers to macrostructures (society, the state and the economy) and micro-structures (individual personality and the family). Neopatriarchy is composed of modernity – referring here to the initial break in history with 'traditionality', which occurred originally in Western Europe – and patriarchy – a social–political structure containing 'a specific value system and forms of discourse and practice, based on a distinctive form of economic organization' where the male holds positions of power (Sharabi, 1988, p. 15). The break with traditionality created an important distinction: traditional patriarchy and modernised patriarchy, essential in understanding the hybrid nature of Arab society:

[A modernised patriarchy] must be viewed as the product of a hegemonic modern Europe; but 'modernization' as the product of patriarchal and dependent conditions can only be dependent 'modernization': dependency relations inevitably lead not to modernity but to 'modernized' patriarchy, neopatriarchy. Modernization, in this context, is the metonomy [sic] of inverted modernity. (Sharabi, 1988, p. 4, emphasis original).

Sharabi argues that the patriarchal structures of Arab society were not displaced nor modernised but strengthened and maintained through 'deformed, "modernized" forms'. He traces the beginnings of neopatriarchy from the Arab *Nahda* (revival) of the nineteenth century, which failed to break down forms of patriarchy and laid the groundwork for a new type of hybrid society and culture which is the current neopatriarchal society (ibid).

Neither traditional nor modern, neopatriarchy is a dependent and non-modern socio-economic structure that characterises an underdeveloped society. Omnipresent in this structure is its inability to perform as an effective or integrated system – whether social, political or economic, lacking 'the main characteristics of modern formations: organisation, inner force, and consciousness' (Sharabi, 1988, p.7). Like patriarchy, the psychosocial feature central to the neopatriarchal society is the father (patriarch). In both society and familial relations, only vertical relations exist, where the paternal will is absolute and 'mediated...by a force consensus based on ritual and coercion' (ibid.). A characteristic of neopatriarchal regimes is a two-state system: the military–bureaucratic structure and the secret service/police (*mukhabarat*) structure. Whereas Sharabi argues that the structures are impotent, the most effective one is the *mukhabarat*, which:

dominates everyday life, serving as the ultimate regulator of civil and political existence. Thus...citizens...are arbitrarily deprived of some of their basic rights but are the virtual prisoners of the state, the objects of its capricious and ever-present violence... (Sharabi, 1988, p. 7).

Additionally, the fluidity of the public and the private domains, of the civic space and the state, provide no escape for ordinary citizens – family, religious sect or the clan enact similar displays of authority and violence. Neopatriarchy is characterised by duality. Legal, material and aesthetic forms of neopatriarchal societies may project an outward 'modern' image, but internally they remain rooted in patriarchal values and social relations (Sharabi, 1988).

Neopatriarchy consists of four attributes. The first is social fragmentation. The basis of social relations and organisation are family, religion, clan and ethnic group as opposed to the nation or civil society. In Jordan, this is visible through the ruling family who have attempted to construct the nation 'not in terms of autochthony and territory but loyalty to the regime and the royal family' (Shami, 2007, p. 228). The second attribute is authoritarian organisation where coercion, domination and paternalism govern familial and state relations, as opposed to equality, mutual recognition and cooperation. The patriarchy is reinforced by the ruling family, who infantilise its citizens and maintain the power structure and political organisation amongst a powerful elite (Hinchcliffe and Milton-Edwards, 2009). The third is absolutist paradigms, where 'a closed, absolutist consciousness...grounded in transcendence, metaphysics, revelation, and closure' (Kassab, 2010, p. 252) characterises politics, theoretical practice and everyday life rather than plurality, openness, diffusion or difference. And, lastly, ritualistic practice, where customs, ceremonies, traditions and rituals govern behaviour, as opposed to the creative, spontaneous or innovative.[8]

A space of possibilities

Arab governments spend heavily on education, but Arab universities operate in difficult circumstances and are mired in inertia. In a region where youth consist of more than 30 per cent of the population, this inertia denies their ability to fulfil their potential. While education is ranked high on the priority list for youth, their faith in it is extremely low.[9] In addition, only 10 per cent of youth regionally place community participation as important. The lack of opportunities available to them limits their vision, and youth turn their eyes elsewhere, desperate to find meaning and hope anywhere but where they are (Selim, 2021).

Reports from international NGOs and agencies call for reforms in higher education, and in research policy and planning to meet the region's current needs, by presenting challenges and solutions such as overhauling governance. They frame the discussion in developmental discourse, where the Arab world must catch up with global standards, but these reports fail to address aggressive neoliberal reforms adopted by Arab governments that fuel these issues. The reports also fail to acknowledge the role of the Westernised university in limited research outputs, or the models of curriculum and pedagogy that are devoid of critical thinking and disconnected from society at large. Moreover, results rely on quantitative measures and provide simplistic sticking-plaster solutions.

This book will illustrate how the design curriculum in Arab universities is outdated and disconnected from its context and milieu (places, people, environments and institutions that individuals encounter, which shape daily life and inform their worldview), due in part to its blind borrowing of curricula from the Global North. More generally, education is an instrument of control by the state, focused on transmission and rote learning, and is a space of academic oppression rather than freedom. The book does not present a history of design education or design in the Arab region, nor does it set out to create a prototype for a curriculum, as the development of a model renders curriculum static. A curriculum is never truly final but open to critical scrutiny, continuously changing, adapting and learning. Otherwise, it

---

8 Historically, Amman was made into a capital city through ceremonial practices rather than the construction of buildings (Rogan, 1996). Recently, this has been made visible in the construction of a 'traditional' image of the city to attract tourism, Islamising the city by building mosques that encourage communal prayers, restoring historical monuments, and building plazas, parade grounds and town halls (Shami, 2007; Jacobs, 2010).

9 In a World Bank survey, which asked young people whether education improved their chances in the job market in their countries, the overwhelming response was 'no' (92 per cent); see Selim (2021).

will never be relevant to its location. The concern of the book is how the actors with the most at stake in design and design education (students, designers and educators) shape it through their ideas, testimonies and viewpoints, and to create an actionable roadmap drawing on their voices. What this opportunity presents is an argument for a locally centric design education, imagining design education and design *otherwise*, a space where 'different narratives [are brought] into contact with each other, allow[ing] the marginalized to reveal their own interpretation, and opens space for accommodation, contradiction, and resistance' (Rojas, 2007, p. 585). It outlines the possible curricular elements that spread across the formal, informal and hidden curriculum that emerge to create space for this possibility through an actionable framework. As a designer and design researcher, my interests are in investigating how students, designers and educators can contribute to creating a design education and design *otherwise*.

This book is a culmination of many years of research and is a contextualised study examining the philosophies, theories, practices and models of curriculum and pedagogy appropriate for a locally centric design education in the Arab region, using Jordan as a case study. It provides an overview of the growing design culture proliferating across the Arab region not due to government funding and support but due to the lack of it. These largely grassroots initiatives dedicated to alternative and critical forms of design practice and education – relevant to their local contexts and committed to public engagement – spread during the new sense of hope brought on by the Arab uprisings in the 2010s. The book by no means purports to provide a comprehensive overview of all design education or design cultures in the region. Moreover, the issues outlined in this book are not all unique to the Arab region; many readers will find the problems familiar to their own contexts. I propose that only through the collective imagining of students, designers and educators can design education become relevant to its context and milieu. What follows is a book about possibilities, presenting an actionable roadmap for applying theory to practice.

Chapter organisation

Chapter 1 is concerned with higher education in Jordan and the Arab region by providing a brief history and laying out the issues and challenges that are pertinent to the development of curriculum and pedagogy. I describe how Arab and Jordanian universities fall under the Westernised university model and mirror the American model of design education. The discussion moves into design education, whose programmes do not reflect the limited industry, itself limited of opportunities.

Chapter 2 deals with the ways the state exercises its power in higher education and the challenges it sets up in the development of pedagogy and curriculum. This manifests through the models of curriculum, the teacher as authority figure, government interference (leading to increased brain drain) and the culture of conformity. The chapter considers how bureaucracy plays out in faculty and student recruitment, admission criteria and resourcing for programmes.

Chapter 3 delves into regional and local design culture(s), defining the growth of design as fetishised consciousness, where the Global North provides the matrix of measurement and validation of all activity. It explores this through the development of design in the UAE and in more grassroots forms, critiquing the modes of 'parachuting in' to more deprived areas and fixing problems through design events, while understanding the efforts of community engagement that combat this mode. It concludes by highlighting the importance of design in creating a connection to the city.

Chapter 4 outlines the teaching philosophies of educators which counter the culture of the authoritarian educator. I explore this desire to redirect teaching practices through two models of curriculum: process and praxis. The chapter examines the skills and strategies for equipping future designers, and concludes by discussing how active participation, mutual respect, challenging students to their own convictions, questioning taught histories and Arabising design are key components to change and develop successful model(s) of curricula and pedagogy that imagine *otherwise*.

Chapter 5 explores the moments of possibility offered for design in the Arab region to be imagined *otherwise*. By asking who design is for, I outline possibilities for shifting perceptions of design away from elitist perceptions and towards more socially engaged and contextually relevant practices, and to develop better ties between education and industry for job creation. Working through the Arab region's current design cultures, it describes different strategies proposed by participants in creating stronger links between education and industry, and in educating the general public, designers, educators and design students on design's value and role in society.

Chapter 6 concludes the book and outlines the main actionable framework for developing a more contextually-based design education in the Arab region, providing the tools to imagine design education and design *otherwise*.

Finally, readers will notice that the Arabic is transliterated using the Arabic chat alphabet. A reference to this is provided at the front of the book. A translation is in brackets, but I wanted to keep the words of the participants as they were.

DESIGN EDUCATION

38 —Higher education and the landscape of design education
40 —The Westernised university
　41 –The Arabic language
44 —Jordan
　45 –Design education in Jordan
47 —A myriad of graduates and limited jobs
　51 –Clients and the design industry
　52 –Education, employment and women

Chapter 1

Discussions on higher education in the Arab region are often centred around educational reforms and human development, concerned with addressing educational developments, goals, quality, problems, policy and privatisation, and present mostly quantitative analyses of textbook content.[10] Studies pertaining to higher education in the Arab region are commissioned and conducted by international donor organisations or NGOs, such as the IMF, the UN, the World Bank and the Brookings Institute, which unfortunately are led by specific agendas, and do not adequately tackle curriculum and pedagogic models. Research on higher education in the Arab region presents an overview of the challenges but is concerned with measurement, 'best practices' and economic factors rather than seeing these economic factors alongside social, political and cultural ones (Al-Rashdan, 2009). In short, research operates within a neoliberal and developmental framework; it avoids issues of power and governance and the effects reforms and privatisation of the last few decades have caused to curriculum development and to learning and teaching (Mazawi, 2005). Moreover, design education is never mentioned.

This chapter contextualises higher education and design education in the Arab region through a brief overview of the cities covered, laying out the issues and challenges pertinent to the development of curricula and pedagogy such as power, bureaucracy, language and access. I describe how Arab universities fall under the Westernised university model discussed by Ramon Grosfoguel (2013), mirroring North American models of design education, before moving into an overview of design education in Jordan and the job market for graduates.

---

10 Report and studies published in the last thirty years include Abi-Mershed (2010); Bannayan et al., (2012); Laabas (2002); Abbas (2012); Zughloul (2000); Masri (2009); Sabry (2009); ALESCO (2008); Sultana (1997); Burke and Al-Waked (1997); Haddad (1992); Al-Newashi (2012); Abu al-Sheikh and al-Khalailah (2012); and Anderson (2001).

Higher education and the landscape of design education

The beginnings of contemporary institutions of higher education in the Arab region have their history from the 19th century, and the first art institute – modelled after the French educational system – was established in the 1830s in Egypt (Shehab and Nawar, 2020). During this period, European and American universities and colleges were established by missionaries or as colonial institutions, with access limited to specific socio-economic groups and those living in more urban areas. Reforms initiated by then ruler of Egypt Muhammad Ali (1769-1849), including the translation of European works into Arabic, modernising the administration, rationalising agriculture, and setting the groundwork for a preliminary phase of industrialisation, attempted to model a state on western lines (Hourani, 1983; Abu-Lughod, 2011 [1963]). The goal of the reforms sought to strengthen the region by catching up with Europe, relying on speed as opposed to quality. Institutions relied on European teachers and content written in European languages tailored for European schools, making it incomprehensible to the native Arab student (Abu-Lughod, 2011 [1963]).

The independence period of the 1950s and 1960s saw many nations establish public, state-run institutions of higher education modelled on the American and continental European models and enacting policies of free education at all levels (Herrera, 2006; Mazawi, 2005). Seen as a right for every citizen, access to education at all levels improved dramatically and jobs were guaranteed to all graduates. Despite the progress during this period, the quick rise and expansion of higher education prioritised speed and quantity and governments were unable to secure the national economies or curb unemployment. The system began to deteriorate quickly, academic standards and quality declined and institutions were incapable of keeping up with growing enrolment numbers.

The majority of Arab governments invest heavily in education, but, despite this, the picture of higher education region wide is a bleak one, with an extensive list of challenges and issues, including lack of accountability, evaluation and academic freedom, poor teaching, outdated curricula, teaching and programme quality, discriminatory admissions policies, high unemployment rates and brain drain, a mismatch of skills required in the marketplace and those taught in universities, soaring demand and high enrolment rates, limited financing options, low expenditure on research and development, small size of graduate studies, lack of community engagement and social life, poor faculty salary, libraries and teaching resources and knowledge of foreign languages, heavy teaching loads and administrative work, pressure to publish for promotion, and enormous logjams of students.[11]

These factors make the case for reforms or drastic change all the more urgent. But privatisation and the mounting debt of many Arab countries mean governments adopt largely market-driven reforms. Agencies such as the United Nations Development Programme (UNDP) emphasise the region's need to build a knowledge society and economy to prosper and compete globally, emphasising the importance of social justice, citizenship and preserving social cohesion in the development of a knowledge society, and the need for an environment to engage these elements. However, there are difficulties with such a position. Its strategic vision for the establishment of an 'Arab knowledge society' concludes that increasing budgets to higher education and research, developing and implementing strategic objectives and action plans and encouraging private sector contribution are the best policies to face these challenges. These 'solutions' downplay power and assume "that the dominant model will readily accommodate" where important elements are "a tokenistic add-on, marginal and barely visible" (Keirl, 2015, p. 162). The neoliberal ideology underlying these reforms emphasises human capital and building a knowledge society where education must develop a competitive workforce by privileging science and technology over other disciplines, such as design.

The connection between power and knowledge informs educational reforms aiming to establish an Arab knowledge society. International agencies offer limited accounts of power and knowledge in the building of a knowledge society, and of the social groups who contribute to the development of a knowledge society – refugees, the poor, women, and the disabled, for example – further excluding these communities from society. Endorsed by social and political movements and international institutions, reports articulate the priorities of an urban and established elite.

---

11 See for example Al-Adwan (2013); Badran (2014); Boissiere (2011); El-Said et al., (2012) ; Galal (2008); Jaramillo, Ruby, Henard, et al. (2011); Kanaan, Al-Salamat and Hanania(2009); Khader (2009); Lamine (2010); Romani (2009); Sabry (2009); Mazawi (2005, 2010); United Nations Development Programme (2009)(2009); United Nations Development Programme and Mohammed bin Rashid Al Maktoum Foundation (2014); and Wilkens (2011).

The Westernised university

Like the primary and secondary sector of education, the university educational models region wide are heterogeneous – a mix of private and public sector institutions. National universities are managed by the state and offer programmes in Arabic and English. In most Arab countries, national universities are competitive and affordable. Private universities take multiple forms, either as local or international. Local private universities offer similar curricula to national universities in Arabic/English and were developed due to the privatisation drives and increased demand from students since the late 1980s. Entry criteria is lower and tuition more expensive. International private universities offer American, British, German or Australian style education, which take the form of satellite campuses (for example Heriot-Watt, NYU Abu Dhabi, University of Wollongong) and American-affiliated institutions like the American University of Beirut (est. 1866) and the American University in Cairo (est. 1919), non-profit private universities established by American missionaries. Whereas in Lebanon and the UAE international private universities prevail, students who attend local private universities in Jordan and Egypt are seen as poorly performing, whereas national universities in are relatively competitive in these countries.

No matter what form they take, the models fall under what Ramon Grosfoguel's (2013) calls the 'Westernised University' – a model that can be found globally, with the same curriculum, the same authors and disciplinary divisions as any university in the West. These institutions promote or diffuse Eurocentric knowledge to produce Westernised elites in the Global South that act as intermediaries between the West and the Global South, and placing Arab universities in a position of dependency with lower academic standards and resources, in opposition to centres with a large amount of resources and high academic standards, dominating knowledge production and distribution (Altbach, 2006). The peripheries are usually dependent on the centres for knowledge, research, teaching, and even organisational structures, a division further cemented with increased use of common course materials, textbooks and syllabi produced by multinational publishers, the internet, databases, and educators who return after studying abroad and bring these ideas with them (Altbach, 2006). The division between centre and periphery is further fuelled by the marginalisation of other languages, as legitimate research and high-impact journals are published in English and research agendas are set by the European Union or the GCC.

For design education, a factor that contributes to the specialised North American model is the growth design experienced in the 1980s and 1990s, in conjunction with neoliberal reforms. These developments reflect an adaptation of a global trend in design during that period, which led to a "convergence between design and other commercial practices such as advertising, management consultancy and public relations" and where design took on a more prominent commercial and public role (Julier, 2014; p. 24). The limited manufacturing and export industry regionally has contributed to the focus on interior and graphic design over other specialisations (although this shifting in the UAE to reflect government ambitions and technological changes). This reflects the economic and commercial changes globally, such as growth of corporate rebranding, privatisation of state industries and services and the growth of corporate finance (Julier, 2014).

The Arabic language

Across the region, the language of instruction is dependent on policy and colonial history. In Jordan, the MoHESR encouraged Arabisation of science and research but made no mention of language of instruction requirements (Hanafi and Arvanitis, 2016). The peripheral status of Arabic as a language of instruction is partly due to dependency on knowledge produced in the Western countries (Mazawi, 2005). Therefore, Arab universities do not generate knowledge, but process it from Western countries, leaving them in a peripheral position when it comes to knowledge production. What is problematic is that the knowledge itself remains foreign to the institutions and the economic and social reality. This is compounded by limited links between academic institutions and industry. Moreover, the marginalisation of the Arabic language leads to poor skills in Arabic and in foreign languages generally; to limited research in Arabic that is disconnected from the local environment; it divides institutions between the centre and the periphery where the latter must rely on models from elsewhere for content; and it creates divisions between local societies and the elites. Teaching in Arabic grounds education in reality – leading to translation efforts and to the development of theories and methodologies (Hanafi and Arvanitis, 2016).

The language of design education in Jordan, Lebanon, and Egypt[12] is fluid, moving between English and Arabic. It is dependent on the person teaching, the students, or the content. Some educators have made

---

12 State universities in Egypt teach strictly in Arabic.

cases to teach a class entirely in Arabic due to the subject matter and some American universities take steps to ensure no Arabic is spoken in the classroom: course evaluations ask students if the teacher spoke Arabic during this class. Due to a lack of policy on language, design education is taught in English and most of the design cultures are in English with bilingual elements. Rita, an educator in Beirut, explains the effects of this dilemma on educators:

We introduced the introduction to Arabic typography [...] but you know I go back and think why am I teaching a course about Arabic typography in English? Why am I explaining to the students 'alqawaa'ed al khat al aaraby' bas bil ingleeseh [the rule of Arabic script in English], you know, like why am I doing this?

Discussions on language and translation referred to an examination of the teaching language and the language of design culture. Participants felt strongly that a design culture that only speaks English is problematic but there are difficulties to translation. Arabic design terminology is an obstacle in both practice and education. Educators deal with the back and forth mixture of English and Arabic in different ways. Khaled, a Professor and former Dean of the School, prefers to use English terms and, for students with weaker English skills, he translates them to Arabic on paper. He begins teaching in Arabic and slowly moves to integrating English rather than imposing it, otherwise, people will reject him.

Educator Maria is disappointed by the low-level Arabic skills of her Lebanese students:

Not taking Arabic as something that is integral to their nationality and to their culture. It's unbelievable what you see at university level, they don't know letters [because] they've been 'ma3fyeen mn el3arabi' [excused from Arabic][13]. Because they hold [...] another passport, the schools let them get this policy. So, you get these students that have never read Arabic or have been tutored special Arabic.

Educator/Designer Karma stated that some students prefer learning in Arabic, and it is necessary to accommodate their needs. She described how students see the language gap and challenge themselves by producing projects entirely in classical Arabic, whereas others play with the language, producing work using *dawaween* Arabic (ghetto/street) over classical. She believes that this is a mutual learning experience, as she learns new terms through student work, and students challenge themselves through language. Karma referred to the importance of

---

13 Refer to the Arabic chat alphabet (Arabizi) on p. 11 for reference.

language in learning, describing an experience she had in Germany, where the German students easily switched to German when they were unable to describe their practice in English whereas Arab students were discussing design in English but were unable to describe their practice in Arabic:

They [Germans] couldn't translate and I was surprised that it's part of the culture. Arabic wasn't moulded to accommodate design. I mean how do you translate design thinking? This affects the awareness of the average person on design.

Fawz – who runs an independent institute for design in Amman – claimed that if her content was in Arabic, she would attract a larger audience, but design terminology is not easily translatable into Arabic, leading to a disconnect with the public. Similarly, the designer Mona launched her design website with English-only content. A few years later, she Arabised the whole site, which expanded her reach to a larger public. When I asked her why she chose English initially, she provided two reasons: she studied design in English, and at the time, Arabic programming code was in its infancy, thus building the site in English would be quicker.

Issues of translation led to confusion. For example, programme names are lost in translation when translated to Arabic. Laila, a student, recounted how three quarters of the students had no idea what the major was:

The name in Arabic is confusing 'alttasmim walttawasul albasri' (Design and Visual Communication) people thought it had something to do with eyesight and glasses! [laughs]

When Baha completed his studies in Graphic Design, he had to complete his Lebanese military service (mandatory at the time). He explains how the army officer did not know where to place him based on his degree:

In Arabic, it's called 'Tasmeem AlTakhteeti' [Design Planning]. Where do they send me to? 'Mudereyat Altakhteet' [the planning department] because the word 'takhteeti' [planning]. But [...] there's nothing about planning!

Amman-based designer Athar argued that introducing more Arabic in design language would help in finding Arabic counterparts for design terminology:

In Latin I understand the difference between logo, visual identity and brand. In Arabic, they all go under the same term: 'Al hawiya il bassariya' [visual identity]. If I re-translate that into English it's visual identity, but branding is not only about a visual identity, that's one component. How will we understand the discipline in Arabic if we aren't taught? I understand why we are taught in English but we need it in Arabic so at least we can communicate about design in our mother tongue.

The end goal for designers and educators working in the region is about generating Arabic content rather than relying on translation.

Jordan

The establishment of the University of Jordan in 1962 was followed by other public universities across Jordan and, while they claim to be autonomous institutions, the reality was that policies were determined by the King and the government (Reiter, 2002). The planning, management, policies and research and development related to higher education is the responsibility of the Ministry of Higher Education and Scientific Research (MoHESR). The ministry imposes a great deal of constraints and supervises universities closely, leaving them with little autonomy. Fully centralised ministry control is similar in Egypt, the UAE and Lebanon, however, ministerial powers are more limited for the latter two.

Despite the progress in Jordan's education system at all levels of schooling, it continues – as the rest of the Arab region – to lag behind international standards such as the number of registered patents, published scientific papers, university rankings, research and development expenditure, and world intellectual property indicators. Although the enrolment rate is high, the country struggles with high unemployment rates amongst youth and graduates.

Growing in parallel to Jordan's neoliberal reforms, education experienced great demand in the late 1980s due to an increase in high school graduates and unemployment, an economic crisis and the first Gulf War. Pressured to create openings, public universities were unable to keep up with growing numbers and this led to the establishment of the Private Universities Act No. 19 in 1989 and the opening of Al-Ahliyya Amman University – the first private university in Jordan[14]. Private universities are profit-driven, with tuition fees as the main source of income, a model that 'threatens to exacerbate one of the major deficiencies in Arab education, i.e. selective exclusion for the rich and powerful in good quality education' (Fergany, 2009, p. 45), further fuelled by limited availability of student loans and financial aid.

---

14 Kanaan, Al-Salamat and Hanania (2009) suggest that demand for the creation of private universities came from students with uncompetitive qualifications unable to secure a seat in a public university, rather than from the public.

Design education in Jordan

The establishment of design as a discipline dates back to the early 1980s[15], with the first development of a programme as a subsidiary of fine art at Yarmouk University. Further universities developed design programmes in the 1990s and mid-to-late 2000s. Regionally, specialisations that dominate are graphic design and interior design, due to a limited industrial infrastructure and a region dependent on services and the construction industry. Moreover, design education remains at the undergraduate level only, with over a dozen private and public institutions accredited by the MoHESR offering design degrees at the university level country wide.

Across the region, design education programmes borrow their form liberally from North America and Europe, with North American style credit systems, and some local public and private universities are accredited by American bodies such as the National Association of Schools of Art and Design (NASAD), established in 1944 as a national forum for visual arts in higher education in the United States. It is almost impossible to pinpoint a structure for any Arab country; one size does not fit all. The best descriptor of the programmes is, to quote multiple participants, 'Frankenstein-like'. Most schools were Beaux-Arts academies, and design as a separate discipline only dates to the late 1970s and early 1980s (mainly interior design and visual communication/graphic design). Models of design education have changed since the Bauhaus was established in 1919, however North American design programmes, and Jordan's mirroring of them, continue the 'universal' structure established by the Bauhaus. These design schools were shaped by different forces that are vastly different from the Arab context. Moreover, many design programmes in North America and Europe are located within stand-alone art and design colleges, institutes and academies, whereas in the Arab region design programmes are located within universities.

Like North American design education, Jordanian design programmes favour descriptive and technical content over the analytical and intellectual. Technique, form, technology and style provide the structure, and an emphasis on foundation courses such as painting, drawing, sculpture, art history, technology, typography and communication concepts enables students to fully develop as market-ready and aesthetically conscious designers. Although these courses are important, they present students with 'value-free' education where everything has a visual solution regardless of the cultural context.

---

15 The origins of design education in the region are documented in the book *A History of Arab Graphic Design* (Shehab and Nawar, 2020). However, Jordan is not mentioned.

Students graduate with portfolios for employability, emphasising aesthetics rather than content or meaning (Bierut, 2007).

Design caters to undergraduates, focuses on professional and traditional industry preparation, and relies on Western theories of design. For example, a separation between History of Art and History of Islamic Art, History of Design and Islamic Design and Architecture, and Western Aesthetics and Islamic Aesthetics. Programmes heavily address technical skills such as software skills and art practice, rarely delve outside of design to engage with other disciplines and contain limited theory and history. Additionally, the design curriculum does not expose students to other disciplines outside of design and fine art, even though programmes are located in universities, leaving them isolated within design and fine art and detached from the context surrounding them.[16] Exposure to non-design-related content is within electives and requirements replicating high school content (for example Military Science and Arabic Language), not content that exposes students to disciplines that inform the work of designers and their engagement with the world. Moreover, few context-specific courses exist, such as Islamic Art History, Islamic Design and Architecture, and Arabic Typography, although this is slowly changing, and course terminology does not reflect contemporary advances in the field of design. If not exposed to culture and other disciplines, design students will continue to speak to and design for themselves and other designers.

A minor shift is occurring towards more critical forms of design education across the Global North, however, the basis of their curricula continues to favour the designer as craftsman rather than the designer as intellectual. Design schools teach a form of design that is largely value-free, placing the client at the centre, and tends to favour a problem-solving and form-driven approach that places value on the aesthetics of the outcomes rather than content or meaning behind the design. While these models are adopted from other countries, the last decade has seen an adaptation to local needs and market demand. For example, illustration is taught within graphic design programmes rather than as a separate discipline and specialisations are eroding in favour of generalist modes of design.

---

16 Exceptions would be universities adopting the US style liberal arts model (to an extent).

A myriad of graduates and limited jobs

Arab youth are over-educated, not well-educated, and their stalled status reminds them of that difference daily. (Mulderig, 2011, p. 3)

What could be classified as the design sector is broad and attempting to confine an industry could not capture the breadth of opportunities available for designers. However, the Arab region has a small and traditional market for design. Education caters to the larger share of interior design and graphic design jobs, with few programmes in industrial/product design or fashion design due to a small manufacturing industry. Arab states are mostly reliant on the construction industry and do not possess competitive private sectors. But construction – which drives the high value interior design market (itself set to grow with ambitious projects in Saudi Arabia) – only creates temporary jobs and is vulnerable to economic shocks. The COVID-19 pandemic highlighted a need for digital skills, where investment in high-growth areas such as digital and green economies requires investment in technical skills to match labour demand and close the digital divide (United Nations Development Programme, 2022). Moreover, the diversification of the economy puts increased emphasis on 'computer coding, computational thinking, problem solving, and design thinking into all levels of educational institutions' (Karakhanyan, 2019, p. 214).

In contrast to most Arab governments, the UAE government acknowledges the need for superior and homegrown talent by investing in higher education, training, skills and innovation capacity (ibid., p. 212), The establishment of the Dubai Institute of Design and Innovation (DIDI) is looking at new market opportunities, focusing on developing technological skills for a new generation of designers. Maher, who teaches at DIDI, tells me how the UAE government established the need for such an institution based on findings from a 2016 Deloitte report, which estimated that 'the region requires at least 30,000 design graduates by 2019 to achieve sustainable growth projections. This suggests the need for a nine-fold increase in the number of design graduates currently produced' (Dubai Design and Fashion Council and Monitor Deloitte, 2016, p. 33). The report outlines that regional economies must 'focus their attention on creating additional pathways into the design sector, such as strengthening vocational education to create diversity in the graduate marketplace' (ibid., p.9).

Relative to other markets, the creative industries contribute only 1.5 per cent to the GDP regionally. Capitalising on design within and beyond the creative industries remains low on the agendas of Arab governments, excluding the UAE, who have taken steps to address the shortage. Despite the small market, there is a significant number of universities offering design programmes, alongside community colleges and a growing number of training centres focused on teaching design software. Educators are concerned with how a small market can absorb a large number of graduates, particularly where higher education regionally is largely disconnected from industry. Indeed, as Hillman and Baydoun (2019, p. 46) show:

Too few universities use external advisors from industry and civil society to gauge the utility of new or existing course. Many courses seem to be established somewhat whimsically in that they reflect the opinion of one or a few dominant personalities.

Finding a job after graduation becomes increasingly important for students paying high tuition fees, and adds pressure on educators to focus on employability, a trend not unique to the region but in many countries around the world. Competition for jobs is tight due to a surplus of graduates caused by the number of students graduating from universities, community colleges and technical centres. Amman-based educator Aws explained the issues this poses for university graduates:

When a graduate with a diploma [community college] wants to work, and a low wage job is offered to him, he accepts it because he isn't too deep in debt, whereas the graduate with a bachelor's degree has studied for four years and accumulated debts won't accept a low wage.

The increase of institutions teaching graphic design has reinforced the perception that graphic designers work on computers (one tool in the production process), and this enables anyone with a few days' training in design software to call themselves a designer, Aws tells me. This is not unique to Jordan or the Arab region, but worldwide, with six- or twelve-week courses offered by institutions such as General Assembly and Shillington Education. The rise of bidding sites such as Fiverr and 99 Designs lead to a blurring between amateurs and designers, where hobbyists who are familiar with design software provide all types of design services, further fuelling the association of design as software. Educator Khaled blamed those who run design studios because they hire graduates for their technical skills rather than to generate ideas, concepts or conduct research. Indeed, the issue is also with educators. Amman-based designer and educator Adam tells me how foreign educators in particular believe students will not amount to anything more than 'a good finaliser'. 'If you have that in the back of your head,' he says, 'then you're going to be teaching oddly.'

Whereas graphic design is perceived as software, interior design is equated with painting and furnishing a room, and fashion design with tailoring. Moreover, interior design graduates face stiff competition from an expansive architecture practice where graduates compete with architecture graduates for jobs, interior design educator Nadine tells me. Nadine describes how interior design is not taken seriously and, because architecture covers several domains, if offered the choice between an interior design graduate or an architecture graduate, companies will opt for the latter. Therefore, half of the students who graduate do not find a job in the profession; students are aware of the lack of jobs and industry in Jordan, and either seek work abroad or leave design altogether, she says.

Advertising is the largest employer for graphic designers in Jordan, Egypt, the UAE and Lebanon. More companies working in graphic design are branching out of printed materials, signage, advertising and logos and expanding to include strategic advice and consultancy. The link between advertising and design is close, and most design graduates understand design as advertising and think this is the only option for them upon graduation. Laith, a designer based in Amman who freelances for advertising agencies to 'pay the bills', argued that not everyone has the willpower to work in advertising, and many of his friends gave up and pursued other careers due to the agency environment. He felt there is a problem with thinking that advertising is the only option, and this is because institutions think of design graduates in the same way as business graduates: confined to an office job. Although critical of advertising, designer Karma believes that advertising agencies provide stability, particularly since there are little options for students upon graduation.

The frustration designers Rami and Laith had working in advertising encouraged them to launch a multidisciplinary studio that centres experimentation. Launching an independent studio in Jordan is risky and requires resources and business skills. While they were both excited and scared of the possibilities, they felt that the positives outweighed the negatives. Providing a space that encourages experimentation can be attractive to new graduates, and operating in opposition to the norm presents young designers with role models in a country without any. But they identify the monetary aspect – which they argue is cultural – as an obstacle to success. Laith explains:

A student might come work with us and not make that much money but [...] sees his friend who tells him I'm working at X and I'm making 1,500JD, are you stupid? In all honesty, he's right. This is a cultural issue, for everything, not just design.

Beirut and Amman are cities with many small businesses that cannot afford to hire big advertising or branding agencies for design work, and this could provide opportunities for smaller studios to build client lists.

Designer-educator Baha, who launched a studio with a partner in Beirut in the 2010s, wanted to place design in the cultural sector rather than advertising to challenge the notion that designers merely execute rather than think with their clients. This is approach is similar to the one taken by Dubai-based studios, many of which work exclusively with the UAE cultural industry.

Khaled points to the disconnect between industry and universities, explaining how the mutual non-recognition – where industry does not recognise universities or their graduates and the other way around – is the cause of the disconnect. He suggested the establishment of a stakeholder who builds a connection between universities and the design industry to clarify the design needs of Jordan and the type of designer required for the future. Otherwise, he argued, curricula will remain copy and pasted from outside models, where universities offer majors such as industrial design without assessing them, and the needs of the country will remain unknown. Educators Aws and Hind believe that if society can comprehend the role of the designer, the field can develop and create new job opportunities. Unsettling political, social and economic problems, and the limited government support given to design, are blamed for a lack of opportunities for young graduates. Like with education, bureaucracy holds both industry and experimentation back, imposing regulations on companies and complicated registration practices for businesses due to 'perennial obsession with security hampers' (Kassir, 2006, p. 21). High rates of youth unemployment, however, are more structural than cyclical (Waterbury, 2020).

Clients and the design industry

Bureaucracy is not the only factor halting experimentation and imposing red tape on designers. The world over, designers express frustration with clients who lack an understanding of the designer's role. Throughout my interviews, designers discussed another element to the client relationship: the culture of bypassing designers. This adds an additional layer to their job: educating the client. Students and designers had a cynical attitude towards clients, claiming clients' views and expectations of designers prevent the growth of a design culture and reduce the role of the designer to a tool. Despite the optimism accompanying an increased design awareness amongst businesses, cultural organiser Sama, and designers Maya and Fairuz, believe bypassing the designer overshadows these small steps. Clients, they explain, are incapable of differentiating between the designer and the production person or contractor, often skipping the designer and going straight to production. They argued that it is part of the local work ethic and they point to storefronts as the most visible sign of this act. Production on storefronts is mostly the work of print houses rather than graphic designers. The work ethic is highlighted by Karma and Rami, who referred to the way clients speak *at* designers rather than *listen* to them, and the low production standards. Karma explains the effects of the work ethic on students:

Stick on stick on [...] this affects how students produce work, how they present it to clients, and what client expectations are.

Work ethic and bypassing the designer led to a misconception of the designer's role, and designers must add an educational layer to their work. Fairuz told me that, in her contracts, she emphasises her role and work plan in the first few pages:

People don't know. They think, just give us the design. Even architecture, an old profession [...] people don't know. And we worked on a project where we got a client and he skipped us and went straight to the contractor... [laughs] we were solving the spatial problem. But for him it was [...] a matter of taste. 'I will tell the contractor; I have good taste!'

In her research for Amman Design Week (ADW), Sama heard similar statements from designers. She found a disconnect between clients and designers, where designers felt obliged to educate the client on their role because clients devalued design. She believes that this is a global problem, but it is pronounced in Jordan as clients often bypass the designer to get the work done:

They won't go to an architect; they go to a builder. They won't go to a graphic designer; they go to a sign maker. They don't go to a fashion designer; they go to a tailor. Design it themselves. Complete misunderstanding of the designer as a critical thinker in the process.

What are the causes of this misunderstanding? Designers Basem and Rami point to the focus on saleability, which they argued hinders the creative process and leads to little experimentation and conformity. Khaled believes it is the recreation of the patriarchal authoritarian figure who pushes a 'you work for me' attitude and contributes to a stifling creative environment, which then leads to increased migration. This attitude forces designers to work in a one-way vertical relationship rather than engage in dialogue and see it as a client–designer relationship. However, Baha thinks this is a two-sided issue, where designers are devalued by clients but themselves devalue craftspeople:

[Designers] do not often value the knowledge of printers and book binders, etc., We seek them for their skills, but we do not consult them.

In the Arab region, there is a narrow-minded view of industry that confines design to advertising agencies and studios, and students have limited awareness of opportunities available to them in other sectors. The market share long dominated by multinational advertising agencies like JWT and Leo Burnett is being challenged by smaller design studios working locally and regionally, and this trend introduces new and exciting opportunities for design and establishing design's value. These studios could shift perceptions and enable non-design industries to begin to see the value of design's placement within their work. Furthermore, it can help with migration and brain drain, and tackling female unemployment.

Education, employment and women

The positive impact of liberal reforms on women's lives should not lead to the assumption that they eradicate systems of domination. [...] The lack of any emphasis on domination is consistent with the liberal feminist belief that women can achieve equality with men of their class without challenging and changing the cultural basis of group oppression (hooks, 2000, p. 21).

The basis of neopatriarchal societies is the oppression of women and the most embodied form of inequality regionally is gender. To overcome inequality requires the emancipation of women, found through access to education, work and economic independence (Sharabi, 1988). However, women have different experiences and agency because they negotiate and bargain with patriarchy differently (Kandiyoti, 1988), therefore access to education and employment depends on relational factors such as race, age, gender, sexuality, ability, class, marital status, education and cultural values and tradition amongst similar categories (Collins, 2000; Al-Ali and Pratt, 2009). Female empowerment cannot be reduced to quantifiable measures or changes of laws. Implementing policies are not enough for change; change must be radical to abolish the patriarchy. Jordan, for example, has reached parity in primary education and literacy and is making significant progress in secondary and higher education. While there is evidence that girls and women are better achievers in education (Fergany, 2009; Ripley, 2017), and women constitute the majority in Jordanian universities, they remain invisible in the workforce, with alarmingly low participation rates.[17]

The student population of design programmes regionally is predominantly female. Low female participation in the labour market is likely due to entrenched social biases and the neopatriarchal state, leading to discriminatory hiring practices, traditional attitudes towards women and weak governmental policies in preventing such forms of discrimination. Despite efforts and advances in freedom, citizenship, education and political participation by NGOs, coalitions, collectives and civil society organisations, there remains an enormous amount of work to be done as women continue to find themselves paralysed as members of society. The perception is that art and design are feminine domains of study, and men are discouraged from pursuing it. Rayan, a designer/educator in the UAE, shares his experience:

Growing up, wanting to do design, I was almost ashamed...because it was always considered a hobby. [...] like art. And it's more something that women would do, not men [...] I didn't know how to tell them [my parents] that I was doing design. So I used to say I was doing multimedia design, it has something to do with computers. But I'd go back home with charcoal on my 'Kandora' [traditional Emirati menswear]. 'Ent tarsem?' (You draw?) I'm like 'Yeah', 'Okay whatever you want to do we support you. Is there a career path for this?' I'm like 'Yeah. There is.' You know, we were young then, we didn't know the potential of design, especially here, like I didn't know anyone that graduated in design back then.

The male taboo leads to a large percentage of male designers being self-taught instead of pursuing design at university. Rayan uses his influential design practice to promote design as a genderless and legitimate career path, in hopes of encouraging men to pursue studies in design. Whereas women are encouraged to study design, they are discouraged from practicing it. Huda recounted in a frustrating manner when I asked about her plans when she graduates:

---

17 Workforce rates are 13.5 per cent in Jordan, 15.4 per cent in Egypt and 20.8 per cent in Lebanon – in contrast to 46.5 per cent in the UAE; see https://hdr.undp.org/data-center/country-insights#/ranks.

I am going to learn to cook. I know a lot of people who have a lot of potential to become great designers. I know someone [...] he taught himself design and I asked him why didn't you study at school, he said people will look at me weirdly. Society accepts women studying but does not accept a man studying arts. Society doesn't help, but if you study abroad, yes. Here I am limited by the company, by people, by society, I can't do anything like I want so I don't have to work. That's how I see the world.

Huda's words reiterate Rayan's by demonstrating how studying design is gendered, and how women view it as an appropriate field for the sake of obtaining a degree. When I asked her if she is going to feed into the role imposed on her, she replied:

I am trying to leave to go to the US. [...] Over there they give you an ability to work. It's not about 'oh you can't do that because society doesn't accept it.'

Huda's comments sparked a debate as her classmates disagreed with her and debated their plans after graduation:

Nawal: But not everyone can go study abroad. What are you going to do just sit around and not work?

Danah: You all want to work, right?

Several female students: Yes!

Danah: That's great! Because many people just want a degree and go off and get married!

Huda: 90 per cent of Jordan!

Nawal: Many people think this way.

Lamees: I want to build myself, have a job, have a career. I don't want to sit around the house cooking and wait for my husband to come home... that's not how I see myself.

A noticeable issue is the ratio of female students to female educators. Educators across universities in Jordan are predominantly male. During one of the focus groups, the students mentioned they had one female educator out of seven and began laughing. Their laughter displayed the absurdity of the situation. Students and designers discussed how some women reinforced design's gendered role. For example, Lara described how some of her colleagues had no idea what design was and many female students 'would say that "I'm in design because I'm a girl!" Imagine how horrible is that!'

Mayar, a designer, told me that when she was a student some of her peers had no interest in working in design and only wanted the degree. Moreover, when she briefly taught design at university, she described how some female students only wanted to graduate and get married. I asked that if these women only want to get married and have children, then why did they go to school to begin with? 'Because they have to. [...] She cooks, she cleans, she takes care of the kids, but she has to go to school and university,' she replied.

The portrait of the design industry in Jordan, Lebanon and Egypt is different to the UAE. Whereas all countries have over 70 per cent female enrolment in design, design studios and managerial positions are male dominated in Jordan, Lebanon and Egypt. In the UAE, design studios are predominantly female run, likely due to the creative industry being female led and the UAE boasting nine female Ministers. The UAE also has a much higher female employment rate.

Jordan, the UAE and Lebanon have bridged the gender gap in universities, but Jordan and Lebanon suffer from a low female employment rate. Yet a university degree is an asset for women to resist and bargain with patriarchy by providing them more employment opportunities and control of financial resources. Education presents women a challenge to the culture of conformity, and empowers them in different ways, for example to obtain necessary skills and make decisions for themselves, including choosing a marriage partner, or to use education for freedom of movement (Nasser Eddin, 2011).

Why then do women still represent such a small number of the labour force, particularly where design programmes are female dominated? Historian Afsaneh Najmabadi (1998, p. 102) points to the woman's role transferring from house to manager of the house, where women became 'the manager of the household...instead of being subject to his [the husband's] management'. Education became important for women because uneducated women were not suitable mothers or spouses (Najmabadi, 1998). Therefore, due to assigned gender roles, the goal of women's education is marriage, and economic activity is secondary to this.

The traditional educational system helps reinforce this notion by teaching students to depend and follow authority rather than guiding students towards 'critical thought...into autonomous habits of mind' (Shor, 1992, p. 13). Transforming curriculum and pedagogy can empower women to form their conception of self and of the world, and through the role of critical educators – females in particular – critically reflect on it and relate it to their own experience, challenging the neopatriarchal society and the roles imposed on them. It can promote equal treatment between genders and address these social biases and discriminatory practices against women (and other socially marginalised groups). To speak of the industry, and a collaboration with industry, is to question the invisibility of women within it.

POWER AND BUREAUCRACY

58 —Curriculum as product transmission
60 —The teacher as authority figure
63 —More than oil and gas in value: brain drain
67 —Challenging the culture of conformity
69 —Chains of bureaucracy
  69 –Box-ticking exercises
  71 –Faculty recruitment
  72 –Faculty promotion
  74 –A middle-class area of studies
  75 –With great wealth comes great responsibility?
  77 –'Design is easy'
  78 –The diploma disease
  79 –Admission requirements, choice and values
81 —Abolish grades, embrace failure
82 —Resources

Chapter 2

Constraints on academic freedom and the monitoring of activities are some of the ways the state exercises its power. The way power operates in higher education sets up challenges in the development of pedagogy and curriculum. I will focus on four areas to understand how these manifest: curriculum as product/transmission; the teacher as authority figure; government interference leading to increased migration and brain drain; and the culture of conformity.

Curriculum as product/ transmission

Neopatriarchal institutions promote a certain type of knowledge and student; pedagogy and curriculum in the Arab region prioritise rote learning and measurable outputs, as opposed to developing the personality, or building social and critical thinking skills. The product/ transmission curriculum model revolves around setting objectives and targets, developing a plan, applying that plan and measuring the outcomes (products). It is usually an elaborate outline with documents for the teacher and the student. The documents provide the teacher with step-by-step directions on teaching and testing. It is the most prevalent model of curriculum in the Arab region.

The teaching action in this model is 'making' action, which implies that the act of teaching is product oriented. The product is the student (products of the educational system), or a material product such as a well-executed artwork or a well-written essay (Grundy, 1987). Skill is making action based on the syllabus requirements – the student is rewarded for their technical expertise and aesthetic competencies – and the success of the educator's work is evaluated by how the result conforms to the specifications set out within the syllabus (Grundy, 1987). In other words, the outcome (material product) 'exists apart from the producer to the extent that it may have been produced by anyone with the same skills' (ibid., p.64). In this model, design is a neutral activity.

The product/transmission model, in line with solutions from international organisations to establish a knowledge society, which emphasises the necessity of setting measurable objectives to capitalise on human capital and to keep up with globalisation, is characterised by the safety of prescribed materials and the transmission of subjects, where students are told what they must learn and how they are going to learn it. In this model, the central component is content, and as such 'organization becomes a matter solely of effectiveness of "delivery" and evaluation is focused on the degree to attainment achieved by the [students]' (Kelly, 2004, p. 15). Moreover, the development of a knowledge society emphasises building human capital and cognitive skills, stresses vocational training and focuses on science and technology that lead to development.

One example of this is through unsustainable credit hour systems, where Jordan, Egypt, UAE and, to an extent, Lebanon require over 25 per cent more hours than other institutions globally, squeezing

---

18   The comparison was made between engineering, social sciences and accounting departments and included universities from Canada, USA, Saudi Arabia, UAE, Egypt, Lebanon and Jordan.

content in the curriculum wherever possible.[18] Heavy workloads and demanding credit hours affect both students and faculty, deterring them from extracurricular activities such as community engagement and volunteerism.

The product/transmission model is designed with behavioural objectives in mind where curriculum planning is based around four dimensions (Kelly, 2004, p.14):

- objectives (what we hope to achieve);
- content or subject matter (what we are planning to cover to achieve our objectives);
- methods or procedures (activities that are most effective in reaching our goals);
- evaluation (the tools and devices to help us evaluate our work).

Setting targets and objectives are not educational principles; targets and objectives are set by governments where the concern is to measure these and use them for statistics. In this method, the curriculum is placed outside of the context and milieu as curriculum construction is the work of curriculum specialists providing instructions on its use (Cornbleth, 1988).

The model is simple, and the sole interest of this model is controlling student learning for the product to conform to the ideas of the original objectives, and to promote a discourse of inequality between the teacher and the student (Stenhouse, 1975; Grundy, 1987). Aggressive neoliberal agendas that emphasise the knowledge economy and building human capital have made simplicity and measurability the norm in higher education. This equates education with usefulness for employment and economic growth, a worldwide trend.

In design, the acquisition of skills and technique results in stylistic prowess and, upon graduation, those with the best skills and aesthetic are the most employable. The road to a knowledge society is paved with private sector involvement in curriculum development and investment in education and partnerships. This road however does not address the issues with this curriculum planning model, nor does it consider students, nor the impact of these policies on them. The pedagogic goal is for students to learn the content offered to them as effectively as possible. In that way, it is similar to the banking model of education, which involves the educator depositing information and narration into the student (Freire, 2000). The student is instructed to record, memorise and repeat without understanding the true significance of what they are asked to learn. It becomes mechanical, turning students into '"containers," into "receptacles" to be filled by the teacher', and limiting their scope of action to "receiving, filing, and storing the deposits"' (ibid., p. 72).

This method, although simple, is linear, disconnected from the act of teaching, and implies power relations where power resides with those who control the objectives (Grundy, 1987) and aims to change behaviour. It provides students with reactive rather than active power.

The teacher as authority figure

Within universities, power interferes in teaching and learning by creating a system of fear where students view educators as prophet-like due to their authority. Within neopatriarchial society, authority figures (saviours/heroes/leaders) are paralysing, offering a 'sense of security to people who are afraid of freedom' to quote Syrian poet Adonis (2006, no pagination). They create barriers, developing an environment that discourages criticism and experimentation, thereby removing the students' opportunity to explore, and act as a scaring mechanism. They work in conjunction with the product/transmission model.

This fear leads to a safe set of outcomes by both students and designers, reiterated by the educator who disciplines, recreating the structures of the neopatriarchal state within the classroom by imposing their authority. Classrooms become sites of maintaining the status quo rather than challenging conventional methods. Students Elia, Maria and Linda described how in practice, and by using specific language, educators framed the classroom as a competition, encouraging students to survey the weaknesses of their peers by openly stating how one student's work was better than another's. A culture of competition should be healthy, but instead it allows the educators to abuse their power in the classroom by using tactics they think are motivating when they are in fact demoralising.

The students I spoke with believed many educators imposed their views and opinions on them, did not listen or engage them, did not consider them as individuals, nor did they respect or comprehend learning abilities, and they instigated fear to establish authority. The students detailed moments where educators destroyed their work during crits to set an example, which led them to produce work the way the educator wanted for fear of failing, denying them the ability to develop their own styles. Elia, a student, recounted his experience of the assertion of power in the classroom:

The Dean was showing us a pyramid which said, 'levels of education' with his face at the top. And he says when you reach that level, you can discuss ideas with me.

Other students reported stories about educators destroying their work to set an example when students respond to the brief differently. The purpose is to instigate fear and establish authority, mirroring the authoritarian and domination of the neopatriarchal state, and bears every aspect of Freire's banking education.

Moreover, educators described colleagues who approached students in a standardised way, unable to tap into the skills and strengths of the students and refusing to acknowledge students as individuals. The effect educators have on students can be detrimental because standardising students is a form of refusing to acknowledge their presence. Moreover, designer Laith experienced educators who wanted to sculpt small versions of themselves in their students. Indeed, some educators admit to teaching in a similar style to how they were taught, but for others the goal is the opposite.

Educators directing a project their way centres student learning on skills and outcomes of material products rather than learning and teaching methods – for example, a well-executed design piece (Grundy, 1987). Interestingly, this appears in a subtle way during the interview with interior design educator Nadine, when she described the role of the educator as one of correcting students:

Our job as instructors is to tell them this chair is wrong in dimensions, its location is wrong, this space isn't correct, this isn't good combination, etc.

By 'correcting students', the class turns into a teacher-centred examination instead of asking questions to 'extend their remarks, providing more of their own words as the foundation of dialogue... giving... contact with the way they think and use language' (Shor, 1992, p.89). Rather than focus on the act and the actor, she focuses on the outcome of the action. The result of the product becomes separate from the producer – anyone with the same set of skills obtained by conforming to the syllabus requirements could produce it (Grundy, 1987). It demonstrates how educators homogenise students by teaching 'universal' design skills emphasised in the curriculum. But this phenomenon is not unique to the Arab world; a master–apprentice model of design education pushes these ideas.

Another form of alienation described was through openly favouring students from 'pure' Jordanian backgrounds. Fairuz, a Jordanian-Egyptian architect and designer, described her experience:

The professor comes, I am in the front row with three friends and he asks the first one, 'what's your name?', 'my name is so and so,' and he says, 'oh from Karak, our relatives, 'ahla wa sahla (welcome)'. The second girl, she is Circassian, 'ahla wa sahla', then the third, Palestinian, 'mmm' he's not so pleased [laughs], then it's my turn...'I'm Egyptian.' 'Shou (what)?' and the whole lecture hall is laughing at his reaction.

The educator imposes a Jordanian nativist attitude (Massad, 2001), opposed to non-native others (despite being Jordanian citizens), and reminding them of their 'inferior' status, thereby establishing her/his authority as not only a teacher but as a native Jordanian. It closes off the discussion before it begins, and alienated students realise that their result in the class is dependent on an educator who has already established a dislike for non-native others. Intimidation and fear imposed by educators is simply the reverse: the teacher is disciplined by the institution, the state and society, and in turn disciplines the students. It leads to people becoming part of a system of inaction, creating a culture that consumes as opposed to producing design. A traditional education with a passive and top-down curriculum evokes negative emotions within students:

Until students experience lively participation, mutual authority, and meaningful work, they will display depressed skills and knowledge, as well as negative emotions. Teachers will be measuring and reacting to an artificially low picture of student abilities (Shor, 1992, p. 21).

The role of the educator is critical, as educators help students understand who they are and make sense of the world around them. Educators that reinforce the neopatriarchal structure in the classroom – acting out the oppressive figure at the centre and considered the authority – 'arouses in many students a variety of negative emotions: self-doubt, hostility, resentment, boredom, indignation, cynicism, disrespect, frustration, the desire to escape' (Shor, 1992, p. 23). This produces negative consequences by interfering with learning and leading to alienation, particularly from civil life (Shor, 1992). Ignoring the students' language, themes, culture and conditions enforces a resistance to learning from the educator. Designer Noor describes outdated attitudes and teaching methods:

When a new professor comes in...he's teaching old stuff[...], the gap between professors and students is very wide. I'm talking about the older ones.

A lot of them they are not ready to learn new things. And if he does, it's the same as teaching a small child[...] He's not professional about it.

Students Ruba and Fareeda were vocal about educators being unqualified and outdated:

Fareeda: we have a lot of professors that don't know what they are doing. [laughs]

Ruba: [laughs] I was just about to say that!

Architect/designer Maya describes them as:

Old School. Stuck in the 1970s. Mostly men[...] Even the way they look at architecture as an aesthetic.

Designer Basem blamed the poor quality of graduates on educators with outdated attitudes towards design, who romanticise the field, reduce it to magazines and posters rather than a strategy and way of thinking, who teach irrelevant content removed from the realities of industry and do not allow students to engage with contemporary issues. 'It's really nice to study about the political Russian poster that happened 200 years ago [...] No one is going to tell me "design a poster inspired by communism,"' he tells me.

The gap lies in viewing design as a form of art rather than functionally, focused on aesthetics instead of the message. Basem described how understanding who he was designing for – where design work needs to speak to a wide-ranging audience rather than self-expression – was one of the hardest learning curves he faced when he began working. Only then, he admitted, did he begin to understand what he learned in university, how design worked beyond aesthetics.

More than oil and gas in value: brain drain

The Arab world is well-known for its thriving culture of academic oppression. Institutions of higher learning became sites of control and policing by Arab governments when 'the potential of the Arab academe engage[d] the interest of opposition parties in establishing constituencies on campuses' (Romani, 2009, p. 3). Academic affairs are severely strained where the government exercises control on campuses over faculty, students and curricula, and through the intimidating presence of the *mukhabarat* (secret service), which, alongside the administration, interferes in everything from scholarly exchanges, to research topics, curricula, travel and employment (Herrera and Torres, 2006; Romani, 2009).

Repression faced by academics and students affects teaching, research and university life. It contributes to the practice of self-censorship, which can be as damaging to academic freedom as direct repression (Docherty, 2005). This leads to brain drain, and 'human capital is among the region's major exports, possibly equal to oil and gas in value' (Hanafi and Arvanitis, 2016, p. 152). Indeed, designer Karma tells me 'we have one issue with all citizens, everyone is killing themselves to leave the country. The new Arabic behaviour let's call it.' The situation is even more dire in Lebanon. Since the economic collapse in 2019, whoever can leave the country has taken the opportunity to do so. Paul, a designer in Beirut, explains:

A lot of professors are leaving, they're taking a year of unpaid leave... doing fellowships abroad to get some money in. They're doing consultancies on the side, and some of the universities accept it, because if they don't do those things, they're gonna leave... academia would be completely empty.

There are several factors behind the brain drain of highly skilled academics: the lack of academic freedom, under-funding for research, conflicts and terms of employment. Regional conflicts drain material and human resources, interfere in the production of research and lead to further repression on campuses. Terms of employment leave professors employed by institutions with little autonomy as the state has total jurisdiction over academic and administrative affairs (Mazawi, 2005). It is difficult to see how reforms alone can address governmental involvement and control imposed on higher education.

Research, an essential aspect of any society, remains a marginal activity regionally. Most Arab universities do not have research budgets and rely on external funding from foreign sources, which are accompanied by conditions. In addition, research centres and private enterprises conduct little research, and the research environment discourages creativity and criticality. Moreover, research is rarely connected to local social and political issues, nor have universities developed spaces for communities of research (journals, meetings, collaborations, training institutions) (Hanafi and Arvanitis, 2016). Bureaucracy and poor governance prevent highly ranked academics from producing work, forcing them to migrate to other countries[19] to seek better salaries, working conditions and tools for research (Altbach, 2006). Furthermore, universities do not explicitly state research in their agenda; the promotion system is not made clear to academics; and there is a rarity of local journals published in Arabic, which are valuable in promoting an image of the discipline in society

---

19 The Arab region has one of the highest rates of emigration amongst skilled academics and researchers in the world. Estimates are around 10–15 per cent for Arab youth and 9 per cent for graduates from higher education – double the global rate (United Nations Development Programme and Mohammed bin Rashid Al Maktoum Foundation, 2014). Hanafi and Arvanitis (2016, pp. 151–152) state the following statistics: '45 percent of Arab students who study abroad do not return to their home countries...and the Arab region has contributed 31 percent of the skilled migration...to the West.[...] Over 200,000 PhD holders (80 percent of all Arab doctorate holders), unable to connect with the local economy, emigrate.'

and provide researchers with a venue for diffusion of activity (Hanafi and Arvanitis, 2016). This issue is heightened for disciplines like design which are handed the same criteria as other disciplines.

Migration is draining the Arab region of its talent, but people who choose to stay and build their life at home are often mocked for attempting to improve things and this is discouraging, Karma says. She explains how 'it affects people's connections to their culture, their country, this affects progress from every area, not just design.' Designers Rami and Laith and educator Raja all shared her sentiments. They described Jordan as a culture of maintaining the status quo; a country that provides nothing to its citizens and, consequently, people seek a better life elsewhere and do not bother investing any effort in the country. This statement is reflective of most Arab countries, although many now attempt to make careers in the GCC countries – high-income countries with more work opportunities – despite never being able to acquire citizenship (because expatriates outnumber locals and the GCC countries focus on their own citizens).

Contributing factors are the narrow outlook of design with a small and limiting design industry, and the low value attributed to design and design education. The situation is even acknowledged by higher ups in the Jordanian government. Raja recounted a story of a Jordanian dignitary whose son studied in the UK:

He went to the ceremony...and he invited people for the graduation dinner[...] he had two other [Jordanian] friends[...] The head of the department was asking the other Jordanians 'are you going back to Jordan after this?' they said, 'no we are staying here.' So the head of the department was asking [the dignitary], 'what do you think of this? Jordanian students got a very good degree here and are refusing to go back, what is your take on brain drain in Jordan?' The dignitary says, 'brain drain is better than brains in the drain.' This is a dignitary and he is thinking this way. He thinks of his own country as being the drain!

Arab governments themselves promote migration to varying degrees, '[b]ecause politicians and policymakers see brain drain as exporting those most likely to challenge autocratic rule' and overseas remittance keeps local economies afloat (Waterbury, 2020, p. 21).

The situation is desperate and demonstrates how those in power are aware of it yet provide no solutions to it. Educator Khaled believes this is what happens when design graduates cannot find an environment suitable for their creative output, leading them to migrate. For example, the 2008 financial crash deeply impacted the Jordan economy due to its reliance on foreign funds and remittances from the Gulf countries. Designers Maya and Fairuz claimed that most of their contemporaries left the country to find work elsewhere during that time, whereas cultural organiser Sama described how difficult it was to hire people on a short deadline for ADW, because qualified people find jobs abroad due to the lack of opportunities. Even if universities reformed curriculum, 'who would be there to implement the changes?', she asks.

Indeed, the structure of design programmes themselves encourages students to migrate as the values and aims of programmes are unclear to students. Designer and educator Maha believes this leaves students unaware of the opportunities available to them and where they can carve their place in less traditional sectors that need design and designers. In my conversations with students, they spoke of graduating and leaving the country. Jordanian design students admitted choosing the German Jordanian University for the opportunity to spend a year abroad, opening doors for them in the future, and female students expressed concern around society accepting their work. For instance, Ruba's interests lean towards car design, but she found no respect when discussing her ideas nor opportunities for work. Ruba believes leaving is her only option to pursue a career. Society is a barrier for women, particularly with low rates of female employment in many Arab countries, but being a designer in a society that does not understand the role of a designer is an issue that affects both men and women.

The low value placed on design and design education from ministries of education in Jordan, Egypt and Lebanon is a hinderance to the progress of the discipline. The UAE is the only government that has capitalised on new opportunities brought forth by design. The designers, educators and students I spoke with all believe that if the public begins to understand design the ministries will follow. There are designers attempting to fight this defeatist environment, however. Designers Rami, Laith, Athar and Adam all launched their own studios to offer something new and innovative in a country that desperately needs it. They yearn to produce design work as they see it and change client–designer relations in Jordan. Similar opportunities are being created by designers in Cairo, a market largely dominated by advertising agencies.

Combatting high levels of brain drain is not easy, particularly addressing bureaucratic measures and government interference in universities, but opportunities through investment in digital and green economies, and introducing new areas of design that match local need, are one direction.

Challenging the culture of conformity

What happens when design graduates cannot find an environment suitable for their creative output? A neopatriarchal society is one that celebrates conformity and discourages people that deviate from the norm. Despite the heterogeneous make-up of its population, participants described Jordanian culture as 'conformist'. Cultural organiser Sama explained that 'because we have a culture that dictates a norm, and we don't have a lot of people who move away from that... people try to conform.'

Jordanian culture, and Arab culture more generally, does not encourage non-conformity. In fact, some people embrace conformity and are proud of it. Designer Mona believes conformity is due to the influx of foreigners who came to Jordan while its culture was developing:

Everyone came in from different backgrounds and ideologies and imposed their cultures into a country that...was still very young. The culture now that you get is so schizo[phrenic], I feel like I have culture shock in my own country. I'm from here I never left!

To counter this conforming culture, experimentation becomes a necessary practice. However, designers and educators alike are aware of the challenges to experimentation due to a discouraging culture of conformity and respect for elders, which they describe as the 'I know better' attitude. Raja attributes this to limited knowledge and cultural production in the Arab region:

We live in a culture that lacks creativity [...] we don't only lack it but the power to produce[...]Arabs in general are extinct. [...] extinct in terms of a culture that lacks creativity, the energy to produce and have an impact on the world around it. This is a big issue when it comes to design [...] [b]ecause we define design as an act of applying methodologies and approaches to solving a broader set of issues and problems in business and society. So, we can't really separate design from society and business, we don't have so much business because the business we have [...] is borrowed business.

His argument relates to what Syrian poet Adonis says about the Arabs being extinct:

If I look at the Arabs, with all their resources and great capacities, and I compare what they have achieved over the past century with what others have achieved [...] I would have to say that we Arabs are in a phase of extinction, in the sense that we have no creative presence in the world [...] a people becomes extinct when it no longer has a creative capacity, and the capacity to change its world (Adonis, cited in Elsheshtawy, 2008, p. 1).

How can change be instigated through design? Raja believes it is about beginning to criticise ourselves rather than blaming others, something he tries to bring to his teaching. But he acknowledges that one's desire for change weakens and 'you become a part of it [the system], conforming to it, or you leave', which he admitted he might do very soon. Design student Ruba also acknowledged this when she tells me 'We need to step down from the pedestal that everyone is... a director, a minister, a King! We need to move away from this.' She blamed this attitude on a population that does not read. If we are to educate the population about the importance of design, then reading is one way to start, she says. Although Ruba is enthusiastic, she is overcome by a defeatist attitude because she does not think society will change. 'Arabs don't read' can be interpreted as sweeping statement, but figures for book publishing and translations are low in relation to the overall population.[20] Despite high literacy rates in Jordan, the UAE and Lebanon, they are low in Egypt and regionally overall where ongoing conflicts and deteriorating safety contribute to low levels of literacy.

The way a culture is affects pedagogy and curriculum. Designer Maya tells me about her experience at university during the screening of a documentary. In the first scene, the camera moves through the hallways and spaces of a spa, then cuts to people's legs moving in the water. She recalls what happened next:

So a bunch of students stood up and they said 'this...is haram [forbidden]' and the professor was like 'I didn't know!' and they stopped the screening. To me, this sums up [my university]! [...] Is this [really] happening?

Mona, who runs a website connecting designers regionally, tells me that religion is 'the most powerful tool I've ever seen in my life.' She believes that religion and cultural conservatism interfere in design and she often must censor herself in the content she posts on her website due to the backlash she receives. Rami referred to the creative limitations that discourage experimentation imposed on designers by clients, leading to 'very literal and boring ideas.' Laith stated that self-censorship is remarkably strong in Amman where people impose the red tape themselves through 'self-policing'.

---

20 The Arab region has a population of 430 million and there are over 370 million Arabic speakers globally. Figures for book publishing and translation are not reliable, however, based on data, they place the Arab region in line with Romania, a country of 20 million.

With the exception of Mona, who pushed a more business-oriented approach to design (designer as service provider) without the embellishment of a philosophy, many of the designers I interviewed championed a more experimental approach as a necessary outlet in an otherwise stifling environment.

Chains of bureaucracy

Thus bureaucracy – in government, the military, education, business – projects a modernized exterior, but internally its structure is essentially patriarchal, animated by an elaborate system of personal relations, kinship, and patronage. These are all neopatriarchal institutions (Sharabi, 1988, p. 131).

In the Arab region, bureaucracy is represented by an over centralisation of public authority due to dominant and overreaching governments. The bureaucratic system is represented by a hierarchical command-and-control approach, characterised by corruption, nepotism, cronyism and incompetence, whose decisions do not reflect the needs, demands or preferences of its citizens (Jreisat, 2009). Bureaucracy affects teaching and learning and the curriculum. An obsession with red tape creates hurdles for educators through admission requirements, accreditation, the recruitment process and classroom content. This section explores the overreaching ways of over-compliant administrators on university design programmes.

Box-ticking exercises

Why is Jordanian design curricula outdated and disconnected from reality? Jordanian educators blamed the MoHESR and its focus on box ticking over curriculum development. Curricula is not only copy-pasted from Western institutions, but the MoHESR does not perform a quality check on curricula, educator Raja told me. He believes that these design programmes fail to speak to Jordan or its people. In her research for ADW, Sama found that some institutions change their curriculum once every ten years and do so only because of accreditation requirements. Referencing their own education, designers Maya and Fairuz described the syllabus as 'stagnant' and unchanged for 30 years: 'even the books assigned are the same'.

A lack of updates is reflected in dated subject titles, and terms used to describe courses do not appear to consider advancements in design or technology. For example, titles like 'Web Browser: Structured programming and scripting', 'Web Design Development', 'DVD

Authoring', 'Multimedia Software' and 'Computer Visualisations', 'Green Building Trends and Technology' and 'Web Page Design'. 'Green' for example, has been criticised in design for being a commercial fad in the 1980s. 'Web Page' focuses on a single page rather than a website that considers user experience, and 'Web Browser' refers to web browsers like Firefox and Chrome. Nowadays, 'Interface Design' or 'User Experience Design' would likely refer to 'Introduction to Computer Graphics', 'Web Page Design' and 'Web Browser'. Because design is treated similarly to any other discipline (a shared sentiment from educators across Jordan, the UAE, Lebanon and Egypt), this imposes irrelevant criteria onto faculty, curricula and students. Even community workshops cannot be conducted without piles of paperwork that complicate external projects and students and educators often miss out, working on projects awaiting approvals. Educator Khaled claimed that a reason why curricula and study plans are out of date is due to the person teaching approaching curriculum design as a 'one man show' that fails to consider dialogue in planning.

The 'outdated' descriptor can be attributed to curriculum being largely copy-pasted from Western institutions. Institutions adopt everything but the underlying philosophy of the design programme they copy. Participants discussed the notion of copying and pasting ideas within Jordan's wider design culture, where everything from interventions to campaigns to ADW are copy-pasted ideas. They described them as disconnected from the local environment. Cultural organisers Zein and Eman referred to the curriculum as something that is not serious, mediocre and trapped in time, and thus education fails to implement practices relevant to Jordan. Khaled explained how curricula in Jordan and regionally are:

Copy and paste from other universities. [...] Even those American universities or European ones who come to teach design in Arab areas, they implement their own but it doesn't work with the local market.

The copy-paste syndrome is evident in this statement from student Ruba, where she discussed the offering of a major without an actual market in Jordan:

You'll graduate and your degree will say BA Design and Visual Communication slash the major that you took. [...] I was convinced I would be an industrial designer [...] the Ministry doesn't have something called Industrial Design, [because] there isn't enough [Professors] to put weight on this certificate, so they put an X on it. This gave me an issue in the Masters in Germany and Italy [for Car Design], England was the only one who accepted because it's within the arts faculty.

Additionally, the major not only suffers from non-recognition from the MoHESR, there is a shortage of qualified faculty to teach these specialisations. A similar situation was described by Anas in Egypt:

The classification is within the university roles if you want to have a degree in graphic design, and so on. But we try to avoid [...] the classification as much as we can. Because also when they graduate, we don't want them to be bounded to the classification.

The exception are universities with foreign accreditation, such as NASAD, who must abide by periodic review processes to maintain the accreditation. Educators become confined to ministries and their inability to review changes to reflect contemporary changes. While calling out the box ticking, they find ways to meet the criteria while evading them in other ways.

Faculty recruitment

When it comes to teaching, practice and research the requirements lead to precarious working conditions for educators. Educators struggle with low salaries and a full five-day work week, which makes running a design studio or practicing design challenging. The situation is even more difficult for educators[21] teaching at universities outside of Amman, where 90 per cent of studios are based (Abu Awad, 2012). Some educators admitted working two jobs because the salary was not enough.

There is a demand from both educators and students for faculty to be practicing designers, however, hiring practices are also confronted with bureaucratic measures. Hiring part-time faculty is difficult (at American universities, the hiring of part-time faculty is more common and easier), packed teaching loads and administrative duties leave little time for practice, and faculty encounter resistance if they manage a studio while teaching from powerful unions such as the Jordan Engineers Association (JEA).

Although encouraged to practice design, educators Karma and Raja described how finding the time is difficult, and they both expressed the necessity for part-time practice as it prevents a disconnect between industry and education and allows them to stay up to date. Khaled describes the recruitment process as unnecessarily complex:

Accreditation laws prevent universities from hiring anyone without a Masters and this causes educators [to] flock to Europe to obtain a Masters or PhDs because they think this is a passport to be an educator.

In addition, the MoHESR rules for accrediting new programmes are detrimental to design's development. To accredit a new programme, universities must have four PhD and four Masters degree holders, a challenge within design, and this demonstrates the failure of the MoHESR to understand what requirements design actual needs. On top of the educational requirements, some institutions require that half of the faculty be Jordanian citizens, limiting external recruitment. At the same time, foreign institutions based in the region prioritise recruitment of international faculty over local and regional staff. In Jordan, students are recruited as teaching assistants, a source of cheap labour, without any support for development. They cannot move up the ranks without obtaining further education and publishing.

Khaled, who at the time of our interview was the Dean of the College,[22] advocated for changes but was unsuccessful. He was critical about the processes imposed on design departments, because it recruited 'unqualified candidates who are not able to improve themselves... [Students want] a tutor who is capable of teaching [them]'. During his tenure as Dean, he attempted to use his position to attract better candidates. He sent promising students on scholarships to Europe to feed the institutions with new ideas, knowledge and thinking. However, his statement demonstrates an inferiority complex, equating sending people to study abroad with the intent of acquiring a more open mind. The statement views the Arab world as inferior, as Khaled told me he refuses to send students on scholarships to Arab countries. However, the dearth of graduate studies in design regionally means that most faculty have completed at least one of their degrees abroad. Without universities supporting both scholars and designers in pedagogical development and research, the bureaucratic measures imposed by educational ministries will cause further brain drain.

Faculty promotion

Promotion is another area hit by bureaucratic measures. The process is more straightforward for educators working in American universities since it follows a similar system, but those who work in state and private universities in Jordan – where educators possess only an MA or MFA degree, and to some extent a PhD – do so in precarious conditions. Although acquiring a PhD or publishing makes educators eligible for a promotion, based on MoHESR laws design practice and what it produces (such as exhibitions) is not considered research, and

---

21 Private foreign institutions offer better pay, but there is a hierarchy in pay scales between locals and holders of non-Arab passports.
22 Khaled sadly passed away in 2021.

the requirements imposed on design means moving up the ranks is difficult. Educator Aws recounted a story:

There are often honorary ceremonies at our university, and we are probably the only department...whose name never comes out...there is a professor who has had his PhD since 1974. He is still in the same role, Associate Professor. Staff are not advancing because of standards that the university have set. He is asking to be raised to a Professorial role based on exhibitions...

The story illustrates how the outdated rules and uniform criteria applied to design hinder research and progression of the field. Moreover, staff are burnt out from administrative duties and teaching, leaving little time for research and publishing.

Relating education to practice through sharing one's experience is something designers and students feel is beneficial to their education. Designer Basem describes his experience as a university student, when he benefitted from faculty running their own studios:

We had a professor who [...] had a studio, he would tell us about the experience. [...] He [is] not the most exposed but at least he wants to give you everything he has. 'Come use my studio, let me show you magazines.' I feel that we have to as [design] studios, do this.

Basem believes educators should be practitioners and that studios and agencies should become informal spaces of learning.

A recurring discussion was how many educators lacked a design background. While things are now changing, many design educators come from fine art and architecture backgrounds. Educators, designers and students all described them as excellent in technique, but lack the designerly mindset, treating design as artistic, concerned with feelings and aesthetics over function, and disconnected from practice. Designer Paul believes this leads to a distorted view of design. He draws on the high design and design art market in Lebanon – largely lead by architects turned designers – who use materials without considering function, only aesthetic form.

In Jordan, as in much of the Arab region, design is either in the faculty of fine arts, faculty of art and design, or the faculty of architecture and engineering, and this presents three challenges discussed by educators:

1. people perceive designers and artists as the same thing;
2. designers are trained at a university with an artist or architect mindset;
3. the lack of respect from architects towards designers and design.

Unlike major professions such as law, architecture or medicine, design's status as a minor profession means it does not have national or industry standards. It exhibits diverse curricula, is not professionally regulated, does not require a licence to practice and design associations focus on promoting design rather than best practices (Heskett, 2002; Julier, 2014). The negative effect of this is that it makes design prone to entryism, increased by the limited value attributed to it. There is a strong desire from participants to see more educators with design backgrounds, who understand what design is, attribute a value to it and instil a passion for design in students.

A middle-class area of studies

Society pays for education but, despite its supposed egalitarian origins, higher education reinforces class privilege and has a bias towards middle- and upper-income students. Public universities attract different demographics than private ones,[23] and have a mixture of students from across the country and region wide. Private universities attract middle to upper-class students due to cost, and foreign/satellite universities are even costlier. If families can afford it, they 'invest more heavily in private lessons, send their children to the best high schools, and frequently send them abroad for university education' (Waterbury, 2020, p. 25). The case is even more pronounced in Lebanon where its citizens make high personal investments in private education (at all levels) with the hopes of better career opportunities elsewhere (Waterbury, 2020). The heterogeneous make-up of universities regionally leads to different class make-up based on university types. However, similar to designers and design students worldwide, designers are often from middle or upper middle-class backgrounds. Karma explains:

One problem with the German Jordanian University is most of the students come from similar classes, unlike the University of Jordan [where] [w]e had people from all around Jordan, all around the world [...] We were exposed to all kinds of people before we went to the market. As for here, I have students who are best friends from school, they enrol in our programme, they graduate together and are still friends.

Student life in the Arab region is not the same as the typical experience portrayed in the Global North. Societal expectations, cultural norms and the importance of family, tradition, generosity and religion dictate students live at home during their studies or study close to home. Many continue to live at home upon graduation. Where parents

---

23 In the UAE, the student demographic in public universities is primarily composed of Emirati nationals.

want quality education but keep their children nearby, the American universities in Beirut, Cairo and Sharjah are a good compromise. Educator Anas explains:

If you count on the Arab culture of having the kids nearby, not send them to Europe or to the US and then having them closer, but they get quality of education, American degree [...] then it's a good formula. However, the type of students you get is of course the one that can afford it.

Maher, an educator based in Dubai, stressed that the general maturity level of the students is low, which interferes with the independent learning he pushes in his teaching:

When you're treating people as professionals, it might work in a European context, but it does have its downsides in the region because [...] the students here are not as mature. [...] They are not autonomous psychologically; they are much more fragile. They need a lot of pampering and handholding and also a lot of reassurance 'oh you did this well, well done. It's a great job' you know. And all of this is coming from the culture in which they are brought up.

When I asked if this was a cultural or class issue, he replied it was mostly cultural. Dubai-based educator Masa describes how this immaturity manifests in a culture of exaggerated celebration and reassurance at the expense of meaningful engagement with the feedback provided. Living at home has its positives and negatives: there is an immaturity described by educators that is inherent in the culture, and for some students limited responsibilities enables a sense of security when studying.[24]

With great wealth comes great responsibility?

The educators I interviewed teaching at American universities admitted their students were financially comfortable. Lack of scholarships skews towards students whose parents can afford the price tag of over £20,000 a year. Recruitment is almost exclusively made up of students who completed private high school education. Anas places the percentage of students from *thanawiyyah ammah* (Egyptian state education) at 2 per cent but describes their GPA as extremely high. He is currently working on increasing the number of scholarships to *thanawiyyah ammah graduates* from across the country, not an easy endeavour because, as his colleague Jeeda explains, 'graphic design is not that popular when it comes to scholarship students, they prefer to study law or economics or engineering'. Those that do pursue design are 'hungry for knowledge...

---

24 The maturity factor is also influenced by the state of 'waithood' due to the youth bulge over the last three decades, and high rates of unemployment leading to wasted youthful energy and potential. The delayed transition affects other pathways to adulthood including marriage, homeownership and civic participation. See Mulderig (2013) and Kabbani (2019).

they just want to just take [anything] and absorb it and use it,' Cairo-based educator Salim tells me. Wealthier students are not panicked about their prospects post-graduation because most of them have secured employment at their father's company, a comment shared by educators across all cities. The silver lining to this is the power and access these students possess to enact change, as explained by Jeeda:

I had [an] average student [...] She found me to tell me [about] her new job [as] the exhibition director of COP27 [...] she's very rich. She's very connected. Her father is the contractor of COP27. She's a sweetheart [...] She was calling me [for advice]. [...] They are [...] so connected to power [...] they can make a change. [...] What do I need to teach the students so they can make a change? I don't care if they're good designers or not. But it made me question my position in this equation. [...] I can use my classroom to put new ideas in those kids' heads, and maybe in a few years [...] they realise something and they can make a change. This is what we need to focus on... she can hire the right people. She can open the important questions on the table and discuss it.

The downside of wealthier students is how seriously the subject is taken and using connections to get ahead. Paul explains the interference of 'connected' students:

In Lebanon, there's a whole 'if I fail this course, my dad will call the Dean and make a small donation. And then I kind of passed the course.' This has happened with me twice. We failed a student for the entire year because they were not good at all. [...] And then we get a call from the Dean...

Masa tells me about the differences between her experience teaching at an American university in Jordan and a national university in Dubai:

My first teaching experience I would write these poetic and amazing briefs, and [the Dean and the Chair] were like 'y6ala3u 3alai shu 3am bte3meli' [what are you doing?], why are you doing this excessive way of working [...] just give them [any] project. [T]he dynamics are very different 'l2ni' [because] it's vocational [...] purely designed for its aesthetics, no purpose whatsoever. Whereas in Zayed University [...] it's different because they're going to work for [...] a very progressive government. So they kind of want to make that change [...] create changes [...] they're not afraid of experimenting, which I love. And you walk into our senior shows and you find they don't have an end result. I love that, because it's more of the experience and the journey of finding yourself and self-reflection, rather than having that end result.

At the beginning, national universities in the Arab region

guaranteed employment in the public service, so much in fact they were referred to as factories for civil servants. This is no longer the case except in the UAE and most GCC countries. The desire to change one's environment motivates Emiratis to experiment in their programmes because the government moves more quickly and is more progressive, unlike the unproductive bureaucrats in surrounding countries.

'Design is easy'

As favouritism and prestige skews towards science, technology, engineering and mathematics (STEM) subjects, design's value on the academic hierarchy ladder is low. It is offered as a study option mostly at private universities, attracting lower-performing students whose grades did not support their entry into public institutions. In student focus groups, students described many of their peers possessing no knowledge or passion for design, with a reputation as an 'easy' subject, where many entered based on low grades or *wasta*,[25] and wanted to obtain the degree with no intention of working in design. Students Rashad and Jenna stated that most of their peers were clueless and only attend university to increase their social rank; only half the class engage with the content, display curiosity and take the subject seriously, while others are just waiting for it to be over. Similarly, designers Lara and Abla describe their former peers as indifferent about design and say that they chose it because they thought it was interesting and required minimal studying. They reported how students would sit in class, bored and disconnected from the content, putting nail polish on each other. There are stark differences between students who enter design by choice and those who enrol only to obtain a degree. People perceive design as an easy major, without much studying or traditional exams. However, design has a demanding workload and dropout rates are high as students progress throughout the degree. Designer Athar recounted how the difficulties he encountered in his first year studying design in Beirut made him appreciate it:

The whole four years are demanding, but you grow into it...and you start to dedicate your whole life towards design. [...] [F]or a student coming from school, I used to cry in the dorms working on a colour project [...] but it made me appreciate design as a discipline. I came back to Jordan during Christmas break, she [professor] has this ritual, she gets underperforming students [...] and said I think you need to reconsider [...] design school [...] you're not gonna pass my class. I graduated top of my class [...] so she had

---

25 *Wasta* is not easily defined with one term, but it refers to nepotism, connections, mediation and favouritism.

an impact on me. She was basically saying take it seriously or leave. Design is not a piece of cake.

Although students began appreciating design while studying it, students described feeling lost upon graduating. Fareeda explained:

You come and go and still have no idea what you're doing or what you're going to do. So students don't know what they are doing, their parents can't understand, so everyone has no idea what they are doing.

She felt that students should be more educated about their discipline and future careers to help explain their studies to peers and parents. Although this is a short-term solution, the main issue is admission requirements, which in most universities do not require portfolios or interviews before acceptance.

The diploma disease

Some students are forced to attend university by their parents, and design is one option for students who are not interested in 'studying' in the traditional sense. Educators described this as the 'diploma disease'. Educator Khaled believes the diploma disease is a social class issue. Students, who are mostly from middle- to upper-middle-class backgrounds, see obtaining a degree in fine arts or design as a luxury that increases their social rank, he tells me. Many of his students do not necessarily pursue careers in design after graduating. The diploma disease could be a factor in the low number of women in the workforce, particularly as design programmes have a higher percentage of women than men.

In Beirut, university expansion plans coupled with a dire financial situation has led to a lowering of standards. Designer Paul explains:

We were accepting a lot of students who were not good from the get-go. Like, really bad portfolios, but [...] the university needed the money, because they were building new buildings...

Educators Baha and Rita describe similar situations at American universities where they are increasing student numbers and lowering admissions standards to attract students who can pay the hefty price tag. Overwhelmingly, designers, students and educators championed portfolios and an interview that asks prospective students about their experience and ambitions, and why they want to study design, which could help educators identify areas of focus for specific students.

Admission requirements, choice and values

Why do people choose to study design? Admission requirements are a controversial topic, and the overall feeling shared was how the privatisation of education has contributed to diminishing standards. The increase in tuition fees and profit-oriented focus has declined admission standards, recruiting students who are not serious about design and preventing certain sectors of society from accessing education. Without change, people will not appreciate or value design and will continue to see it as a discipline that intakes failures.

Imposed criterion from educational ministries do not consider design's needs. For Jordanian universities, students who attended public schools must complete *tawjihi* and *thanawiyyah ammah* in Egypt – a traditional exam based on rote learning and memorisation that requires students to possess knowledge in the courses undertaken in their secondary schooling (Badran, 2014). The exam splits students into tracks, and their grades dictate their applications.

These admissions procedures are centralised and regulated, and students are distributed in programmes based almost exclusively on this score. Centralising the process may seem to provide equal opportunities to all with its non-discriminatory and uniform criteria, but this is hardly the case. Centralising admissions with the *tawjihi* score as the major criterion usually leads to inequitable distribution, as all students are subject to unified criteria (Lamine, 2010). The higher your grades, the more prestigious programmes you can enter, and design is low on the scale.

In addition to the grades barrier, there is exclusion to students from certain sectors of society based on their cultural capital. The designer Laith tells me about his interview at Yarmouk University in Jordan, where they asked him if he went to museums or knew of any. When he replied, no, they rejected his application. He describes feeling 'uncultured' at that moment. The interviewer assessed Laith's cultural capital and denied him entry because he did not possess enough of it. He must acquire the right culture to be legitimate. When students' culture is valueless, it can be alienating. What is the 'correct' way to behave in design? Further fuelling this is the limited exposure to forms of art and design education in elementary and secondary schooling, mostly in public schools. Some universities have a drawing entrance exam, which can act as a form of exclusion to students from certain sectors of society. Maria, a student, discusses her experience with the exam:

> *The entrance exam [...] was around a box and make it into perspective, but students did not know because schools don't teach this. [...] I did not know what perspective was. The exam was hard because I was unaware. [...] We don't do portfolios because students do not understand what this is, as the people conducting the exam told me.*

The story illustrates that students are unaware of basic art and design terminology, depending on their high school education. American universities normally take large cohorts into foundation, and require a portfolio when students declare a major in the sophomore year. Rita, an educator in Beirut, explains how she worked on establishing a foundation year to prevent exclusion of students without access to art and design in high school:

> *It's unfair to ask for a portfolio when you have some students who went to schools where design and art is offered and others where it's not. [...] [T]he way we resolved this issue was to establish the foundation year, so students get into the university, they take a foundation year, [...] to build a portfolio, present a portfolio and then upon their portfolio, we accept them or not.*

Unclear values and aims of design programmes, alongside poorly designed websites, lack of information in high school and programme names lost in translation when translated to Arabic lead to a lack of understanding of what students go on to study. Student Leila blames university websites containing little information regarding majors for the confusion. The only way to acquire information is in person by asking either the faculty or current students, she says. Leila felt it is the responsibility of both the university and schools to inform students on their options, a point emphasised by other educators, designers and students.

Knowledge of what design is before choosing a university major can be beneficial to students who might be interested in design but do not necessarily understand what it is. As Ruba explained, she always had a passion for problem-solving and making, and design was exactly what she was looking for, but she was unfamiliar with the term, and her interest in technology and cars was interpreted as mechanics and engineering because that is what people knew. When I asked educators Khaled, Aws and Nadine why students chose design, they stated four main reasons: design entails a good salaried job and social rank; rejection from other disciplines; perceiving design as 'easy'; and students need a degree 'to hang it'.

The student Fareeda obtained a high tawjihi score, placing her in the faculty of pharmacy. Her sister was studying graphic design and she became intrigued with the work and the process. After auditing some classes, she changed her major to design. There is an absence of choice for students – exam scores and familial pressure dictate the routes for most, particularly those studying at public universities.

Abolish grades, embrace failure

Most Arab universities base entry to university programmes on grades. Exams like *tawjihi* and *thanawiyyah ammah* put incredible pressure on students, where their fate in higher education is based on their performance on one test. This obsession over grades drags into their approach to classes. In Jordan, the MoHESR prioritises grades over portfolios in design, and this does not support student progression. Former educator Karma, who is now a full-time designer, outlines how this obsession is a problem for both community- and client-based projects. Students are engaged until they 'get their grades and they go', leaving projects incomplete. The challenge is for students to take the projects beyond the classroom, their peers and tutors. Karma cares about the students' experience working on projects more than the actual assessment, but how can students understand the value of something beyond their grades?

Architect and designer Camilia pointed to the problem of how educators and students focus on the results rather than the design process:

We were not taught how to get to the solution through process. Focusing on process can open up a discussion.

A grades-oriented approach is synonymous with the product/transmission curriculum model – where the product is the well-executed project – whereas a process model is critical and provides alternative and more relevant ways of assessing design work because it is focused on understanding the subject as opposed to grades. If students had less pressure to get good grades, they could see the value in their projects and continue working on them, Karma tells me. Similarly, designer and educator Maha pushes to foster a culture of failure, one that understands failure as a starting point rather than an end. For her, the idea of vulnerability is key: professors do not share vulnerability, they project an image of perfection, and this is a problem. How much you share determines the make-up of the class. But for designer and educator Raja, the teacher-as-prophet viewpoint breeds a culture of fear and is the reason why there is a fear of failure.

Resources

Arab universities lack resources (human and capital), and despite the high tuition fees students do not receive access to necessary resources such as studios, workshops and computer labs. Universities have limited access to computer labs and facilities for making that are relevant to specialisations. Poorly stocked libraries and limited access to printing and design software can be costly for students. Lack of facilities penalises the students most in need, and access to computer labs remains crucial for collaboration during school projects, particularly if teams are made up of men and women due to cultural norms (students cannot just get together at each other's homes).

Students argued that the lack of tools and labs required to complete design projects limits their work. For example, although there is a 3D printer at her university, Ruba told me students are not permitted to use it. In addition, clay modelling is a necessity in industrial design, yet this was not available. While completing her graduation project, Ruba made a car but had to experiment with different materials resulting from lack of access. Cultural organiser Sama argued that the lack of resources causes a gap in learning, as designers cannot make and do not understand materials:

How many of [these universities] have workshops and how many of them actually build models? It's shocking.

Driving experimentation requires the necessary labs, materials and technology and fewer restrictions for use, as well as access to workspaces. If universities do not provide resources, students are forced to seek alternative spaces at a huge cost to produce work. They also miss out on aspects of learning how to use the tools to create their work.

The absence of resources increases the division between designers, clients and craftspeople. Designers cannot find manufacturers for their prototypes, and few craftspeople are willing to experiment and manipulate materials due to the 'it does not work' mentality in the country, cultural organiser Sama argued. In Dubai, while resources exist to create prototypes, it is often too expensive for the manufacturer to devote time and labour to support it, designer Dalal tells me. She explained issues faced by designers:

Designers who were trying to manufacture prototypes in Dubai, you were dealing with the likes of 99 per cent of manufacturers who were doing the doors and windows for towers and developments. Stopping their factory for an hour to manufacture your prototype? It was worth thousands of dirhams. So they made life hell for young designers who were actually trying to create. And that's where the likes of Tashkeel are so vital because they would give you the space and time and the experts and the machines to make something. [...] [B]ut they didn't always have the person who could help you actually make it.

In her research for ADW, Sama found that product designers tend to outsource their production, which slows down their process. She cited this as one of the reasons the first edition of ADW (2016) chose to focus on digital fabrication and 3D printing.[26] Other options for students would be Design Institute Amman, which has a product design studio and a jewellery making studio, but courses cost upwards of 300JD, a price tag that is unaffordable for many. The Arab region represents a small percentage of the global 3D printing market and has some FabLabs, but outside of the UAE universities do not always have the necessary facilities for students. Furthermore, students and educators reported a lack studio spaces for students.[27] The absence of studio space and labs dismisses the formal and informal spaces of learning, crucial to contextually-based design education. Once the classes are over and the buildings close, students must go home. However, a university space, as Allaq (1997, p. 95) argues:

is the lecture halls, the corridors, the parks, the façades facing them, the restaurants, the clubs, the libraries, the reading-rooms, the laboratories, the playgrounds, the hostels, the smell of books, the intimate talks, the free interaction [...] the dialogue of minds [...] It is all these details that help students to mature mentally, psychologically, and physically and to grow into strong, effective citizens imbued with the spirit of initiative.

Early closure, in some cases as early as 4pm, and lack of spaces dismiss other parts of the university that contribute to learning and point to a traditional outlook towards spaces of learning. No studio spaces mean students are often scrambling to find places around the university to complete work. To work after hours, students described how they must apply for permission, faced with piles of paperwork and waiting for approvals to meet deadlines. Adam, a designer and educator, told me how he would see students 'working on projects in cafes wherever they can, and my heart just sank for them.'

---

26 Jordan initially banned individuals from owning 3D printers, see Al Nawas (2016).

27 This was not an issue for American universities in the Arab region.

Not only do opening times regulate the hours of learning, but students require staff supervision when using the spaces. The need for a staff member to be present puts the students' studying time under constant observation. Designer Athar describes the importance of the design studio in design education:

[It is] an enriching part of [a] design programme [...] if I want to be with other[s] [...] to bounce ideas off and brainstorm, work together so I don't feel alone and I need feedback, I would pull all-nighters with others and I had easy access but here they don't. At 6pm school is done you go home.

How can spaces of learning be fostered if students cannot find places or time to work once class is over? Additionally, students not only battle to find materials and places to work, but they struggle to find a crucial resource: books. My research revealed a consensus that books and magazines on design in both Arabic and English are lacking, causing issues for research, self-learning and class readings. Designers and students described the poor state of the libraries and how people only have the web as a resource.

Academic Jamil Jreisat claims that Arab bureaucracy has failed to harness 'the positive potential of the bureaucratic model as an instrument of managerial precision, promptness, and efficiency', but has 'experienced most of the unintended consequences and dysfunctions of the classic bureaucratic model' (2009, p. 592). In this chapter, we have seen how dysfunctional bureaucracy has negatively impacted design and design education – from admission to hiring to resources. The curriculum as product/transmission pushes rote learning and blind obedience to the detriment of critical thinking and independent learning. Yet, as the next chapter will show, the region's growing design culture may be one catalyst for change.

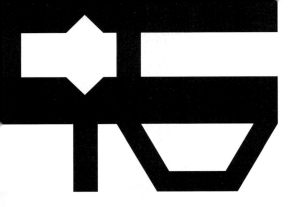

REGIONAL AND LOCAL

88 —Fetishized consciousness
88 —Design culture(s)
    89 –Global ambitions: the growing influence of GCC capital
    93 –Another side of the coin
95 —Elitism and design
96 —Meaningful engagement or parachuting in?
    97 –Design weeks
    99 –Community engagement
    104 –NGOisation and international expertise
109—Milieu
    113 –The city that always sleeps

DESIGN CULTURES

Chapter 3

Design culture(s) across the Arab region have witnessed monumental growth in the last 15 years, in parallel with the Middle Eastern and North African (MENA) art market, partly due to the establishment of the Art Dubai fair in 2007. An increase in university design programmes was accompanied by initiatives including design events such as design weeks, fairs, exhibitions, institutes offering workshops and short courses, new cultural spaces, independent design studios, a rise in local and regional brands and more attentiveness towards branding and the design of products and spaces. It is difficult to pinpoint one reason behind this growth, but we can identify a few reasons beyond the art market boom. Design became more accessible and affordable, aided by technological advancement, the accessibility to design software and online resources, and through brands like Apple and Target (Millman, 2013), meaning new generations of students are more aware about design. Another reason is the grassroots nature of its development in Amman, Beirut and Cairo, where a generation of designers who graduated during the 2008 financial crisis and impending recession found themselves without any prospects for employment and began organising events, competitions and talks around design and architecture. Governments and municipalities capitalised on the rise of initiatives, where design-led regeneration projects saw urban planning, design and visual communication used to encourage investment and the flow of human capital, injecting value into cities through the facilitation of improved infrastructure.

The growth, however, has been informed by a fixation on the outsider gaze, and many design initiatives are funded by foreign organisations wielding soft power. Moreover, the city plays an important role in the development of design culture(s), whether through design-led regeneration projects or through events that organise design interventions across different neighbourhoods of divided cities like Amman, Beirut, Dubai and Cairo. But how does this public engagement affect perceptions of a discipline considered trivial and elitist?

Fetishised consciousness

When full political independence was achieved [...] cultural decolonization did not accompany it. Indeed, with independence began an indirect [...] somewhat different but more pervasive-form of cultural colonization, whose hegemonic hold derived not from direct political or military control, but from the penetration of a new patriarchal elite by Western education, and from the domination of society by Western mass media and the values and wants of Western consumer society (Sharabi, 1988, pp. 80–81).

To understand the growth of design education and design culture(s) regionally, we must first define the matrix of measure and validation: the West. Co-existing with the neopatriarchal organisation of society is a fetishised consciousness, a fixation on the West where everything is translated and appropriated from Western models, leading to a consumerist society and contributing to the absence of knowledge creation (Sharabi, 1988). Fetishised consciousness exhibits imitation and passivity in ideas, actions, values or institutions, which are validated (or invalidated) by reference to a model instead of through criticism.

Everything is mimicked on Western models – from primary to higher education, to lifestyle, thought, literature and consumption. American influence was further imposed through soft power[28] by establishing educational and philanthropic foundations, which targeted technical training, academic research and extracurricular activities. The greater number of people educated in Europe and the USA post-independence facilitated and continues to facilitate the work by creating an English-speaking intelligentsia (Sharabi, 1988).

Design culture(s)

Activities such as national design policies, design education programmes, international exhibitions, establishment of museums, design societies and specialist and professional magazines make design part of the landscape by establishing its value, and are important factors in industrial competitiveness (Sparke, 2013). Moreover, the structures, design policies and activities implemented – ranging from taste education to promoting certain products through design institutes – varied between governments and were crucial in influencing the direction design takes in a particular location (Heskett, 2002; Gimeno-Martinez, 2016). While this occurred in Europe in the nineteenth and twentieth centuries, it did not occur in the Arab region.

---

28 The ability to get preferred outcomes through the co-optive means of agenda-setting, persuasion and attraction (Nye, 2004).

The state's relationship to design presents a series of paradoxes (Gimeno-Martinez, 2016). The first is how the instrumentalisation of design for different ends enables the state to take a position and participate in the design discussion. The policies it enacts (or what is approved) influence the promotion of design and give meaning to the materiality it supports; design weeks are one such example. Amman, Beirut, Dubai and recently Cairo host or have hosted design weeks prior to the COVID-19 pandemic, each at different scales, and each under some patronage from the Ministry of Culture. The second paradox is the national design discourse versus the country's actual material production (Gimeno-Martinez, 2016), for example crafts. Craft traditions were influential in linking design and national identity, particularly in the early twentieth century where European countries searching for their modern national identities through design tied their craft traditions to more contemporary preoccupations. Promotion organisations helped revive crafts, embedding these in design education.

Crafts caters to tourism, one of Jordan's biggest industries, where demand for souvenirs has stimulated traditional skills by local craftspeople (Abu Al Haija, 2011). Amman Design Week (ADW) launched in 2016, featured a crafts district that aimed to highlight the work of craftspeople and their inspiration on contemporary design practices (see Figure 3). However, this is an invented tradition; Jordan's craft traditions – aside from the Byzantine and Umayyad mosaics in Madaba – are more recent than historic in comparison to the neighbouring cities of Damascus, Aleppo or Cairo. Although the tourism industry has helped develop a higher standard of crafts, the focus on crafts is less about drawing attention to a neglected industry and more about constructing a national design identity and design-led regeneration; particularly when ADW's patronage comes from the state: it forms a Hashemite version of the narrative. Jordan's tourism strategy is the heritage Biblical type, and more recently there is a move towards pushing tourism to Amman by capitalising on design, while its focus on crafts continues to promote the country within the Western imaginary of an idealised 'local'.

Global ambitions: the growing influence of GCC capital

Amman and Dubai have capitalised on this form of design-led regeneration. In Amman, through the creation of a visual identity for a city (the FF Amman typeface);[29] in Dubai, by capitalising on the

---

29 For Amman's centennial in 2009, the Greater Amman Municipality (GAM) hired Syntax, a local design agency, to develop Amman's visual identity, which was accompanied by an unofficial typeface created for Amman called FF Amman, featuring 22 weights, two styles (sans and serif), and upright and italic corners. It was the first Arabic family with actual italics rather than slanted oblique typefaces, and the first typeface created for an Arab city, although it was never commissioned by the GAM. FF Amman soon found its way on bus stops, street signs and outside people's homes.

creative human capital of a city by concentrating cultural production and consumption into creative quarters, such as Alserkal Avenue in Dubai (see Figure 4). Dubai has long divided the city into 'districts' catering to specific consumption patterns, for example Al Quoz for art, Deira for historic Dubai, Business Bay and the purpose-built Dubai Design District (d3). The district strategy was used during ADW, when the creative quarters became sites of cultural production and consumption. Similar to the growth of a design scene in parallel with the art scene in Dubai, Jordan is attempting to define its design culture through a negotiation between a local identity and being 'global'.

It is no secret that GCC interests dictate terms in other Arab countries. The establishment of cultural activities such as design weeks are a strategy to promote cities like Amman as modern. In design, the lion's share of the labour working in the GCC creative industries comes from surrounding countries, particularly from Egypt and Lebanon – the latter even more pronounced since the economic crisis. But the nature of design initiatives in Dubai promote an exclusive form of design connected to elitism and embellishment: 'high design' and 'design art', further alienating design from the public and reinforcing 'the popular stereotype of design as a superficial, stylistic tool steeped in consumerism' (Rawsthorn, 2015, p. 41). The design works are highly expressive (centred on authorship), produced in limited editions (collectable) and emphasising craftsmanship (creating the best artefacts using the best skills), which is all about displaying wealth (Dormer, 1990).

Dubai's design culture is connected to the growth of the city's art market, and is much more global in scope, reflecting the context and ambitions of the city. Its main art fair, Art Dubai, 'position[s] itself as a globally relevant yet regionally aware art fair' (DeTurk, 2020, p. 162). Whereas Cairo, Amman and Beirut's design scene all have global ambitions, they are not as pronounced as Dubai. Moreover, Dubai's population make-up and economy are vastly different. Dubai's ambition to become a centre of culture in the Arab region and globally has meant capitalising on the 'creative industries', with strong governmental support behind it. Between 2012 and 2015, the city saw multiple events spring up dedicated to design, such as Design Days Dubai, a fair dedicated to collectable and limited edition furniture and design objects from international designers; Downtown Design, a curated trade fair focusing strictly on industrial design; d3, a district dedicated to design that includes commercial spaces, co-working spaces and retail; and Dubai Design

Figure 3: Entrance to the Crafts District at the first edition of Amman Design Week, September 2016, photo by Danah Abdulla.

Week (DDW), a platform for regional design featuring a design fair, exhibitions, installations, competitions, talks and workshops.

Dubai's design strategy could be categorised as hyper-commercialised and elitist; the prices, the focus on craftsmanship, the sponsors and the retailers in d3 illustrate a sense of exclusivity associated with high design and design art. And the 'Dubai bug', as designer Athar referred to it, has caught on. Designer Paul explains the situation in Lebanon:

You have these collectives, you have these organisations who do product design [...] And all they do is furniture pieces that are limited editions that cost an arm and a leg has zero functionality. They're just, you know, expensive. And just because they're expensive, then they're 'good'.

He acknowledges the appeal of creating a small number of collectable pieces for a high price, where the sales would ensure the designers making them are covered for the year, but he thinks it sets a bad example and has overtaken the Lebanese market.

High design and design art (encompassing product, furniture and fashion) are pronounced in the Arab world, mainly in Dubai and

Figure 4: FF Amman in use on a bus stop in Amman, Jordan, photo by Nathanael Arnott-Davies.

Beirut, despite the Arab region possessing few university programmes teaching these specialisations. The shortage of fashion programmes has not deterred Lebanon, a country with a thriving fashion scene where big name haute couture and bridal brands as well as independent ready-to-wear labels operate. The GCC is focusing its energies on developing fashion and itself is boasting a growing market for it, with the Arab Fashion Council[30] based in Dubai, and Dubai Fashion Week (formerly Arab Fashion Week) hosted there. The latter's ambitions are to be recognised next to London, Paris, Milan and New York Fashion Weeks.

Whereas the design weeks and festivals attempt to engage the public through programming, the location (d3) acts as a form of exclusion. These locations feel disconnected from other areas in the city and are, as Elsheshtawy (2004, p. 172) shows, 'exclusively associated with "elite" global elements – those that can afford the multi-million dollar [...] price tag associated with these'. This disconnect relates to the exclusionary development within the city itself. Similar to regional building developments, Dubai's public sphere is segregated economically. Instead of driving efforts towards making the city more liveable, solving social problems or the concerns of the lower classes, Dubai responds to global trends, tourism and attracting business investment and large-scale events.

An analysis of the language used across all these initiatives emphasises being global, becoming the platform for design in the

---

30 The Arab region's fashion industry is valued at $89 billion USD. Dubai hosts or has hosted a multitude of fashion weeks including Fashion Week Dubai, Middle East Fashion Week, Dubai Modest Fashion Week and the Islamic Fashion Festival.

MENA, supporting local talent and furthering the growth of the industry regionally. The irony is how most Arab passport holders cannot enter the UAE without applying for a visa in advance. The initiatives claim to further public education on design and want to influence policy, however, they continue to rely on the brand name appeal, for example the branches of the Louvre and Guggenheim in Abu Dhabi, the luxury brand stores in d3 and the satellite campuses of established institutions from the US and the UK. Even the launch of the Dubai Institute of Design and Innovation (DIDI) in 2019, the region's first university dedicated to design and innovation, has a curriculum developed through a strategic collaboration with MIT and Parsons School of Design.

Introducing international brand names reinforces the argument that the Arab region is a consumer society, as opposed to a society that is simultaneously productive and consumptive. Whereas the establishment of DIDI shifts from importing talent to nurturing it at home, the initial strategy 'privileged an expatriate brand of art and culture that may be regionally inflected but is far from local' (DeTurk, 2020, p. 169).

The emphasis on the global leads to a measure of design quality that is 'anomalously Eurocentric' (Aldersey-Williams, 1992, p. 11), illustrating more of a dependency on the 'global' and an obsession with catching up instead of understanding societal needs based on context. Despite growth in design culture and initiative that draws on the unique visual culture and practices regionally, what becomes the narrative must be 'global' or is produced by a designer residing outside the region – the émigré designer[31] – many of which are not necessarily part of the design culture but become the only representatives from the place they are originally from.

Another side of the coin

Dubai's goals of being a place of convergence will always remain, but in more recent years it has pushed to develop its local talent rather than import it. No other Arab country has placed value on design like the UAE and provided the industry with support both through funding and space. Both Maher and Rayan credit the tech industry for aiding the government's understanding and support for design. 'But I mean art, design, innovation, emerging tech, AI, all of these...they [UAE] really like it here and they try to implement it as much as possible,' educator Maher tells me.

---

31 I discuss the concept of the émigré designer in my contribution to the BIPOC Design Histories lecture series (Abdulla, 2023).

Designer Rayan, who received government support to run a large-scale design event, tells me 'every time I would have a conversation with the government, or any kind of official entities it's always that there is support, and there's always encouragement...I was never ever pushed away'. Dalal, a designer who worked on DDW agrees and commends the UAE for their work. 'The ability to make these types of spaces available just in an otherwise poor Arab environment in design [pause] is really something [...] they do support designers in every possible sense,' she tells me. Residencies by Tashkeel and Fikra, awards like the Audi Innovation Award,[32] and the Van Cleef & Arpels emerging designer award are open to designers region wide, and the Global Grad Show, the world's largest education event, is open to design students globally.

The design culture began by focusing on collectors and expensive products through Design Days Dubai (which ran alongside Art Dubai), and Dubai Design Week became more design and creative-industry led. Dalal discusses DDW's evolution:

Design Week [...] improved year on year, in that it involved more local/regional rather than international stars [...] Which I believe is what drove the success of the events eventually.

As the week matured, so did the scale of what Dalal describes as 'capacity building':

If we look at the [...] smallest scale, it was the free workshops you could attend. [...] Where you genuinely learn something, or a talk that was free to attend. Then...it was [...] small scale sponsorship [...] with international brands. Be anything from a tile brand or a toilet brand...and this was something that we cared a lot to do was 'you have to work with an Arab designer of our suggestion' [...] I was responsible for finding the person who deserves the opportunity. [...] Next [...] you had the design competitions. [...] [T]hen it was participating in either Abwab or something called Iconic City. We picked one city from the Arab world we wanted to celebrate [...] Eventually, we started inviting [...] regional design weeks to participate in Downtown Design.

Masa, an educator in Dubai, admitted that while these design weeks can be exclusive, they are useful in helping the Arab region define what design means for that context within a supportive environment. A regional approach could be a win-win situation for both the UAE and the Arab region, because it reduces reliance on US and European funding, it allows the nurturing of local and regional talent, and provides designers with an opportunity to shift from the prevalence of high design and design art and introduce new discourses about what design could be in this context. Only if the UAE begins to enable a grassroots movement to occur, however.

Elitism and design

There exists, across the Arab region, 'design bubbles' that consist of the same people who attend events, architect/designer Maya tells me. Centred in the bigger cities (Amman, Beirut, Cairo, Dubai), bubbles ignore larger communities of design and architecture practice in other parts of the country. While designers acknowledge this bubble, they also acknowledge how difficult it is to get out of because some of these spaces cannot exist outside of the neighbourhoods in which they are based. Maya does not think the bubble is intentional, but exists because it is difficult to engage the public whose perception of design is one of luxury and elitism. 'People don't feel like they need it or deserve it,' she says. She refers to Amman's status as a refuge city, where generations have relied on necessities, and thus design is not considered a need but a luxury, a perception she argued is transmitted from generation to generation. In contrast to Cairo and Beirut, where people have grown up with a sense of craftsmanship and design, it is not a part of Jordan's identity, and therefore it is rejected, she concluded. Amman, she claimed, is entirely about necessity, and the need for design is only now being grasped. Maya's claims that designers are unable to escape the bubble recall art historian and critic Helmut Draxler's argument regarding design's middle-class origins, which is why designers often raise the issue of responsibility. This concept of making things better is a typical middle-class impulse, an expression from a position of privilege, and consequently designers come in to find problems and fix them (Gretzinger, 2012). This frames design as a luxury and elitist, fetishising poorer communities.

Expanding design's 'reach' has been a mission of design weeks; at times this can be positive, and at others it becomes fetishising of people from lower classes, and dealing with symptoms instead of root causes. Fawz, the founder of a design institute, admits that her workshops and short courses in design fill an educational gap but suffers from dealing with symptoms; most courses are attended by wealthy housewives due to cost, affecting the nearby lower-income community.

Moreover, the tie with elitism is how design represents luxury when it enters more affluent areas in Amman; people perceive design as something that comes from elsewhere – Milan, Paris, New York or London – making it more 'valuable' because it is not local. This

---

32 Interestingly, despite the majority of design students in the UAE being women, the Audi Innovation Award 2020 judges were all male.

perception of design enforces a fetishised consciousness, and people consider design from Jordan as substandard in comparison, Mayar tells me. She believes that changing how people see design begins with people accepting each other socially and psychologically before they can begin seeing design and its uses.

Meaningful engagement or parachuting in?

Terms such as social design, design activism, humanitarian design and design for good (or 'social design', as I will use going forward) are new formulations of design that have been appearing in greater frequency. They describe a form of design that seeks to investigate the designer's role in society by tackling community, political and social issues that contribute to human well-being. Community engagement and social responsibility were high on the list of designers, educators and students who believed that designers should work alongside communities and conduct more relevant projects with them. Since the early 2010s, the 'do-good' bug has infested design practice and education. Moving from 'objects, images and spaces to the investigation and provision of relationships and structures' (Julier, 2014, p. 5), designers are tackling new problems and engaging in issues like climate change, unsustainable consumption, and social and economic inequalities. Although efforts are made to push more socially engaged definitions of design that step away from outcomes and highlight process and encourage research, design education does little to support more informed social engagement in design when sending students into new neighbourhoods to find projects. This leads designers to address symptoms rather than confront causes to problems, parachuting in design solutions without attention to context.

Steeped in aid discourse, design solutions are often technological fixes, utilising methods provided by the numerous toolkits devoted to the subject, rather than an investigation of the source of these problems, often rooted in imperialism and in neoliberal restructuring (Johnson, 2011). They have little understanding of the context they are in and capitalism is rarely critiqued. In neglecting the role of productive relations and state policy in producing inequality, do-good design often performs the grassroots ideological work of neoliberalism by promoting market values and autoregulation among poor constituencies. Within the humanitarian–corporate complexes, the global poor are construed as objects of elite benevolence and non-profit largesse, rather than as historical subjects possessing their own unique worldviews, interests and passions (Johnson, 2011, p. 448).

Social design projects assume the right to intervene in a space deprived of problem-solving capacity by imposing design requirements and imaginaries provided by other parts of the world. In other words, they act in the world without the need to know what is going on *in the world* using generalised methods like IDEO method cards (Keshavarz, 2020). Although social design aims to be inclusive of design worldwide, its Eurocentric approach frames design from the Global South outside of the main discourse.

Design weeks

When it comes to Dubai Design Week and others, the problem with that setup is that it renders design as a noun, as a luxury, and not an action or a verb. And so people when they think of design, they think, 'oh, it's going to be a luxury product'. But, at the same time, it was good to have these events because it rendered design as something that we should invest in and explore.

The consensus around the emergence of design events was positive, because they provide new experiences, networking opportunities, economic possibilities and present design in a more public form to society. They also centre social design. The beginnings of Beirut Design Week (BDW) were socially oriented, as Paul, one of the founders, tells me:

The whole idea was that we wanted to show [...] different aspects of design, not just things. [...] [W]e could tackle social issues [...] to show design as more of a social tool or like a creative problem-solving tool, not just aesthetics...

BDW operated as a non-profit and reliance on participation fees and sponsors meant it started leaning more towards commercial endeavours and lost its ability to push the conversation forward.

Similarly, Amman Design Week's organisers steered the event in a different direction from its initial purpose. The event was originally called DesignerJO and was spearheaded by Her Majesty Queen Rania Al-Abdullah's office, who had an interest in promoting the creative industries. Initially, the plan was to host the event in Abdali (the 'new' downtown), and focus on exhibiting products, jewellery and furniture. Unsure of their vision for the event, the Queen's office approached cultural organisers Layalle and Sama to begin defining the project. They conducted research over two months, which gave them an overview of the problems and challenges and the industries that required the most attention. The research helped produce the mission and vision for what they called Amman Design Week. Sama explained how her 'condition for doing it [was that it should be] primarily in Arabic, and it cannot be an elitist exhibition event, not just jewellery for the elites of Abdoun to come in'. Part of their mission was to 'reactivate' spaces around the city, celebrating Amman by focusing on the local and revitalising the city through 'interventions'. The goal was to 'ge[t] to people's neighbourhoods rather than expect them to get to the exhibition,' she tells me.

The overall intention was, if design was more visible across the city and its value in opening possibilities highlighted, it could be both an inspiration to students and a way of including communities that feel excluded by design due to its perception as luxury and elitist.

In some cases, centring social design led to an approach called parachuting in, where projects attempting to 'inject' design into the city succumb to the traps of elitism and exclusion. In the first edition of ADW, the team attempted to tackle social issues by prioritising the reactivation of spaces for public use, addressing problems such as traffic, parking, public transportation and the pedestrian experience. One way they addressed parking and public transportation was through branded ADW buses provided by the Greater Amman Municipality (GAM) to take visitors across destinations. For some Amman residents, this was likely their first experience riding in public transportation in a city with more cars than people, and where a massive stigma around riding public transit exists. The question is, how many people saw it as an 'experience' that fetishised the working-class way of life, as opposed to having a discussion on the importance of transit?

Some designers and educators I interviewed commended the effort by the organisers to diversify locations because it directed them to visit other neighbourhoods or cities (the case for BDW), but the critics of ADW highlighted the problematics of investing money into a week-long event by developing a platform to exhibit works but without the infrastructure to support it, and parachuting in concepts from West Amman into the East, reinforcing class structures and design as luxury and elitist. Cultural organiser Eman was positive about ADW's effect on public perceptions towards design, however, she disagrees with spectacles that have a small impact. Both Zein and Eman would prefer genuine engagement, to invest the funding in new, long-term design projects, a chance to experiment with something different rather than to apply an existing concept. They would like to see the GAM, who are working with

ADW, using the systems put in place after the event is over rather than 'fixing' problems and leaving without any true engagement. Cultural organiser Zein explains how 'this could [...] be part of like a long-term project, where eventually after three or four years, we have ADW. The results of years of work and research and try to understand what needs to be done. Not just copy paste.'

Since the event was under the patronage of Queen Rania's office, we cannot dismiss the role of bureaucracy and control over ADW's content and, like the government's use of design as a device to brand and promote Amman for tourism rather than reflecting a genuine interest in design, this likely introduced some challenges. Copying the design-week model wholesale rather than rethinking it provides an easier solution than imagining a more effective way of injecting design into a city.

The 2017 edition of ADW, titled *Design Moves Life and Life Moves Design*, was all about 'design for change' and 'immersive experiences'. Referring to our current times of 'transformative movements that could not be foreseen', the copy references mass migration, climate change, technology and mobility. It places design as 'a driving force through which we strive for physical, mental, or emotional freedom through "motion"' (Amman Design Week, 2017a, no pagination), and designers are the saviours at the forefront of solving these problems. Alarmingly, the depoliticised copy appears to disregard the Jordanian context. Mass migration has always played a role in the region, and in Jordan particularly, and climate change affects the MENA region significantly (Farajalla, 2013). These should not be described as unique to this era, nor should they be separated from the fundamental issues that cause them. Furthermore, like design discourse, the copy includes buzzwords such as "transformative", "innovating", "conscious", "creative" and "impact", catering to a specific class of people. In a similar way to the knowledge economy discourse, placing designers as 'saviours' does not acknowledge that design consists of 'very different collaborators, quite different commitments, and more or less tolerable forms of compromise' (Tonkiss, 2014, no pagination).

Community engagement

In surveys with Arab youth, community engagement is ranked a low priority for them, attributed to weakness in governance and institutions and poor citizenship education. Low levels of community engagement amongst students leads educators to push them to engage

Figure 5: Installation in the Crafts district at Amman Design Week, first edition 2016, photo by Danah Abdulla.

with unfamiliar contexts. Paul explains the effects of this in the Lebanese context:

> I think [...] the students [...] don't really know what the Middle East's context is. Like [...] understanding of society and how everything functions [...] it's also directly linked to the university that you go to and how privileged you are. [...] [O]ne of the things that I really struggled with [...] [teaching] in the graduate programme is that the students, they don't know the difference between this area, where we will have to do field research, and then this one that's next to it, and it's completely different areas. They come from different backgrounds, different languages. They do not have the understanding or the awareness that the way I would conduct research here would be very different than the way I would conduct there. [...] They don't have enough knowledge of the history of Lebanon and [...] the societies, the communities within Lebanon to be able to become, I would say strong social designers.

Educator Salim explains how his goal is to be the connector between Cairo's multiple 'bubbles' and 'communities', specifically the university design students and the self-taught community. He admits there are:

Language barriers, cultural barriers, economical barriers [...] There are a lot of mistakes that will happen and are happening [...] of [...] worlds mixing together. But this is a healthy thing, that these mistakes will help us become better and produce something more representative of what Egypt is and this diversity.

His intent is to push these barriers between two seemingly disparate worlds to allow 'cross pollination to happen'. When I ask him how he enables this, he replies that it is through a participation grade for attending design events, talks and workshops, and through immersive projects at the foundation level:

One of the projects is to go and explore specific neighbourhoods in Cairo where they have to do research online and then go offline and then document with pictures and text and videos. And they like they are now 18 or 19 years old that's never been to downtown 'fe 7yat'hum' [in their lives] like ever.

While well intentioned, the problematics of the designer gaze of design tourism (Maudet, 2021) are at play when he describes a student and her mother's first visit to the Al Azhar area:

They went all tourist style, like getting the henna, getting their name written on [...] a grain of rice. I mean, they lived the whole thing and they were blown away. Okay, so this just gives you the image on how big the gap is, and how secluded now the younger ones who grew up in [Tagamo3 (5th settlement) or Sheikh Zayed]. That our topics need to bring them down to downtown and even Heliopolis now recently with the Design Week.

Students that are interested in conducting community projects are increasing in number, and educators acknowledge the danger of superficial engagement with complex issues. To counter this, educator Rita assesses projects and attempts to direct students towards more realistic aims, whereas educator Anas attempts to encourage students 'to continue the project after graduation', by seeking funding and partners for support. Both Anas and Rita believe in involving communities in the process to change perceptions. Anas explains how the community must be involved with the process, 'not just sending them the outcome to consume'. He organises a semester-long project where students must immerse themselves in a local community where they work together on a projects and students 'interview [locals], they talk to them, and then

Figure 6: Pop-Up Waterscape by LOOP (Listen Observe Organize Prototype), photo courtesy of Beirut Design Week.

they show them [works], they test them [works], help them [...]with the production and getting local material'. Involving people in the process allows the people to understand design by being involved. Designer Lara was critical of student-led community engagement projects because they often produced superficial projects. She cited the painting of the downtown Amman stairs and the umbrellas suspended on top as an example. The umbrella project was initiated by design students from the German Jordanian University (GJU) as an attempt to engage with the community, but the idea was copy-pasted from the Centro Abierto de Actividades Ciudadanas project in Cordoba, Spain. In Cordoba, the installation aims to connect the local neighbourhoods, the railway station and the urban areas. Equipped with a drainage system to help the city deal with water issues, the parasol provides shade during the day and light in the evening. Amman's version is merely aesthetic with umbrellas suspended on top of the stairs. The project, Lara says, was unrelatable due to the use of umbrellas and because the idea was copy and pasted from another context. She described it as an aesthetic exercise instead of a researched and viable solution with no relation to the neighbourhood and not a functional one.

Students I interviewed expressed an interest in engaging with community projects, but they also described uneasy feelings towards them. GJU student Rashad told me how educators ask students to go downtown, choose a store and rebrand it. Shop owners are not pleased with this and are sceptical of student intentions. Jenna recounted how community work around the university often brings up class divisions:

Where are you coming from? It's like we are an upper-class people that we see ourselves above them and it's hard to escape it. [...] [S]o they have this attitude towards us. [...] People are defensive asking what do you want from me, etc.

Rashad believes the university is more concerned with itself than bettering the community. He tells me how the university's location creates a gap between the students and the community, negatively affecting the surrounding area. While meant to be more strategic, he believes that the relocation of the campus has displaced local businesses. This displacement has worsened the situation for the community rather than allowed the university to engage with their surroundings. To have the design school located in an older area of Amman, where craftspeople still work, should encourage the students to seek out new collaborations and make it easier for them to produce their work. So far, this has not been the case. Ruba believes that isolation will continue because of the social class of the students. The majority come from more affluent backgrounds, and she described the negative effects this has on the local community:

[Students] consider the area cool but they don't engage. We will always be closed. [...] If we want to go down to the high street, we [fear] the people on the streets. I wouldn't go down to a shop unless the Queen went there for example. I feel we are still stuck with this. [University projects] asked us to go down and engage. So we worked on projects to get involved but then we close and go back to our own society.

Students are aware of the difference between their own milieu and the one they find themselves in. Most students were enthusiastic and empowered about the projects, but this enthusiasm is not enough to sustain a project. In Zeina Maasri's (2013, p. 120) discussion on her class at the American University of Beirut (AUB) 'Design in the Community', where graphic design students engage with society through issues of concern to them and their community, she claims that 'mark[ing] the city their voice' and granting with the ability 'to act on the very structure that dismissed them as rightful citizens' empowered students. However, she understands that classes like these may also lead students to believe that only design can change the world, and they must learn that change is only possible if coupled with action:

Design needs politics [...] to effect any change in society, and designers need to collaborate with others and immerse themselves in realities outside those of their own profession (ibid).

Community engagement provides a crucial avenue for Arab students who are often denied the ability to participate in decision-making at school or community level or engage in extracurricular activities. However, the role of contextually-based design education that considers its milieu in changing perceptions is evident, and stressing the value of design and its role in society requires a relevant methodology. It cannot be through the blind borrowing of terms and methods developed elsewhere, nor through a superficial notion of empathy towards the vulnerable individuals and groups designers engage with by using trendy terms such as 'mobilise', 'participation' or 'collaboration', nor through placing designers as problem-solving saviours but rather acknowledging the role designers play in making this world unsustainable and redirecting their practice (Fry, 2007).

NGOisation and international expertise

Foreign funding and consulting are a form of soft power and are often accompanied by an agenda related to wider geopolitical, economic or cultural objectives in the region. In the Arab region, generating knowledge and providing technical assistance – in varying sectors – is largely left to foreign consultants, institutions and publications, leading to a contextual disconnect. Initiatives by the European Union (EU), the British Council, Institut Français, Hivos and the Goethe Institut are part of the NGOisation of society, dictating the type of work produced in Jordan, Egypt and Lebanon. NGOs work to demobilise and legitimise unjust systems, pushing their own agendas based on their funders' interests (Spade, 2020), while at the same time lack of government funding means private initiatives are critical to the survival of the cultural scene (Khan, 2013). Cultural organiser Eman admitted these soft-power initiatives tempt practitioners and small organisations without access to money from other sources.

Design weeks are often launched in third-tier cities to stimulate the knowledge economy: a tool for design-led city regeneration, which aims to make the activities visible on a global scale, regardless of cost. Accompanying every design week is a global programme, because design weeks are part of building a knowledge society, and international recognition and acknowledgement is key:

Conceived to be global from its inception, Amman Design Week adopted the 'Design Week' name in order to plug into a network of creative events around the world, while focusing its efforts on building and sustaining a creative movement with social value (Amman Design Week, 2017).

Some governmental support is provided for ADW and DDW, whereas BDW – which no longer exists due to the economic crisis in Lebanon – was under the patronage of the Ministry of Culture but acquired funding via embassies, l'Institut Français, Goethe Institute and private businesses. Cairo Design Week (CDW), launched in 2022, is funded through corporate sponsorship. Local events are accompanied by international programmes, where embassies sponsor a designer to deliver a talk, a workshop or an exhibition (as is the case for ADW and BDW). Paul tells me how embassy sponsorship for BDW helped sustain the design week and deliver the socially oriented projects BDW was created for. As embassy funding decreased, BDW began relying on participation fees and cultural relations organisations:

British Council would come and say, I would sponsor two people from the UK to come and speak at your conference, like they would just pay for the tickets and accommodation. Or Goethe Institute would do the same. So this is how – we did not have actual money from them, we just had people.

In March 2016, ADW organisers invited me to attend an event hosted by the British Council where the director of Sheffield Design Week (SDW) shared his experience. After his presentation, some members of the ADW team, the SDW director, a British Council employee and I went to one of the royal palaces for a meeting where they both 'consulted' the ADW team on what they should do. The context of the two cities could not be any more different. However, rather than understand Amman's context, they treated it like a standard design week. Sharing experiences between design weeks is beneficial and provides key learnings, yet its placement within the British Council frames the discussion where the expert (SDW) is consulting the developing city (ADW); a third-tier European city would mark the matrix of measurement. The most illustrative example of soft power during the 2016 ADW was the Education UK Design Mini-Fair (sponsored by the British Council), where university representatives from seven UK institutions answered questions about studying design in the UK. Another example is the Female Entrepreneurship Programme (FEP) in Design, organised by the MENA Public Diplomacy Hub of the Dutch Ministry of Foreign Affairs. The programme, which took place in the Netherlands in April 2016, had the goal of empowering female entrepreneurs and/or decision makers aged 25–40 with a talent and passion for design. The former encourages brain drain rather than allow Jordanian universities to seek out potential candidates; it provides the space for mostly privately educated students to seek places in UK institutions, further reinforcing a fetishised consciousness where education abroad is always the better option.

The education fair uses institutions to shape preferences and the FEP example frames itself as a sort of exchange and dialogue, however, the Dutch expertise in entrepreneurship and design is seen as superior to the Jordanian one. Moreover, many designers study abroad and return to practice or teach at university, bringing with them ideas, beliefs, perceptions, preferences and values from countries where they studied, without realising the effect. Joseph Nye (2004, p. 13) articulates the effect of relational power:

Commerce is only one of the ways in which culture is transmitted. It also occurs through personal contacts, visits, and exchanges. The ideas and values that America exports in the minds of more than half a million foreign students who study every year in American universities and then return to their home countries, or in the minds of the Asian entrepreneurs who return home after succeeding in Silicon Valley, tend to reach elites with power.

International recognition is associated with the outward gaze, and during workshops participants highlighted this obsession as one of the reasons why Jordan is a consumer culture without thought leaders, more concerned with achieving something like the international style rather than focusing on the local.

Agenda-setting by foreign governments and fetishised consciousness is also present in examples relayed to me by Yazan, a Professor in Amman, when discussing the development of a design lab in Jordan funded by Japanese and American sources. In 1993–1994, a representative from the Royal Court approached Yazan and told him they were conducting a study to develop the Jordanian industry to export products to the European market. He described how he was first visited by an Irish expert followed by a French expert. The French expert sent him an extensive report, the conclusion of eight months of research:

But the conclusion was, that [...] for Jordan to improve its industrial production and be eligible to enter the European market, the products should be designed by Jordanian artists, not foreign artists[.] [...] If we can guarantee this, and guarantee the quality of these artists, then we have no problem entering as Jordanian industry in the European market. Because they thought

Figure 7: *Tawleh at Sanayeh Park by Architecture for Change, photo courtesy of Beirut Design Week.*

that [...] to look different, the European market, you have to be genuine with yourself. [...] I really respected that [...] because this would give us, people in fine arts and design, a credit. And would make the government [...] realis[e] the value of our education. And that would give us a niche where we would really gain some [political] support.

Yazan explained that the report made no statement for creating a promotional body for implementing design policies: for example, how Japan used modern variants of mercantilist principles to build their industry, which moved from producing imitation goods to world-leading, well-designed and technologically superior products, a model successfully followed by Taiwan and South Korea (Heskett, 2002). Would this lab rely solely on foreign funding? This could expect Jordan to produce stereotypical products, influenced by the cultural policies of the countries involved, particularly by using words like 'to look different'. The Royal Court hired outside experts to conduct research that the university could have undertaken as they are familiar with the local design industry, the content of their curriculum and their alumni. They could, at least, have involved the university in the research. Yazan's conclusion of making the government value design and art education demonstrates the effect of fetishised consciousness where an 'expert' from Ireland or France must pinpoint this to be taken seriously. All these activities promote, in one way or another, migration and brain drain.

The beginnings of most design programmes are largely the work of foreign consultancies and accreditation, and the knowledge of the region or experience of the consultant is irrelevant, as long as they are foreign, some educators tell me. American universities require accreditation by the NASAD. In Jordan, Yazan told me that the department at Yarmouk University – the first to offer design in Jordan in the 1980s – was largely the work of a Nigerian, two Brits, an American and himself. Educator Maria told me how the curriculum at Notre Dame University in Beirut was revalidated by a British academic from Middlesex University. Most recently and explicitly is the development of DIDI, whose curriculum developed through a strategic collaboration with MIT and Parsons School of Design. Maher explains Dubai's strategy:

'Ok I want to create the best institution in the region' and to do that we just partnered up with whoever does this best out there and it was MIT and Parsons, so our curriculum was developed by MIT and Parsons and they gave us this raw curriculum that we had to work on [...] it to make it fit the local need.

Interestingly, MIT does not have a design school,[33] yet was suggesting how to develop one. When I asked Maher the extent of their involvement, he explained:

[MIT and Parsons] provided us most of the programmes, content, lectures, syllabi. And also to facilitate eventual possibility for our students to continue their education in these institutions [...] but we had to take [the curriculum], re-adapt it, change the names, do a lot of work on it as faculty. You couldn't apply it as is because it also needs to fit the local culture, local needs, local industries and what not.

Surely, the DIDI faculty is perfectly capable of developing their own curriculum based on their understanding of the local context, with support from Parsons and MIT, rather than a blind borrowing that requires adapting.

---

33 The Morningside Academy for Design at MIT was launched in September 2022, three years after the launch of DIDI, and is more of a research hub than a design school.

Milieu

The disconnect between design education and the milieu (the places, people, environments and institutions that individuals encounter that shape daily life and inform their worldview) leaves one key ingredient in how people perceive design unaddressed: relevance. The milieu influences people's engagement and understanding of design, and the value placed on it, and this affects perceptions of design.

The Arab region is one of the most urbanised areas in the world, where over 59 per cent of the population live in cities. The cities can be described as a sea of visual pollution, due to the lack of attention from regulatory bodies and development that does not consider 'the effects that unregulated commercial signs had on the aesthetics appearance of the city' (Abu Awad, 2012, p. 1). The phenomenon is worse in cities like Cairo due to haphazard urban sprawl. In short, there are no systems in most Arab cities; a visually polluted landscape signifies a lack of value attributed to design and detracts from the appearance of the city. Earlier, I discussed some of the historical conditions that have contributed to Amman's 'schisms' (Innab, 2016) and hodgepodge urban solutions, and the way in which spaces cause 'lost space' and excludes certain members of the population. Amman's visual pollution and lack of identity influence people's perceptions on design.

The visual culture of Amman, Beirut, Cairo and Dubai are all different, but each share – with Dubai being the most regulated – irregular visual formations: overwhelming commercial signage, mismatched architecture, public art and street furniture, likely due to rapid urbanisation. The visual environment of a city affects people on a personal level. Amman is a city that lacks cohesion, composed of random things piled on top of each other, including its street signage system. Few cities in the Arab region have a coherent street naming system or a proper transportation system.[34] While this adds to the uniqueness of the place, it can be frustrating when no straightforward route exists, in a city accessible mostly by car rather than foot.[35]

Ruba, who was studying design at the time, compared her experience in Amman with her year studying abroad, where she described amazement at how valued design was:

[A] system [...] you don't know the value of it until you actually live in it [...] designers are appreciated, there's respect for human beings.

Ruba's year abroad made her realise how the visual environment of a city affects people on a personal level. She described how the city

---

34 For discussion on signage and visual clutter in Amman see Abu Awad (2012).

35 In 2016, the design agency Syntax developed a transportation map for Amman in collaboration with the citizen-led advocacy group Maan Nasel (arriving together). The volunteer project attempts to map the city's public transit network using a colour coding system, see http://maannasel.net/map/mapinstructions/.

was alive, filled with museums, galleries and historic places; unlike Amman, where much of the city lacks cohesion, composed of random things piled on top of each other. She referred to something as simple as the shop window displays, which were inviting and produced properly, unlike in Jordan.

Similarly, student Fareeda highlighted the ease of navigation through the signage and mapping system in cities she visited compared to Amman, which she described as absolute chaos:

If you take a Jett Bus from Irbid to Amman, if you want to stop somewhere, you have to ask more than one person, ask the driver, it's not made simple at all.

Ruba and Fareeda's examples demonstrate how they see and interpret the experience through the artificial (design and the designed): wayfinding, signage, mapping, window displays and architecture. The examples identified the importance of a practice that engages the public with design; how design interacts with the city and allows citizens to navigate and experience the city; and how design education curricula should consider practices and theories around people. It also relates to public engagement with design and how their experience of it within the city could potentially increase value and appreciation of design.

Cheap/bad design sends an unconscious message that one is not of value (Dilnot, 2016). Design remains elite and for people that are 'higher class', as though people are undeserving of quality – related to aesthetics or 'taste of necessity', where people perceive design as luxury and elitist and they do not feel they deserve durable 'good design'. One issue that contributes to this is the bypassing of the designer and a poor work ethic.

The universities themselves reflected cheap/bad design through a lack of attention to design. The environment where students study design is itself not concerned with design and branding.[36] In my own reflections on campus visits, I noticed stark differences between the appearance of universities. Private universities had proper signage and were easier to navigate and had better facilities and newer buildings. The external aesthetic appearance of the campus is more of a concern for the university than teaching, the student Lamees tells me, and is a tactic used to justify high tuition fees to parents, she thinks.

On one of my visits to a renowned public university, I was shocked by the state of the design building. This was a new building, but it looked dated. Graffiti filled the beige walls, people hung out in the

---

36 I do not confine branding to the realms of service and retail, but an experience that provides people with an ownership over something you can touch and feel (Millman, 2013).

staircases due to a lack of spaces to sit, the smell of stale cigarettes filled the air, wayfinding and signage were non-existent, and the toilets were in a terrible state. Students told me how the toilets and buildings were without electricity for an entire semester.

The designer Basem was critical of university branding and how future students and the public interpret it. He described everything from the logos to the advertising materials, to the signage, the wayfinding and the websites as 'horrible'. This lack of attention reflects how universities feel about design and their disregard for it, he argued. Educator Raja referred to the brand experience more directly when he discussed the security gates located at every entrance of every Jordanian university, which 'separates the city from the institution'. No one knows the reason behind the gates, but Raja believes a university should engage the community and society and be open to the public. '[It] should be a place of knowledge, one where you go [to] be enlightened,' he says. '[Instead] they close them [...] I'm alumni at Yarmouk University but I can't get into it. Can you imagine? [laughs].' The gates are a reminder of state control; a sense of being watched. Rather than providing a space of openness, these gates lock students in and confine learning to the university walls during designated hours, which are between 8am and 6pm. Designer and educator Adam shares a similar story of teaching in Cairo where the university closes workshops early:

I think there's – 'feth8afat alta5ween' [the culture of believing the worst] which is they're always thinking bad like: 'oh, you're up to no good [...] you want to fondle underneath the staircase, or you want to vandalise...'

The branding of these universities reflects the experience students have: one of control that confines learning strictly to the classroom rather than acknowledging the informal spaces of learning, a metaphor for the curriculum as product and transmission model.

In a region with hundreds of design programmes and thousands of design graduates, why is there such little attention to design and visual pollution? The designer Laith blamed the admission requirements and bypassing of the designer by businesses for cost purposes. He referred to the café where the interview took place as an example of what happens when people do not understand the value of branding and bypass the designer:

[This café] he wanted to work with us. We gave him a price [and he went to Fiverr]. [...] The price of coffee hasn't changed, it still sells, it doesn't matter to him [what] the logo [looks like]. But it makes a difference, you leave

Figure 8: Sidewalks in Beirut with obstacles, photo by Danah Abdulla

the store and it leaves no mark on you. It looks clean and nice and there's a brick wall but it's not enough... Branding is important. [...] Branding is made by the owner, we make the visual identity, and we help. It's an image, presentation [...] the image is important.

The designer Mayar was more critical in her discussion on changing perceptions through more design engagement:

No matter how hard people try, it's out of their hands. Because they have no taste. Look at the roundabouts, they are hideous. Everything has to do with 'wasta', or it's commercial. There will be some that appreciate, but the [whole] country [...] I don't know. [...] I hate being this way, but this is how I feel, no matter how hard they try, it's ugly, it's hopeless. When I lived in San Francisco, like the numbers, the colours, the type, you sense there's a sense of taste. Here it's hasty [...] It's unimportant. They don't see it as something beautiful.

The absence of a strong design culture and representation for designers, alongside governments giving no regard for design, contribute to these issues. The post-war periods in Europe saw social, cultural, economic and political perspectives directly influence decisions on street furniture, for example. Eleanor Herring (2016, p. 2) details how injecting 'objects as ubiquitous as litter bins, benches and bollards' with a modernist visual language and materials was so important, 'because it was through such objects that Britain's new social and cultural agenda was given physical expression, and good design was deliberately introduced in people's everyday lives'. Contexts at the time were vastly different. Whereas fast-paced industrial development in the nineteenth and twentieth century led to anxieties about taste, system, class, nationalism and snobbery (Herring, 2016), the Arab region is not afforded the same anxieties. Like the curriculum, cities like Amman become a patchwork with little aesthetic cohesion, supported with the trend of bypassing the designer, where clients alter most design work after the designer has completed it. The city's visual culture also brings up the absence of an Ammani identity. In Chapter 1, I discussed how Amman is not a city because its inhabitants constructed their identity in reference to their cities of origin (Shami, 2007). Despite growing design culture(s) and youth feeling more connected to the city, Amman's lack of identity hung over everyone's heads. Could design help shape a connection to a city?

The city that always sleeps

Cairo is the largest city in the Arab world, one associated with history, and a centre for Arab cultural production. Its sheer size and history mean it is almost impossible to compare it to its neighbours, or even describe its design culture in the singular. Beirut still lives on its reputation as the Switzerland (or Paris, depending on who you ask) of the Middle East. Dubai is known for its Las-Vegas-like look, luxury, starchitect buildings, and a centre for trade and finance. But unlike these cities, Amman has a reputation of being identity-less, a boring and sleepy city. Cultural producers, however, refer to this as an advantage for experimentation. In my conversation with cultural organisers Zein and Eman, they describe this as an opportunity to experiment, keeping it more grassroots and interesting. However, the aid system in the country presents a sort of boundary towards freedom and dictates the type of work produced, Eman tells me. She is happy that Amman attracts little interest from curators and larger institutions, although this is changing, because it allows experimentation in a more grassroots way. They referred to the art and design work coming out of Amman as more 'real', because artists and designers 'have to deal with the reality of the situation' but feel what it lacks is demonstrating Amman's diversity, mainly due to the work being more 'discussion based', with less of a drive to become 'famous and internationally recognised'. When our conversation moves to how people connect to the city, Eman argued, 'I think our generation [millennials] is one of the first that has these ambitions of connecting with the city. Our parents, not at all.'

Unlike their parents, most Millennials and Generation Z have more ambitions to connect with the city and shake the transit-city reputation. But Amman as an inspiration and a backdrop remains a long way away. Because art and design are taught in a way that is disconnected from the city, artists and designers are not as interested in engaging with it, making the work produced by many Amman-based artists and designers disconnected from the milieu.

Designers Laith and Rami felt that the growth of design has failed to contribute something *Ammani*, unlike neighbouring cities in Syria, Iraq, Egypt and Lebanon, which they felt had distinct identities and styles. Laith argued that Amman's visual culture does not provide designers with inspiration that could translate into something visual – aside from the old stencilled street signs. Although Amman has a bit of every community that lives in it, identifying one visual is difficult. Amman's growing design culture however is generating a sort of *Ammani* design identity. Lifestyle brands such as Jo Bedu (launched in 2007) and Mlabbas (launched in 2010) helped develop a Jordanian identity by translating Jordanian street lingo visually, and these have expanded their brand regionally and internationally. Although these brands have been successful, Jordanian designers were very critical of the identity promoted through these brands, who they claimed capitalise on trends and cater to *ajanebs* (foreigners). The landscape of design-led brands in Amman has evolved beyond a focus on graphic T-shirts to include furniture, jewellery and fashion, combining local craft techniques and design, and an increasing number of independent studios are making their mark both locally and regionally.

The growth of a local and regional design culture has been significant in the last 15 years, developing a grassroots culture of design. However, unlike Dubai, it has failed to demonstrate real value to the government, or establish power through associations, and designers continue to be overlooked and under-appreciated by government, institutions and clients. Societal recognition and understanding of the designer's role are crucial, which requires a change in the culture. The people I interviewed pointed first to the importance of defining what design means in their own context; a design beyond the vocational, beyond the commercial, a definition of design that resonates as more relevant to daily life.

CRITICAL [DESIGN] PEDAGOGY

118—Teaching philosophies
122—Decolonising education in the Arab context: alternative curriculum models
    123 –Curriculum as process
    124 –Curriculum as praxis
    125 –Student centred pedagogy
    126 –Arabisation
    129 –Global bilingual outlook
130—Milieu is everything
    131 –On the sly
134—Equipping future designers
    134 –Writing as practice
    136 –Histories
    138 –Where is our history?
    142 –Design research and thinking
    144 –Eroding specialisations
    146 –Typography
    150 –Experimentation to break the phobia
    152 –Business and communication skills

Chapter 4

Earlier on, I discussed the curriculum as a product/transmission model that is prevalent across higher education region wide. The model fails to consider the context in which it is located. In this chapter, I highlight the importance of milieu in forming the university's curricula and establishing its relevance in society by discussing the models of curricula and pedagogy appropriate for developing contextually situated design education. Through insights from participants who discuss their desire to counter the dominant structure of the neopatriarchal state by placing the student at the centre of education, I outline the role of the educator in this process, the skills and strategies for equipping future designers, and conclude by discussing how active participation, mutual respect, challenging students to their own convictions, questioning taught histories and Arabising design are key components to change and to develop successful model(s) of curricula and pedagogy that imagine *otherwise*.

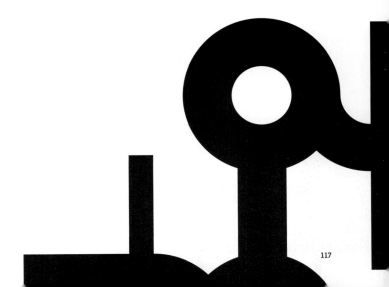

Teaching philosophies

During my interviews with educators, I asked each of them to describe their teaching philosophies and teaching approach. Overwhelmingly, educators put students at the centre of their practice, moving away from the teacher as authority model towards supporting students to become critical thinkers and change agents. The journey towards this approach is not easy, however. Educator Raja defeatedly tells me how 'you start off by having a philosophy but then you become part of the system, you become more of a robot or a machine'. He argued that educators start with different philosophies, but they quickly become institutionalised due to the power of the system. In his approach to teaching, he attempts to break this line of thought by refusing to be part of the system:

[I think of] designers as entrepreneurs, change agents in society [...] Teaching [...] can't be a relationship between an employer and an employee [...] Then you become a machine. You teach the class then you leave. There isn't that spark of innovation and creativity which is [...] what we should teach in design school.

Raja does not believe in a one-way relationship with students. Instead of being a machine, and in turn transforming students into machines (i.e. by approaching them as future employees), he resists integrating them into the structure of oppression, preferring to transform that structure so that they can become 'beings for themselves' (Freire, 2000, p. 74). Once students enter the classroom, he describes how, together, they share their 'own thing':

I try to break [...] this idea of being a teacher and you [must] stand in the middle [...] we have this vision in the Arab world that the teacher has to be like a prophet. [...] I should have the freedom to talk to them because I'll be making mistakes, they'll be making mistakes and it should be a collaborative effort. Sometimes I fail, others I do a good job. [...] This is the beauty of teaching, you can [...] try to experiment with your students.

He admits that students are afraid to challenge his authority, but that it is important to meet in the middle because, with time, students become accustomed to it. Raja tells me how sometimes students themselves are maintaining the system, and they feel *he* should be maintaining the status quo. He tries to challenge this idea but told me it is ingrained in their minds culturally. He relays his own experience of finding himself without opinions while a student in the US, where he was shocked at how openly students disagreed with readings:

It was because of the educational system and my relationship with Qur'an or the idea of Qur'an because we think of any book that it has been written by God. This notion of not criticising comes down to this notion [...] And I have this issue with my students. Sometimes they come to me and say, 'it has been said in that book you can't do this!' I reply 'well that author said it, what do you think? What's your take on this?' It's really hard for them to get out of their comfort zone and not get used to that idea or to get used to a different idea.

Educator Masa describes a similar experience when she studied in the US:

I remember when students would disagree with the professor, and it was more of 'Oh, my God, they're disagreeing. How is that possible?' And it was an eye-opening experience for me, because at the end of the day, you are an individual, you have your opinion, and it's okay to, to disagree or agree.

She describes how the Arab education system and Arab households as having 'one-way communication' where 'children are not allowed to think on their own. It's more of a culture of agreeing with whatever that professor or the leader is saying no matter what'.

Both Raja and Masa's experience demonstrates the transformation of their *conscientização*, where they recognise their conditioned consciousness when finding themselves without an opinion and acknowledging it. A meaningful praxis however must accompany *conscientização* (hooks, 1994; Freire, 2000). Raja grounds his philosophy in the belief that teaching challenges prescribed worldviews and ways of thinking, and introduces students to new worldviews to make them think critically about their work. While he believes in preparing students for industry, this is not equated with employability. He views and approaches students as change agents to enable them to take power and question their responsibility towards society, encouraging them to be collaborative critical thinkers and develop alternative collective futures. Raja acknowledged the difficulties of his job because he is surrounded by a discouraging environment.

Educators Nadine and Hind described the importance of sharing their experience as part of their teaching philosophy – centred on the idea of changing students' perceptions of design and their role as future designers. They argued that educators who relate and share their own experiences with students cultivate excitement towards the subject and a desire to learn. Student–teacher camaraderie, and teacher as facilitator, best categorises former educator Karma's approach. She tells me how the studio environment of design classes forces educators to approach teaching by becoming friends with students:

[I trained] to be a facilitator rather than impose my ideas or tell them what to do. It's always about asking questions and telling them things that prompt them to reflect.

Student–teacher camaraderie is an attribute of Freire's (2000) horizontal dialogue where there is mutual trust between dialoguers based on love, humility and faith. Karma looks at students as 't-shaped thinkers'.[37] She related their competencies to a doctor: specialised in one field (vertical) but slightly knowledgeable about other topics (horizontal). Contrary to Freire's (2000, p. 73) banking concept, Karma does not claim she 'knows everything and the students know nothing'. Since design is now more accessible and affordable, aided by technological advancement, accessibility to design software and online resources, students are more aware about design and more comfortable using certain tools than she was as a student. Her approach demonstrates that she respects her students and sees teaching as a dialogue, where she learns from them as they learn from her. She tests out ideas on her students, attempting to stimulate an experimental environment, and she introduces different practices and understandings of design to expose them to clients, industry and multiple scenarios.

Educator Khaled believes in training students to be problem solvers that possess different competencies. He bases his philosophy on conceptual thinking where he encourages students to 'think more about generating ideas and implementing tools for execution'. Khaled attempts to create an environment where students can develop their own identity as both an intellectual and a craftsperson. Therefore, critical and conceptual thinking must complement technical skills. Khaled called for dialogue within teaching, where the teacher's voice is not the dominant one and learning becomes an open process through student participation (Shor, 1992).

In his reflection on his teaching philosophy, educator Ali told me how his time as a student and lecturer in the UK inspired his 'talk 10 per cent, listen 90 per cent' approach towards education. The 90/10 philosophy aims to encourage students to learn independently by giving them a small part of the content but pushing them to work hard independently and to learn and share knowledge with each other. Knowledge transmits in a circular way:

---

37 See Guest (1991) and Hansen (2010).

We try very hard to learn, even if we hold a PhD, it doesn't mean we just finished studying, we are still learning and [we continue to] read, and we have to give this policy to our students that you don't eat the information from the spoon. I found it really hard from the beginning and now our students or let's say my students, they know my philosophy.

He argued that this is the fundamental difference between students in Jordan and the UK. He describes how students in the UK would often work independently, whereas in Jordan this approach was more difficult to implement. He told me how students in Jordan understand it is important to learn from themselves and each other, and this creates a healthy competition amongst them. Furthermore, Ali emphasised the necessity of learning outside of the university, and for healthy links between industry and the university. These links prepare students for the world of work and allow for different points of view, which are an important part of the learning process for both educators and students.

Educators were conscious of their influence and the perception of the educator as authority figure. Maher, Anas and Salim all described themselves as guides or mentors, supporting students in a professional environment, pushing them to discover themselves. Ali, Raja, Khaled and Karma's teaching practices challenge the traditional forms of learning. They all emphasised participation, which Shor (1992) describes as a door to empowerment by enabling students to see themselves as knowledgeable, championing their aspirations and trusting them with responsibility. Overwhelmingly, designers, students and educators promoted a more horizontal approach to teaching, demonstrating that educators and students should be on the same level.

The contextual, the critical and the interdisciplinary aspect of design was at the centre of Adam, Jeeda, Rita, Maria and Zainab's teaching philosophies. Rita tells me her students often question if what they are teaching is design because 'the students come in and think that design is about aesthetics, and I want them to think beyond aesthetics'. Similarly, Jeeda pushes students to consider 'using design as a way to understand their context and to rebuild a relationship with context that they lost connection with'. Interdisciplinary definitions redefine terms and help 'link [design] or reread history to speculate the future to understand what's happening now'. Rita tells students 'that I teach politics' to challenge their definitions of these terms and contextualise design to Lebanon:

The definition of politics in Lebanon is watching the news and which minister visited which minister and I tell them that this is not [the] politics I teach. I teach something [...] [where] they read between the lines when they read their books, and sometimes I give them examples as in reading a paragraph in a book, that really there's a clash because the book does not address us as Lebanese or students [...] it addresses mostly the American general public.

Designer and educator Adam encourages students to address, acknowledge and challenge issues by giving students the space and ownership:

You're already in a position where you're being put as like this idol [...] they might have far more things to offer towards [...] their own learning than me being in that position of [...] hear what I say and take it as is!

Space and ownership, enabling students to bring their own stories to the classroom, was at the core of Jeeda's teaching philosophy:

To create space for students to express their interests because they're coming also from different backgrounds. [...] It's just like what kind of stories they want to tell, and this is very important for me.

Similarly, Masa centres the experiences of students where she pushes the archival of their work and encourages 'students to get excited about certain aspects of design and create platforms for this discussion to surface'.

Decolonising education in the Arab context: alternative curriculum models

In Chapter 2, we saw how the product/transmission curriculum model is heavily dependent on changing behaviour through objectives. If the students (product) fail to measure up to the desired outcomes of the objectives, it is the learning process that is revised rather than the objectives themselves (Grundy, 1987). In a neopatriarchal society, change is difficult. A key question is how design education (and all education) can provide people with the opportunity to contemplate their environments, be critically aware of the issues and mobilise them to work towards changing these realities? The last section discussed the teaching philosophies of educators teaching design across Amman, Beirut, Cairo and Dubai. Overwhelmingly, their statements demonstrated a commitment to counter the culture of the authoritarian educator. The desire to redirect teaching practices by challenging the traditional educator role in a neopatriarchal society can be supported by two models of curriculum: 'process' – associated with British educational thinker Lawrence Stenhouse (1926–1982) – and 'praxis' – linked with Brazilian educator and philosopher Paulo Freire (1921–1997).

Curriculum as process

Curriculum as process views students as active learners, concerned with how students learn and their growth and development as human beings. The process model is not a set of documents or a syllabus to cover but translates and tests an educational idea or action in practice (Stenhouse, 1975). The educator plays a central role in the process model; a critical person who is 'trying to achieve some degree of mutual understanding and respect between identifiably different human groups' (Stenhouse, 1975, p. 131). Educators propose actions for educational encounters to encourage dialogue and 'conversations between, and with, people in the situation out of which may come thinking and action' while constantly evaluating their process and its outcomes (Smith, 1996, no pagination). In other words, action is generated between subjects rather than upon them (Grundy, 1987).

For Stenhouse, this constant interaction enables critical testing as opposed to immediate acceptance and leads to enquiry and discovery. He uses a recipe analogy to describe approaching a curriculum:

It can be criticized on nutritional or gastronomic grounds – does it nourish the students and does it taste good? – and it can be criticized on the grounds of practicality – we can't get hold of six dozen larks' tongues and the grocer can't find any ground unicorn horn! A curriculum, like the recipe for a dish, is first imagined as a possibility, then the subject of experiment. The recipe offered publicly is in a sense a report on the experiment. Similarly, a curriculum should be grounded in practice. It is an attempt to describe the work observed in classrooms that it is adequately communicated to teachers and others. Finally, within limits, a recipe can be varied according to taste. So can a curriculum (Stenhouse, 1975, pp. 4–5).

Curriculum is a process of exploration and trialling ideas through practice. The studio/classroom becomes a laboratory. Therefore, a curriculum cannot be packaged off and delivered anywhere (Cornbleth, 1988; Stenhouse, 1975). This means that behavioural objectives developed for specific outcomes are not the defining feature of the curriculum, rather the content and means are developed collaboratively between the teacher and the student. In a process model, the attention is on learning, where the actions initiated through deliberation and understanding 'emphasiz[e] interpretation and meaning-making' (Smith, 1996, no pagination), how students are able to apply the skills they learn and make sense of the world around them (Grundy, 1987). The danger is in actions becoming ends and processes becoming products. In design, an example of this is the emphasis on problem-solving. By focusing on solving a problem and by following a certain process to solve it (such as design thinking), designers forgo critical engagement with the context and milieu and are not making sense of their actions and how these affect the people they are designing for.

This model has its limitations, as Stenhouse himself outlined it as a 'critical model, not a marking model' (1975, p. 95), and with more emphasis on grading it becomes more difficult to implement. Another limitation is teacher quality, as the entire process model rests upon this factor.

Curriculum as praxis

Committed to emancipation, the praxis model is not just informed action but *committed* action (Smith, 1996). It shares many of the traits of the process model as it developed from it, but for process to become praxis (action that changes the world and our understanding of it), it requires a transformation of consciousness (*conscientização*), 'learning to perceive social, political, and economic contradictions, and to take action against the oppressive elements of reality' (Freire, 2000, p. 35, note 1). Like the process model, the curriculum is 'constituted through an active process in which planning, acting and evaluating are all reciprocally related and integrated into the process' (ibid., p.115), rather than a product or plans for implementation. As a form of praxis, this model focuses on collective understanding and action as opposed to individual.

In opposition to the neopatriarchal society and the banking model of education that dismisses students, the praxis model values student expressions and contributions, viewing them as active rather than passive learners (hooks, 1994). It is a transformative and emancipatory space of critical engagement and engaged pedagogy that critiques perceptions and assumptions, and educators allow students to speak differently and to engage critically with the consistencies and contradictions of their experiences, challenging them to their convictions, to argue the 'why' by being respectful of differences in ideas and positions (Freire, 2004).

Open-minded, particularly towards criticism, the praxis model enables a language and design problems and possibilities that speak *with,* rather than, *for* others. As emancipatory and transformative, it encourages students 'to cross ideological and political borders as a way of furthering the limits of their own understanding' (Giroux, 2005, p. 25). Its engagement with the political and social realities means it is situated, relevant to place, context and milieu. As Ira Shor (1992, p.15) states, 'education is more than facts and skills. It is a socializing experience that helps make the people who make society.' Empowering and critical education emphasises participation, enabling students to acquire skills for work and to become 'thinking citizens who are also change agents and social critics' (Shor, 1992, p.16), all requirements for building a healthy society, and a healthy engagement with the community, particularly with those surrounding the institution.

Like the process model, educators play an important role in the praxis model as they empower students and enable opportunities for transformation. In this model, the teacher is a researcher who tests theory in practice, while constantly evaluating their work to develop and improve it. Teaching becomes a political act – one where the teacher emphasises human agency and emancipation – and teaching becomes 'an exercise in critical praxis [...] and the construction of political identity and action' (Lavia, 2006, pp. 289–290). Therefore, these teaching approaches allow for professional self-development and self-study that invites the critical testing of ideas based on the setting, ensures that everyone feels responsible to contribute and views the classroom as a community (hooks, 1994).

Student-centred pedagogy

Through conversations with students emerged a vocalisation of their learning philosophies. The student Lamees, for example, expressed frustration with educators allocating too much time for students to produce design work. Added pressure and tighter deadlines would better prepare students for careers in industry:

When we finish our work, we [must] show the professor because there's mistakes or no mistakes, but in the working world, there isn't this type of thing. The professor usually says no to everything.

Her classmate Tala added to her statement, claiming that the entire four years could be completed in one year:

There are some things that have no use, and things that are supposed to be of use were not taught correctly.

When I asked how the teaching could improve, Tala replied that educators should be open to discussion and provide valid feedback to students.

Students believe learning requires a dialogue with educators. However, the students' statements frame the dialogue within a skill-set: a material product. This is the effect of a teacher-centred pedagogy, where students are not seen as individuals and where educators impose their views and ideas on them. Students believed that the design studio in university should emulate the design studio or agency. Their feelings towards their learning demonstrated an unhappiness with the work they produced, because they were incapable of developing their own style. Being provided time to produce work should allow students to focus on conceptual issues.

The students argue against a teacher-centred, banking model of education that denies them the ability to engage in mutual dialogue. The emphasis on dialogue could be that educators themselves fail to provide students with meaningful knowledge where they link the content of the course with the students' experiences (hooks, 1994). Or they fail to engage students with different meanings of design beyond design as a service provider. What emerges in student reactions around time allocation and how educators identify the flaws of their work is the denial of a problem-posing approach. Students are unable to think critically about their work or engage with 'knowledge as a field of contending interpretations' (Shor, 1992, p. 15). Placing students at the centre of the learning process gives them purpose and the ability to establish a culture of mutual respect in the classroom; in other words, a sense of responsibility to share and build a community within the classroom.

Arabisation

Teaching in Arabic grounds education in reality, leading to translation efforts and to the development of theories and methodologies (Hanafi and Arvanitis, 2016). The use of the English language for teaching design education regionally is a setback. Most university students (except for in Dubai and Beirut) attend public schools, where they teach in Arabic with English as a foreign language. Despite its introduction from school, research concludes that both Arabic- and English-language skills among university students are extremely poor and a cause for concern when it comes to students comprehending the materials taught, using foreign references and engaging with research in another language.

Arabic is notorious for its difficulty. The vocabulary is diverse and rich and the grammatical possibilities are immense, making it 'an uncontrollable beast [...] that makes it a problem for Arabs themselves to learn' (Hammond, 2007, p. 59). There have been previous efforts made to render the language less complex, however, it remains a big challenge.

Language is the vehicle for innovation, knowledge and creativity, but, if students lack this ability, how can knowledge transfer occur and how can this knowledge be localised? This presents problems for designers attempting to develop an Arabic design culture, including building an Arabic type library. Work by designers on mechanising typefaces based on Arabic calligraphy forms has been ongoing for some time, however, the library of Arabic fonts remains in its infancy stages. To increase the presence of Arabic online (such as preparing texts for electronic processing), creating technological typographic solutions is crucial. Additionally, developing software for the creation of typefaces that meets the demands of the Arabic script (rather than constraining it to the requirements of Latin) is another urgent focus, and can be accomplished through a collaboration between designers and software engineers.

Poor Arabic skills amongst students is not only attributed to the education system, slow translation efforts or difficulties adapting to Arabic type new technologies; the use of language as an instrument of power in a neopatriarchal society is another possible explanation for poor Arabic skills amongst students.[38] Hanafi and Arvanitis (2016) propose that universities should depend on Arabic as the language of teaching alongside courses in foreign languages to ensure students can use references in both languages and to advance research. Students gaining proficiency in at least one foreign language allows

him/her to explore all realms of human thought and knowledge and to enrich their country's knowledge and add to the overall human knowledge. [...] The key is to strategically combine two languages, while not undermining the Arab national identity or creating walls of isolation between elites living in the same society in the Arab region (Hanafi and Arvanitis, 2016, p. 252).

---

38 Design academic Huda AbiFarès (2017, pp. 197–200) discusses Arabic language literature for children and young adults, and publishers who publish books targeting youth that learned Arabic in a rigid and conservative manner.

The proposed strategy becomes more important with growing design cultures in the region, which are largely skewed towards English, and marginalise the Arabic-speaking, largely autodidactic community.

The language of design education in Jordan and the Arab region at large is fluid, moving between English and Arabic. It is dependent on the person teaching, the students or the content. This fluidity poses several challenges, as outlined in Chapter 1. Participants argued that a design culture that only speaks English is problematic and leads to a disconnect with the public, but they all acknowledge the difficulties to translation.

Arabic design terminology is an obstacle in both practice and education where educators deal with the back-and-forth mixture of English and Arabic in different ways. 'All the discussions, everything is not happening in Arabic. Ourselves, we're working in the business and our decks are fully in English,' Adam tells me. The dearth of design content in Arabic limits a designer's toolset, student Ruba tells me. The goal should be to create content in Arabic rather than translate it. She feels this would create something called '"Arab" design' because when she looks at her own work, and work across Jordan, the Arab element that reflects her identity – beyond the stereotypes of calligraphy, camels and *mansaf* (the national dish of Jordan) – is missing. Moreover, there are few books written exclusively in Arabic about design. The books used in universities are mostly translations, and many bilingual books are written in English and then translated into Arabic.

Educator Salim believes the Arabic language as a unifying force is an important idea to introduce in design. Design in Arabic first, then bilingual, then English, he says. He argued that most people who have access to technology and information have weaker Arabic skills than the public, the very people they design for. Salim felt that education should require designers to *work in* Arabic properly rather than to translate into Arabic. Here, Salim is arguing for a re-envisioning of the language of design in the Arab region – a design education and design *otherwise* – where Arabic is not marginalised but brought to the forefront. He suggested using Arabic *with* other languages rather than at their expense, as research requires students to be proficient in both Arabic and a foreign language (Hanafi and Arvanitis, 2016).

Salim's sentiments about Arabic are shared by many. Conversations about language and translation led to an examination of the teaching language and the language of design culture. Arabic should be as important as English and work on developing terminology was seen as urgent.

Global bilingual outlook

We've always looked to the West, we've lived in the Western bubble all the time. And this is what we actually exported 'lal5eleej enu al5eleejya kanu ya5thu el lebnanya' [to the Gulf, that the people from the Gulf took Lebanese] because they always looked Western. They had Western outlooks, they knew the language, they had the taste, they were a well cultured, rounded people. [...] But now I think we're at a disadvantage if we don't shift and looking into it much more internally. [...] And I think in our psyche, we're always looking to Europe, Europe is where we are, where we want to be where we are much more comfortable with. (Maria)

The previous section discussed the language of design education and the marginalisation of the Arabic language. Many of the people I interviewed were proponents of designing in two languages but emphasised the necessity of designing in Arabic first, then in English. There is an advantage to promoting bilingualism in design. Education should require designers to work in Arabic properly rather than to translate into Arabic: this approach re-envisions the language of design in Jordan and regionally, where Arabic is brought to the forefront rather than marginalised. Research requires students to be proficient in both Arabic and a foreign language, therefore Arabic should be used *with* other languages rather than at their expense (Hanafi and Arvanitis, 2016).

It was evident that designers, students and educators wanted to become part of the international community by engaging in both Arabic and English fluently. Familiarity with both languages (or Arabic and another foreign language) was considered an asset, as designers could translate relevant texts from other languages into Arabic and create new resources in Arabic. Designer and educator Rayan explains how questions around what a bilingual design looks like are being addressed:

We started having these questions, which revolved around what would the bilingual identity look like, [and] where would it exist. How would it communicate with the masses? How many different cultures exist in the UAE? The nationalities? How [and where] would this brand exist? And how would it behave and interact with the community?

Bilingual design has an additional layer in the UAE, where multiple communities speaking languages other than Arabic exist. Educators teaching at American universities in Beirut and Cairo emphasise the global context while respecting the local culture. Anas, an educator in Cairo, describes the approach:

[Students] are very conscious and aware of what's happening in the world of design. When [they] graduate, [they] can work in London, in Dubai, in Cairo [...] [students] work in the international or regional market and this makes them [...] really unique.

The same cannot be said about students in the Global North, who are rarely required to engage with another language or design in another script. Perhaps it is because the West dictates the design industry and is considered the design point of view that students do not feel the need to learn about other cultures beyond the superficial.

The promotion of an Arabic and bilingual design language is supported by important elements such as research, writing and typography. The task of beginning to decolonise education – through challenging and dismantling conventional ways of thinking (that design is taught in English) – is not an easy one. It requires a fundamental shift in primary and secondary schooling in the teaching of Arabic and foreign languages to materialise fruitfully. Educators and designers can begin through minor gestures (Abdulla and de Oliveira, 2023): teaching in Arabic in universities, working collectively on creating a vocabulary, developing new modules for writing in Arabic, encouraging students to Arabise content, creating presentation decks and presentations in Arabic, and forging new connections with Arabic-speaking design cultures. Within this development is a crucial task: to ensure Arabic itself does not marginalise additional languages (Berber, Kurdish, Somali), dialects or other minority languages spoken regionally, but rather embraces the peculiarities of these.

Milieu is everything

What constitutes the most relevant theories and practices for design education to be more relevant to its milieu and context? The theories and practices we draw on must be reflexive and not a blind borrowing of Western concepts and ideas that become oppressive tools if not reflected on.

That the Arab region is a culture that consumes rather than produces design is a recurring statement.[39] Aside from the historical and contemporary causes of the consumer society, there are three other factors with relevance to education we can attribute to this:

- Designs based on opportunities disconnected from the needs of the society.

---

39 A case for this can be made with a fashion industry valued at $89 million (Maki and Schneider, 2023). The Arab Fashion Council was launched in 2015 in an attempt to take advantage of raw materials, manufacturing and design capabilities to grow a regional industry; beyond organising a fashion week, this remains to be seen.

- An absence of resources where students are not able to create prototypes.
- A conforming culture that discourages experimentation and entrepreneurism.

Amidst such an environment, educators and designers attempt to challenge the status quo, encouraging students to be change agents and act as their own role models to create new opportunities for themselves and society at large rather than settling for the limited options available, an approach that pushes design in different directions. For designers, this takes shape in deviating from existing patterns of conformity and experimenting with design approaches that are not confined to a traditional view of design.

Changing one's environment within design becomes more challenging within a discipline that has an ambivalent attitude towards authority, where they too easily agree to clients. Power, as design theorist Clive Dilnot (2016) argues, is that which designers are terrified of but are not taking, and yet moaning about not having. But design without power remains peripheral; a mere service provider. Boxing design as only a service provider dismisses the role designers have had in making the world unsustainable and does not enable it to become a serious contender for challenging the status quo. Questioning design's relationship to capital requires a shift in perception of how designers themselves view design. Grasping a certain amount of power and engaging in experimentation requires resources, both human (labour) and capital (money, tools, equipment), which are lacking regionally.

On the sly

The concept of making design and design education relevant to milieu is to also understand its limitations. In other words, there are topics that cannot be directly addressed for fear of repercussion. Understanding this and how to navigate it within one's context is paramount. Earlier, I discussed the stifling creative and conforming environment design graduates find themselves in upon leaving university (and within it). Educators admit to practicing self-censorship, particularly as warnings and interference from senior management are commonplace. Syrian playwright Saadallah Wannous believed that to be experimental is to find an effective interaction with the people, one that can be found in their habits. This applies to sensitive topics and in relating design back to people's lives. Educators are themselves introducing ways to challenge students by addressing sensitive topics in the studio, or when students themselves want to discuss something deemed un-safe. I discuss two examples shared by participants. In making design relevant to the daily lives of students, Karma integrated critical design as a way of thinking. Critical design 'uses speculative design proposals to challenge narrow assumptions, preconceptions and givens about the role products play in everyday life' (Dunne and Raby, 2007, no pagination).

In critical design, design is not meant to solve a problem or provide a service, but to entice thinking, to raise awareness, to expose assumptions to provoke action and to spark debate (Dunne and Raby, 2007). Although critical design can be a valuable method for envisioning future scenarios, its critics describe it as passive, safe, privileged and lacking criticism, recommending it 'be held accountable for its political and social positions [...] to escape its narrow northern European middle class confines' (Prado de O. Martins and Vieira de Oliveira, 2014 no pagination).

Karma told me that students pushed their projects in radical directions, critiquing social and cultural issues such as sexual harassment, noise and child labour. Some projects dealt with personal issues in powerful ways. She referred to a project by a male student who drew on his experience as a victim of rape. The student created a recipe-style book about raising children designed in the aesthetic of religious books. Moreover, she encouraged students to engage with the public when producing work. She cited an example of a student who worked with a garbage collector:

[The garbage collector] said that what bothers him is that people pass him and they close their nose [...] but it's their garbage not mine. So she did her whole project on this one comment. She made a perfume. The whole class she was soaking garbage [...] The whole design was fancy, it's called 'Prejudice' but you open it and it smells like garbage, but all of it is filled with this information of the chemicals he's inhaling and how it affects his health.

This project used design to create awareness around prejudices the public has towards essential workers. Introducing critical design as a theory within the classroom engages students with criticism, enabling language and design possibilities that speak *with* rather than *for* others. Karma's description of student projects addresses modes of individual and social agency. It becomes non-prescriptive and committed to inclusion, encouraging a commitment and desire for change. She encourages her students to cross borders to further their own understanding in a safe, nurturing and experimental environment (Giroux, 2005).

Karma told me how using critical design as a framework to debate proposals actively in class made student begin to see 'everything as critical design!' She believes critical design and similar methods allow for experimentation. What is interesting to note in her examples is how students focused on contemporary situations grounded in reality, rather than imagining future scenarios, centred on technology as is often the case in critical design projects. Critical design provides an experimental practice that could be appropriate for curricula in the Arab region to engage its milieu and context. Notwithstanding her desire to move away from design as a service provider, the pressure of employability draws her back to design as service provider. Karma was conscious that she cannot teach critical design constantly because 'I won't prepare them for the market because critical design is in the museum, it's not sold.' Therefore, when integrating critical design in her classes, she asks students to 'find a problem, create a solution, then market it and sell it.' During the workshops, students, educators and designers called for the 'necessity to work with current problems,' suggesting a 'more expanded set of topics in design, questioning and experimentation' and 'a focus on critical thinking and open-minded practices'. Participants emphasised questioning and experimentation that 'supported radical ideas where educators push students.'

Designer and educator Adam tells me how he navigates being monitored by the head of department and the Dean, who asks him to see student projects. He establishes a lot of trust with students in order to 'hide things that talk about gender or harassment. [...] And I hide these projects away and I just deal with the student and be like: "this is really good for portfolio, but we don't have to tell anyone, you know" [...] it's very important [pause] to get away with certain things.'

UAE-based designer and educator Zainab, who admits to a lot of self-censorship, uses her studio to provide a safe space to counter that:

A safe space where students are allowed to speak up their mind, explore different topics, but I also make them aware of the consequence of what they're saying [...] And this is one of the challenges of us [...] as designers that you can say it but you have to figure out a way that doesn't sound like you are pointing fingers or in a very aggressive way.

I observed this at play firsthand on two occasions: while a jury member at a Jordanian university when a student wanted to discuss the body through performance, and the lecturer swiftly warned her of the dangers of this approach, instead guiding her into a safer direction; and when I was interviewed for a job at a private university in Cairo. Despite being approved by the search committee and the head of department, my appointment was denied due to the political contents of my magazine *Kalimat*.

Equipping future designers

The World Economic Forum Future of Jobs report (2020) outlines key skills for 2025 to aid towards the future of digital transformation, including analytical thinking and innovation, active learning and learning strategies, complex problem-solving, critical thinking and analysis, creativity, originality and initiative, leadership and social influence, technology design and programming, reasoning, problem-solving and ideation, user experience, systems analysis and evaluation, and persuasion and negotiation, among others. These are key skills since current curriculum models focus on the bottom three of Bloom's taxonomy pyramid: remember, understand and apply (Sebaaly, 2019). The Arab region has the world's highest unemployment rate, and digitalisation presents a unique opportunity for job creation. While the process and praxis curricular models are an approach towards developing these within students and increasing educational quality, overall digital transformation is only possible if the whole university shows progress towards this (Sebaaly, 2019).

Educators highlighted student interests leaning towards an exploration of identity and culture – specifically the Arabic language and Arabic typography, gaming, fashion design, and local materials and crafts. The next section explores skills, theories and practices that become important contextually-based tools for educators, designers and students.

Writing as practice

In Chapter 1, I discussed the ambitions of design regionally to emphasise Arabic while also becoming a bilingual endeavour. Design writing becomes an important element to achieve this because designers can begin to research and write about their work in both languages and generate new knowledge. Writing, however, is given little attention in design education. The issue lies in the design briefs themselves. Wherever you study design, writing is seldom part of the brief requirements. In her article 'What has writing got to do with design?', Anne Burdick (1993, p. 4) asks why design students and professionals are resistant to writing. She writes:

Graphic design [tends] to view historical work for its interesting surfaces while overlooking the contributory elements that make those surfaces interesting. [...] In the shadow of that agonising contradiction between design rhetoric and practice, where designers profess to admire one thing (culture) but base their practice on another (commerce), too little attention has been paid [...] to the relevance of writing to graphic design.

Karma and Adam, who taught in Amman and Cairo, described how students were not required to write about their work and instead discussed concepts and design decisions superficially. Maher, who teaches in Dubai, told me how students are completing a final capstone project while simultaneously learning to write. This writing expectation, however, comes in their final year when it is already too late. Students are resistant to writing, causing anger amongst students, Karma says. She tells me how the final thesis is no more than ten pages, and educators do not provide students with any intellectual tools on how to write it, a view shared by many educators. The rise of independent publishing both online and offline has led to an increase in regionally produced content. However, well-researched design publications and documentation remain rare in the area. Although participants described a lack of Arabic design content, encouraging students to write about their work is critical as '[w]riting can feed the profession in two ways: through the challenge of critical analysis and through the exploratory freedom of self-initiated work' (Burdick, 1993, p. 4). Writing creates a discourse, a dialogue, and enriches the design culture of a certain place and a field (Burdick, 1993).

The limited attention to local and regional histories was attributed to disinterested students, uninformed educators and an absence of research, resources and documentation. Several generations in the Arab region are unaware of their intellectual and artistic contributions as these are not taught in schools or universities. The duty of writing and disseminating these is crucial. Publications are forums, spaces to pose questions where designers can challenge and reflect on their work. This 'critical introspection' is a requirement as it 'can help broaden our understanding of what we accept as natural. We can then choose to accept it as it is, or to change it for the better' (Burdick, 1993, p. 4).

The last ten years has witnessed a growing interest in researching and writing one's own history to combat the little room allocated to local and regional histories in design curricula region wide. The release of *A History of Arab Graphic Design* by Bahia Shehab and Haytham Nawwar, for example, was cited as necessary and a step in the right direction. Therefore, the role of writing as a practice in design programmes and in publications becomes crucial in documenting local design culture and history, and develops a forum for students, designers and educators to share ideas and write about design.

Histories

Amongst educators and designers, there was an interest around archiving and writing histories of designers from the Arab region, to reclaim the narrative and grow the body of work. Educators described curricula as starved of local content, where students learn little about design history or art history beyond the Western canon.[40] 'We developed a [class] called the history of graphic design in the Middle East,' Rita tells me. Educator Salim started purging the content of the foundation classes when he saw all the references were American or European, adding people from Egypt, the Arab region and other regions. 'I kept trying to push, put in people from different places so they all get exposed kind of equally, *la katha* [for multiple] source[s],' he tells me. Anas places Egypt and its cultural industry as a source of inspiration in his history of design classes; after all, Egypt is a centre for film and music regionally, dating back to 1896. While Egypt's influence has waned throughout the twentieth century, it was the hegemonic power of the Arab world. Anas tells me:

We try to give [the] global context of graphic design that people they can be conscious and aware about what's happening in the world of design. [...] So we look at different alternative history and then they look, they dig down to the heritage and then learn from the heritage. What could be inspiring or could be a tool, what could be a new method [...] It's really very important to stay connected to the culture where they are. [...] So we are reconnecting them again within the design study.

More resources now exist, supported by a growing cultural scene regionally and, whereas some universities have introduced similar classes, in others resistance remains. Zainab explains:

[T]here's resistance injecting it because the current faculty who are responsible for history courses have taught the discourses in a specific way for so long, they're not willing to open it up for discussion. But I try to inject it to other courses, [because I am] aware of the lack of regional references in history courses.

---

40 Two educators told me the main book for design history classes was Philip B. Meggs's *History of Graphic Design* (2016).

Zainab tolerates the resistance due to her locale (an American university) but understands the importance of students relating to the content and the effect of history on them.

Students described the teaching of history and theory courses as disconnected from larger social and historical issues, rendering them incapable of relating their own experience to the knowledge presented or enabling any form of questioning towards this knowledge. Moreover, they described how theory and history classes are taught by rote. Thus, educators deposit knowledge into the students, in contrast to a problem-posing approach that:

offers all subject matter as historical products to be questioned rather than as universal wisdom to be accepted. From this perspective, the central bank is viewed as exclusionary rather than inclusive (Shor, 1992, p. 32).

Within traditional forms of curriculum, rote learning is the main teaching technique, where students are taught concepts and theories but never how to apply them. Projects should illustrate a sense of reality and be more applicable, Huda, a student, tells me:

They should give us the basic idea and not [...] when someone was born, and where [...] [i]t needs to be more about design rather than the designer himself. How he came up with his ideas, rather than his personal history.

Similarly, student Nawal struggled with learning theory and history classes by rote. She resists learning within traditional pedagogical processes that deposit facts into the 'central bank'. Both Nawal and Huda were unable to see the relevance of the theoretical and historical topics because they are not taught in a way that connected with their own experience or with design practice – removing their presence in the classroom. Designers had similar sentiments when discussing their experience studying design and art history. Laith tells me how he learned about art deco and the Bauhaus, but the relevance of these movements to design and design practice were never explained to him, rather 'it's by heart, by rote'.

Teaching design history by rote goes against the aims of a history of design survey course. As design historian Sarah Lichtman (2009, p. 342) states, design history should not 'be taught [...] as a series of illustrated historical events to be memorized, but rather as a network of cultural systems integral to the histories of aesthetics, technology and materiality.' Furthermore, it should always be relevant to design practice to be relatable.

Where is our history?

When we speak of context and milieu, content was generally seen as disconnected from the daily lives of students, where the Arab narrative had little room in the curriculum. Dalal, who studied Interior Design at an American university in Beirut, describes her experience:

I did not study about a single Arab architectural designer. I had no concept of it even existing. [...] The elective that I took, which was Islamic architecture, had it not been for that elective, I would never even have known [...] there was a single Arab architect, even though I was studying interior design.

Concerned by how little Arab design students know of their own design history, designer Jad asked:

Where is our Arab school in graphic design? Who are these designers, who is [Mohieddin] Ellabbad, how did he contribute to design, where are his books, how can I benefit from his ideas, how did he motivate the youth? [...] This is an aspect I am sure is completely absent from universities. When we talk about Jordanian universities, are we going to have special designers? I am convinced that 99 per cent of them, their understanding of design is foreign. You're in an Arab university, and Arab community, where's your touch that is related to the community? That's relevant to here?

Many designers I spoke with shared Jad's concerns. They expressed an interest in being able to reference where the inspiration for their designs came from historically because it provides the story behind the creation of the work. Designer Athar reiterated the issues around students being unaware of their own designers:

People need to know who Hilmi al-Tuni is, who Ellabbad is [...] Tarik Atrissi, Nadine Chahine, Pascal Zoghbi, students need to be informed because they become role models [...] whether we like, agree, disagree about their work, that's irrelevant.

He cited how a design history class during his undergraduate studies in Beirut inspired him, equipping him with knowledge on works originating from the region relevant to his own milieu. Another reason for the absence of an Arab design history is because it is largely the story of graphic design and interior design, both on the margins of design history. While the content of history classes in Arab universities revolve around the Western canon, at the University of Jordan former students Karma and Mayar describe an education that strongly emphasised Arab and Islamic art history, including organised trips to regional sites. They attributed this to Princess Wijdan Ali, an educator, artist and a diplomat, and the founder of the department. Karma describes how three mandatory art classes she took in her undergraduate changed her life:

I didn't have an identity, [I] didn't know the difference between an Arab and a Muslim, all I knew about Islam was what the textbook taught me and people on television and my atheist parents! It changed my thinking in an unbelievable way. [This educator] is considered controversial. She prays but doesn't wear the hijab. I was like wow! I didn't know there were people like that. She always wanted to show us that the stereotype we grew up on is false and that we were an intellectual and open society historically. The issues that we have with ourselves came from outside not from us.

Although Karma's experience of learning and engaging with her history were transformative, this is not the norm. It was evident how little students, designers and even educators knew about their own designers, artists, architects, design culture and histories. A fetishised consciousness (more interest in teaching a Western canon) and an absence of resources and research were to blame. Zainab explains her experience learning history:

History is such an important thing to revive, because it really plays with the students' head. I remember my first art history class here [at this uni], the professor starts the lecture by quoting, Churchill, 'History is written by winners.'[41] You know, this quote? And then we go through the curriculum and the history of the Arab world stops at the Ottoman Empire. Anything beyond that is neglected. You go out of the lecture thinking that, 'Arabs suck at design, or Arabs suck at art.' You can't help but think this way. So this has to change, but we're trying to inject it through other courses, like in the Arabic type course. We prepared a series of six lectures that speaks of the history of Arabic script and how it's used in contemporary context. But now we have no excuse. There are so many resources like Khatt Books.

The origins of design education in Jordan and the Arab world are not published. The history of Jordanian design education was orally transmitted to me through Yazan, one of the professors who taught on Jordan's first design programme. Student work is rarely documented (except for at the American University of Beirut) and few design publications exist locally or regionally, leaving students, designers and educators without easily accessible references. Moreover, students are unable to see the relationship between design theory, history courses and their own experience. With design cultures in the Arab region becoming more prominent, the small body of literature on design has focused on displaying design work in the form of coffee table books rather than research about design and design education. The exception is Khatt Books, a publishing house established in 2010 focused on design and visual culture from the Middle East and

---

41 The quote, wrongly attributed to Churchill, is 'History is written by the victors.'

Figure 9: Khatt Books covers from the Arabic Design Library, photo courtesy of Khatt Foundation

North Africa region. The publications are bilingual, and their Arabic Design Library series highlights the work of Arab designers and illustrators throughout history. Khatt also produces *Khatt Chronicles*, a podcast aimed at a younger audience, featuring designers, illustrators and researchers from the Arab world, which supports new ideas, enhances networks and provides educational resources (see Figure 9).

While work around the area is taking shape, content remains relegated to Instagram accounts featuring historical images of Arab visual culture, accompanied by brief text featuring the designer's name, the year the work was made and a short bio. Maria explains how this limited information renders teaching difficult:

We [ask] the students to research pioneering typographers and type designers, and [students] do a 10–15-minute presentation. '6ayeb ya jama3a badna' [right, you guys we need] we need Arabs. Who do we put? [My colleague] wanted to put Mohieddine Ellabbad, Hilmi Al-Toumi [...] I mean, the names are amazing but at the same time, how do you do equate? You have [Nicolas] Jenson, [John] Baskerville, Paul Renner, Herbert Bayer, and all of these names are European, and maybe North Americans. We put Iranian designers like Reza Abedini, Studio Kargah, Homa Delvaray. We were deliberating, what is the theory behind this work? What can [students] show beyond the Instagram page that they pick up? There is no scholarly work that talks about that work, how it is produced, the context, the background. So we tried it, and what [students] did is just go on Instagram, get a few images from Studio Karga's work, and then put it there and talk about what they read from Instagram messages. That's not going to cut it. On Jan Tschichold you have books and books and books and websites. [...] The point is, that students *who have Tschichold will not have the same experience as the student who has Kameel Hawa or [Abdulkader] Arnaout. Now there are some books and thank you to Khatt Books for doing them, but it's not enough, we need more context to the work.*

Maria believes the solution is more scholarly writers, and local and regional Masters programmes to develop writers and researchers as opposed to only focusing on design practice:

Whatever research funding I get or research lab I have, I don't have research assistants. I have a very hard time finding research assistants, because they'll all be A Level students, and if I get the architecture [students], they're not going to be as invested in what we're doing as someone from design, graphic design background...

Educator Rita believes now is the best time to produce these works:

There is this interest of archiving these designers work and writing about them. I think this is the time because these designers who worked in the 1950s/60s/70s, some of them are living but they're 80 and 90 [...]. I think this is the time to do interviews that we should do to rescue all these [...] and maybe build history. I think it's important for local designers, for example, in Beirut or in the Arab region to know what was happening in Beirut in the 1960s and 70s. Who were the designers, what they did, how they dealt with design.

Are students interested in these histories? When I posed the question to Anas, he replied that when students get exposed to it and reflect on how little they know, about '95 per cent get so interested'.

Participants did question and contest the teaching of a 'universal' canon and dominant forms of knowledge, but the excitement around generating new knowledge, without questioning the form it takes, took precedence. The danger in these new histories being written is that they pose no challenge to the discipline's Eurocentric orientation and historiography. Time remains linear, empty and homogenous, and it develops yet another 'canon' – what is valued, worth saving and excluded. Design history's attention to the one (often male) designer and his style, to the work of modernist designers, objects (the chair in specific) and industrial design, and a heavy focus on architecture, fine art and what constitutes 'good' design contributes to creating 'conditions of marginality' (Fry, 1989, p. 15). Ira Shor (1992, p. 32) cautions how canons are historical choices set by groups in power who set the standard:

[Canons are] delivered [...] as a common culture belonging to everyone, even though not everyone had an equal right to add to it, take from it, critique

it, or become part of it. This body of knowledge [...] is society's essential facts, artifacts, words, and ideas. [...] It represents them [students] as deficient, devoid of culture and language, needing to be filled with official knowledge. The transfer of this knowledge...is thus a celebration of the status quo which downplays nontraditional student culture and the problem of social inequality.

The opportunity presents itself to decolonise the teaching of design history by not presenting standard canons that are universal, excellent or neutral, but in how students bring their experiences to this writing of design histories and question the so-called universal wisdom.

Design research and thinking

The low production and contribution of research from Arab universities – and the obstacles around it – is well-documented. Constraints on academic time, and universities discouraging academics from maintaining a practice, contribute to the lack of outputs. In design, the limited avenues for publishing, time and the quality of teaching staff affect research. Educator Khaled has been working on attracting qualified faculty to encourage research at his university. To accomplish this and raise the university's research profile, he offers 1000JD (more than a month's salary) to any educator who publishes in a reputable international journal. His challenge, however, is not to get educators to publish for the financial incentive and base research on 'strategic' objectives, but to implement curiosity-driven research.

Approaching research in this way is important because design faculty generate poor research outputs. The irrelevance of studies relates to who controls research and knowledge. Both Raja and Karma complained of limited research and knowledge production, and a lack of information and avenues for publishing where studies are not related to the Arab context or society. They attribute this to the low number of design-based academic journals and an absence of graduate degrees in design. If the very people who teach research are not taught research, nor conduct any, how can the uninformed teach the uninformed and expect students to appreciate and respect it? The limited knowledge production regionally (across disciplines) poses a very real problem to educators in design programmes across Jordan, Lebanon, the UAE and Egypt, as is the absence of graduate studies.

Like writing, research and design thinking were missing from the design curriculum. Most programmes centre the vocational, or focus on corporate identities and branding, but the integration of design into daily life is not taught, designer Abla tells me. The design as service-provider focus in education 'prevents designers from pursuing community work,' she says. Abla believes a proper application of design thinking in finding problems and solutions, to be able to communicate these and motivate people, should be curricular priorities. Her colleague Basem tells me how design thinking has shaped who he is and taught him to break down problems into the smallest increments before piecing them back together to discover an innovative solution. Design thinking is not taught in universities; instead, educators use a literal approach that strips the students' imagination.

In her research for ADW, Sama cited the lack of knowledge around design research as one of the main findings. Research is not defined nor understood properly, and the case was bleaker when discussing design research. Karma reported how she went for an interview at a design agency in Jordan, and when she explained her work, the owner told her 'I can't hire a design guru that comes every morning fills the wall with post-it notes and goes home.'

The experience discouraged her, but a year later, the same agency advertised a post for a design researcher, demonstrating a shift within the industry's understanding of design research. The design researcher as someone who pins sticky notes on the wall in a conference room during brainstorms has paralleled the prevalence of design thinking. Rather than understanding design research as part of the design process, research becomes a simple set of tools. Moreover, it reduces design thinking to a scientific method that revolves around tools and techniques to get desired results. But design thinking is about providing a different way of thinking about design that invites critical thinking into the practice.

Educator Aws stated that no design department in any university requires undergraduate students to produce research. He told me that students often copy and paste from online websites described as 'Pinterest Fetist' and they equate research with Behance. Designer and educator Rayan blames social media for quick online searches where 'students can't necessarily identify what is good and what is bad design,' and focus on trends rather than context. The use of online sources in the design process can inspire students when they are stuck. Examples and tutorials provide quick and easy ways for designers to share ideas and obtain feedback beyond their immediate network. Social media acts as an important supplement to the design process, and videos can be important tools for learning about design and software skills to execute ideas. Aws explained his own struggle with the absence of research and how he taught himself:

The research we learned in school was copying from textbooks [...] and now our students copy paste from Wikipedia. But there's no understanding of the concept of [...] research...had I not [done graduate] education I would never have learned.

Educators and designers blamed the curriculum's focus on the designer as craftsperson rather than critical thinker for poor research skills amongst students. Demand for research skills was vocalised by educators, students and designers, particularly with an interest in viewing design as an interdisciplinary practice away from outcome-based work. What is important is for educators to emphasise the different forms of research to make students aware of these, and teach them how to conduct research, including research ethics.

Eroding specialisations

The emphasis on research and thinking reflected the shifts in design practice and pedagogy in the last 15 years. Design, an outcome-based field, often overlooks the requirements of the brief in favour of making a thing. But the design process is equally important in the journey. As I have written elsewhere:

Expanding design to encompass theories and practices from other disciplines has long been debated. However, most of these discussions revolve around incorporating different methodologies and practices from other disciplines, or developing another '-disciplinarity' in design, rather than eroding the borders between different specializations within design. Specifically, while Bremner and Rodgers describe design moving away from disciplines and into issue- and project-based work, there is no discussion of the how, what, and where we think in design (Abdulla, 2021, pp. 227–228).

Educators across the four cities expressed their desire to push process-based work over outcome based, to expand beyond the confines of the disciplinary borders if designers are expected to deal with complex wicked problems. Rayan explains his approach with students to make them understand that outcome is part of something larger:

The outcome is extremely important, especially in university where students have to make something. [...] [B]ecause they need to learn how to make it. That's part of the process. But I what I try to emphasise in my teaching [...] is that the outcome will happen anyway, it's a process that will lead to the outcome.

Anas encourages his students 'to understand design differently, to grow the definition of design for them'. He cites the privilege of having wealthier students for his ability to experiment, because they are not stressed about finding a job post-graduation. He believes the lack of rigidity to the idea of graphic design advantages the programme:

It's more of the process of design and the methodology itself, using design as a methodology and the research behind any topic and any product at the end. And then outcome is a matter of practice and then it will work right in the future.

Showing process is catching on in the design industry. Educator Masa explains how this evolution is visible at DDW:

'Mathalan lamma balash' [for example when it started] Design Week, it was very polished. It was finished product and no one really understood, but today you walk into Design Week and you find the process, find the designers there explaining their struggles.

Rayan, whose design studio runs a design residency, describes how the focus is research-based, emphasising connections and the journey rather than outcomes. 'For us, it's not an end product,' he says, 'it's more of the process, nothing is supposed to be final. It's the conversations that are happening.'

Beirut-based educator Rita explains how she encourages students to think in an interdisciplinary way:

I get [students] to this point to say design is not about producing a logo or corporate identity, a manual or [...] a brochure or a website or an animation, it is about the thought behind this, the process and the way we thought about the needs of the end user. And [...] this is why I believe [...] design is very interdisciplinary, that they need to learn about different disciplines to understand [this].

Interdisciplinarity within design programmes regionally is reflective of the context. While design programmes are more defined and specific now, their origins inhabited a space between art and design, which designer Baha believes allowed him to 'branch out and to consider design within a kind of wider scope'. Rita, who teaches at an American university (accredited by NASAD), describes how the academic who validated her university's programme reacted to the approach:

They came in and they were surprised that we, we focus on illustration in a graphic design programme, and for them, these were separate [...] you don't teach graphic designers illustration. I realised that in Lebanon, that's how we teach, because of the limited opportunities for graphic designers, we try to branch out.

Similarly, Raja described the curriculum at a Jordanian university like a colourful and flavourful salad – with cinema studies and cinematography, computer graphics, design methodology, branding and animation. This is because most majors do not necessarily fit in Jordan, he tells me, so diversity provides students with options. Adam described a similar approach to the University of Jordan's programme, who produce more interdisciplinary designers who teeter between disciplines. Cairo-based educator Anas refers to how his programme attempts to avoid the classification of just 'graphic design' and move towards 'design'. Salim's work with the computer science department at his university capitalises on the emerging market of gaming, currently devoid of designers. '*Fa belnesba lal studios elle mawjooda houn* [so for the studios that exist here] they think of the designer as a luxury. "We can't afford to hire a designer",' he tells me. They produce UX/UI on their own and copy existing works. Salim is looking to create new pathways, to integrate designers within the sector and 'focus on games that have impact and local and regional relevance.' Gaming and UX/UI are growing areas regionally, educator Maher tells me, and the UAE – through the launch of DIDI – is focusing on generating talent locally rather than importing it to feed these new emerging markets.

The safety of the specialisation comes from the fear of the unknown. Despite eroding disciplinary boundaries, generalist programmes are considered not marketable, particularly with economic uncertainty rife in the region.

Typography

Design champions itself as a universal problem-solving discipline, and the Islamic and Arabic descriptor demonstrates the power of design's 'universal' language. In typography, the universal is Latin, and it renders everything else as non-Latin because it is not part of the canon. Typography is a practice that 'was once a fluently multilingual and [a] multicultural calling' but the last hundred years has seen an increase in 'typographic ethnocentricity and racism [...] and much of that narrow-mindedness is institutionalized in the workings of machines' (Bringhurst, 2015). Typographer Robert Bringhurst (2015, p. 89) shows there are alphabets that have histories longer and more intricate than Latin, and 'typography and typographers must honor the variety and complexity of human language, thought and identity, instead of homogenizing or hiding it'. Categorising Arabic as non-Latin implies a hierarchy, an outdated method that ignores the multilingual audience, and some designers have called for abolishing the term. Recent advances in technology and desktop publishing have rendered the creation of special characters easier, but the 'non-Latin' category remains in place, and machines are embedded with this binary.

Nowhere is this marginalisation more evident than in the structure of design programmes region wide. In four years of study, students are offered only one class on Arabic type and one on Latin type. On the other hand, students can take up to three typography courses at US universities. In the latter case, all three courses are devoted exclusively to Latin type, whereas in Jordan and other Arab countries (a region that speaks Arabic), students can only take two courses for two completely different languages, and these courses prioritise Latin over Arabic. While we cannot dismiss the importance of bilingual learning, it is often at the expense of Arabic. Why does a university located in the Arab region call it Arabic typography rather than typography? Is Arabic truly so alien that it requires its own special study, even amongst the people who are Arabs themselves? The privileging of Latin over Arabic in an Arab country makes the case for decolonising typography, to change the terms of the conversation, where liberating Arabic typography from its narrow confines and restrictions would unsettle the space.

The situation is rendered more complex in American universities, however. Zainab, who teaches in Dubai, tells me the difficulties she faced when proposing an Arabic typography class, which was rejected twice:[42]

A lot of people were against this idea of teaching Arabic type for some reason because it's thought of as not being inclusive, because not all our students speak Arabic. And we were shocked; I can't believe a white person is telling me 'You're not being inclusive'. But [...] the Arabic script doesn't mean the Arabic language. Our students speak Urdu or Persian or Arabic or Swahili, all languages around us use the Arabic script, it doesn't mean you have to know Arabic language. [...] [I]n this part of the world [...] when you go out and practice, you will always deal with bilingual content.

Attempting to force a one-size-fits-all American definition of inclusion fails to understand the context of how cultures operate. Even if the university is American, it should not 'forget that it's in the UAE, and that the context also has to be addressed in the curriculum,' Zainab tells me. Student demand and support for the class has been strong, allowing Zainab to bring forward the case to make the class a permanent part of the curriculum rather than an elective. Throughout

---

42 Since the interview, the class has now become mandatory.

my conversations, participants concluded that the teaching of Arabic typography was inadequate. Designer Athar explains:

They are not doing it [typography] properly [...] we need to follow a Western system even in Arabic typography, we need to encode our glyphs, although the language and letterform is different. And the arrangement of letters with four variables, three to five variables for each letter we're just stuffing it into a system and tweaking that system for it to work rather than create something that functions for us or caters to our language.

Athar believes that a well-rounded understanding of the subject is necessary to further the design discipline, particularly by creating systems relevant to the complexities of the language itself. Educator Maria tells me how she struggles teaching Arabic type:

[W]e are also superficial in handling our Arabic type. [...] I struggle with my type classes to give them the anatomy of Arabic type...there's no sheet in a book. So I had to do it on my own. But it's based on calligraphy. It's not type per se. [...] Slowly [...] we turn it into a type practice. And we call things by their name as if they were called in the calligraphic dictionaries.

Teaching type requires solutions for Arabic typography, not simply basing it on calligraphic principles or principles from Latin type. 'Who actually studied the length of the line? What is the best reading line length? [...] How many characters?' Maria asks while calling for more in-depth research into Arabic typography. Principles for Arabic type, and space for experimentation, present new opportunities for creating new and relevant typefaces – as opposed to the 'Frankenstein' trend of using Arabic fonts based on the Latin alphabet, which use disconnected letters copy and pasted from Latin letters, or Arabic companion fonts that are made to fit an existing Latin typeface. Designer and educator Rayan describes how this approach led to disconnected design work:

when I was working at a branding agency in Dubai [...] and brands that existed back then [were] one dimensional in terms of developing Arabic typography [...] they would work on the Latin and then have the Arabic be secondary. And if they were thinking of the Arabic first, then it was specifically about the typography, and not necessarily think[ing] of the culture in which they design.

The increasing economic power and influence of the GCC has escalated demand for new visual identities and typefaces. High levels of brain drain means GCC countries are one of the main recruiters of design talent from Jordan, Lebanon and Egypt. In addition, GCC employers are demanding a command of the Arabic language, including writing

Figure 10: 100 Best Arabic Posters travelling exhibition at La Locanda Boutique Hotel, first edition of Amman Design Week in 2016, photo by Danah Abdulla

emails in Arabic, which many students struggle with, Maria tells me. The increase in demand for Arabic content transforms typography into an important practice. Moreover, if Arabic is to become the language of design – within this philosophy – typography is crucial. Participants concluded that familiarity with Arabic is a necessity due to the importance of digitising publications, developing new technologies and methods for Arabic typography, and creating type libraries.

Indeed, Arabic programming code remains in its infancy, thus building websites in English is a quicker process. Whereas technology has progressed, education has not kept up, and training in typography is behind. Opportunities are scarce. If a native Arabic speaker would like to pursue further studies to focus on Arabic typography, their only option is to enrol in a Masters programme in Europe. Designers region wide are making up for the absence of Arabic type education through a series of summer schools. The Amman-based design studio Eyen Collective held The Arabic Letter Lab in Summer 2022, Lebanese designers Lara Captan and Kristyan Sarkis hosted three editions of Arabic Type, an

Figure 11: Eyen Design Arabic Letter Lab 2022 workshop, photo by Hussam Hasan

intensive six-week typography workshop in Beirut, and Tunisian-French designer Naïma Ben Ayed developed an openly available programme for a multi-script type design education, featuring principles for learning and assignments (see Figure 11).[43]

Experimentation to break the phobia

Rote learning (a method of banking education) is prevalent at all levels of education in Jordan and regionally. This form of pedagogy has its roots in the Qur'anic schools, which formed the educational system until the modernisation of schools. Classical Arabic plays a fundamental role in the manner in which people raise their children and in the educational practices of society, two factors that shape the milieu and attitudes. The Qur'an is where children first encounter classical Arabic, which they are often taught to learn by heart. Through memorisation and rejecting forms of questioning, children experience the break 'between *learning* and *understanding*' (Sharabi, 1988, p. 85, emphasis original). Rote learning becomes the standard for acquiring ideas and 'internalizing values', and is a form of learning and understanding that persists throughout education and socialisation.

---

43 The proposal is available on Futuress, see https://futuress.org/stories/letters-words-stories/.

The Arab region uses a form of classical Arabic that is 'practically unchanged as its basic means of bureaucratic communication and formal discourse' (Sharabi, 1988, p. 85). The rift between the classical form and the colloquial form has reinforced traditional social divisions, transforming knowledge into an instrument of power. The structure of classical Arabic, prioritising speech over writing and rhetoric over dialogue, has significant implications. Sharabi (1988) illustrates this implication through the example of printing. Printing made the Bible widely available and allowed Europeans to read it, therefore spreading the Protestant revolution as it enabled the 'transition from rhetoric to hermeneutics' (Sharabi, 1988, p. 87). Printing made the Qur'an widely available in the Arab world in the nineteenth century, however, reading the Qur'an was never promoted. The Quran is recited, repeated, but very rarely is it *read*. Interpretation of the text[44] is the special privilege of religious officials, because reading is subversive and liberating. It is attained through 'reading (interpretation), understanding, criticism' (Sharabi, 1988, p. 87). Reading leads to the production of knowledge, to innovation and change, whereas speech represents stability and the status quo.

It is no wonder that Arabic and Arabic typography instils fear in designers. Zainab explains her interest in focusing on Arabic typography and implementing it into her classes:

It's a struggle. Again, I graduated from AUS with zero knowledge about the Arabic script and I came out with this phobia from touching the script, because, for me, it's such a sacred thing that I can't touch or experiment with. And I felt that I have to make sure that my students don't graduate with this mentality that it's okay to break the rules. It's okay to play with it.

Designer and educator Adam explains:

there's such a fear from the design students from the Arabic letter because there were so many instances where they were slapped on the hand whenever they had the desire to try to play with it. We do believe in the power of play and experimentalism and this is why we kind of wanted to be like: 'Okay, 5leena nekser el rahba [break the fear].'

Maria describes a resistance from students in working with Arabic typography and difficulty in learning the language, and the fear is more applicable to Muslim students:

Notre Dame University because it's Christian, and it's really clerical there, the students have no attachment. They don't see Arabic as anything sacred. They just see it as something that is third grade. And it's not cool. [...]

---

44 The Egyptian thinker Nasr Hamid Abu Zayd (1943–2010) discussed the Qur'an and its hermeneutics and called for subjecting the Qur'an to new interpretations in his writings. In 1995, an Egyptian court accused him of apostasy.

We don't need it, who needs it? I'm going to go and travel to the US and I'm going to go to Europe who's going to talk in Arabic or use it or.

The dismissive attitude means students struggle to comprehend the importance of reading and writing in Arabic to work in the GCC market, which the Lebanese universities largely cater to.

Business and communication skills

Business skills are defined as both management (instrumental skills) and an understanding of basic economic theory. In other words, they are the ability to communicate with clients and aid designers in articulating their value. The absence of business and communication education in design education negatively affects designers who choose to start their own businesses, or even have to price their work. How to price work is a question designers around the world grapple with. In the data collected for Designers' Inquiry, an investigation into the social and economic profiles of designers living in Italy, the research reveals that 'young designers are primarily applying somewhat arbitrary measures in order to define their fees and often undersell their labour-power thus lowering the general perception of the money-value of design work' (Elzenbaumer, 2013, p. 97). Freelancers are particularly affected because of the absence of an accessible scale of fees that is adaptable to a range of work levels (Elzenbaumer, 2013).

Establishing better relationships with clients would increase value attributed to design. Designer Maha argued studios and agencies are incapable of tapping into the talent they possess due to management issues. How can we surface talents and skills to generate self-awareness and awareness of others to create effective collaborations? She asks. In other words, how are designers effectively adapting to challenges and opportunities?

The location of design programmes in universities presents opportunities for cross-departmental collaborations. Although they operate in silos, the placement of design programmes provides an easier opportunity for educators to break these silos and introduce students to new methodologies and epistemologies from other disciplines. Design is now taught in business programmes, in hopes of teaching business leaders the design process and design thinking. But why not the other way around? Designers need business and communication skills to develop and run successful businesses. To seek new clients and convince them of their ideas and articulate design's value, designers should be persuasive, especially if they are trying to present something new. An important element here is teaching designers to communicate and work with clients. As Japanese designer Takuo Hirano (1991, p. 58) mentions:

At least half of a designer's time is spent meeting and working with everyone from the company president to the machinists who finally assemble the product. If a designer is not only to convince decision makers about new design ideas but to promote full understanding, which leads to total commitment and effective follow-up, then working with people will take an inordinate amount of time. Without the recognition and comprehension of this designer role, I see little chance for even the best design to be realized.

Hirano's (1991) point highlights the importance of writing, speaking and presentation skills. In Chapter 1, I discussed the issues with client–designer communication. The integration of business and communication skills – including both theoretical and practical practices from the fields of organisational communication, management and economic theory – are necessary for preparing designers to work in industry.

SHIFTING PERCEPTIONS ON DESIGN

156—Design's role in society
    157 –Possibilities: community service
    158 –Possibilities: outreach
    160 –Possibilities: open studios, workshops and libraries
    163 –Possibilities: design advocates

165—Establishing new forms of practice: who is design for?
    166 –Possibilities: dialogue
    167 –Placements, internships and educators with ties to industry
    169 –Local and regional connections
    170 –Possibilities: defining design
    172 –Possibilities: generalist and graduate studies
    173 –Possibilities: design vocabularies

Chapter 5

In this book, design is viewed as an opening of possibilities through negotiations with the given, not a problem-solving, solution-oriented field (Dilnot, 2005). What are – to borrow Palestinian architect Yara Sharif's (2017) term – the moments of possibility offered for design in the Arab region to be imagined *otherwise*? This chapter asks who design is for by outlining possibilities for shifting perceptions on design, away from elitist perceptions and towards more socially engaged and contextually relevant practices, and to develop better ties between education and industry for job creation. Working through the Arab region's current design cultures, it describes different strategies proposed by participants in creating stronger links between education and industry, and educating the general public, designers, educators and design students on design's value and role in society.

Design's role in society

The weakness of Arab education lies in the quality of curriculum, namely outdated content lacking in relevance to labor-market needs. Also lacking is a culture of lifelong learning and community engagement (Badran, Baydoun and Hillman, 2019, p. 9).

Community engagement and social responsibility were marked as important elements for participants who believe that 'designers should integrate themselves in society', to encourage 'more relevant projects with the community', to include 'voluntary service', and to 'work alongside and connect with communities'. Design education, however, does little to support more informed social engagement in design, leading designers to address symptoms rather than causes.

Discussion on community engagement projects and research in Chapter 4 demonstrate that educators should make their intentions clearer, and teach students how to approach the community in a more sensitive way through an official dialogue between the university and the community. What is obvious is not only a lack of research, where students jump to solutions without first addressing the fundamental issues at hand, but that design is depoliticised. Instead of targeting symptoms, both educators and students should confront complex problems and be aware of the time involved in understanding the political, social, economic, historical and geographical challenges of the community, of the milieu and the context the students are rushing to work in.

'The problem is not in design as much as it is in society,' educator and designer Raja tells me. 'Design in its simplest definition is not just form and function but a comprehensive vision of humanity,' he continues. In stating that design is a comprehensive vision of humanity, Raja goes against a traditional view of design. When students begin working, they find themselves in agencies where their role is merely about giving form. When society does not understand design, he continues, design becomes alienated and stereotyped as an aesthetic exercise. Raja blamed designers and their inability to communicate their work to society and felt that the work of changing perceptions is the duty of the design community.

The inability of designers to demonstrate the value of their profession to society is a communication and representation issue. Unclear intentions and elitist connotations further contribute to the dismissal of design. A new opportunity arises when the design field redefines itself beyond a mere service provider connected to a traditional industry.

What happens when designers start to integrate their practice into communities, and connect social responsibility with the surrounding location into the design curriculum? There was a general consensus that for people to see the relevance of design to daily life and appreciate its value, it must speak to them. In other words, designers must stop speaking to themselves if they want to make design relevant to people's lives.

Community engagement plays a significant role in contextually-based design education. Its goals, aims and implementation, however, must be genuine. Here is where the value of research methods and of eroding specialisations becomes evident. Emphasising research throughout the curriculum can create links between different social worlds, class, locations, places, interests and objects (Hanafi and Arvanitis, 2016), and could enable students to think differently about the multiple worlds that make up the Arab region.

A range of suggestions was made for engaging the public, including news coverage, campaigns, events and public talks. I will focus on community engagement, open studios, workshops and libraries, outreach and design advocates as moments of possibility.

Possibilities: community service

The designer Jad is all about the vernacular of the city, bridging design worlds, instilling a sense of responsibility and promoting access. Part of his Amman-based design practice provides pro-bono design services to the community for free by applying creative interventions and introducing these to share them with the public. Jad feels that these interventions are 'important in a culture where "design" as a concept is not a priority. In many communities, it is an unaffordable privilege, and therefore almost completely absent.' Moreover, the project aims 'to redefine and reshape the city's identity' and stimulate the public to talk about design and 'respond to these creative interventions'. Jad tells me about a workshop he conducted at a university in Saudi Arabia that encourages students to contribute community service hours every year. He suggested Jordanian universities should make community work a condition for the completion of a university degree. He tells me how one of the students was inspired by his workshop and pursued her project as part of her community service, working with women-run stores across Jeddah, a sensitive topic in the country.

Mandatory volunteering could help students use design to understand their surroundings and the local political situation. Furthermore, the action could initiate conversations and opportunities for change. Additionally, mandatory volunteering – framed as community engagement to emphasise a longer-term commitment – could encourage students to continue working on community-based projects beyond the allocated class time or seek projects out themselves. But instilling a sense of community service is not so simple. Young people across the Arab region have low levels of trust in the government and public institutions to varying degrees. The clear disconnect between the youth and public institutions contributes to feelings of hopelessness and waithood (OECD, 2022). There is hope, however. Distrust leads youth towards civil society organisations, community-based projects and informal associations, important partners for genuine community engagement for students and designers.

Possibilities: outreach

Access to publishing tools, video tutorials, social media, portfolio websites and other online resources have increased engagement with design, but these are often centred around software skills or sharing work for feedback, catering to designers and enthusiasts rather than the public. How do you capitalise on the media to integrate design into more mainstream conversations? This is the question that preoccupies students. Educators acknowledged that the level of understanding of design in students is far superior than it was ten years ago. '[S]tudents are much more aware [of design] and they're like, "oh, I went to this exhibition, and I saw this and it inspired me to think about this and it was" [...] We didn't have that back then,' Rayan says. But they also acknowledge the dangers of information overload. How do you address them so the public can listen?

Outreach in the form of design events – whether through design weeks, biennales, public talks or workshops were cited as effective methods of public engagement. Educators Salim, Jeeda, Anas and Rita praised design events for providing a more vibrant cultural scene and exposure to their students. Attending these events has become part of their participation grade to push student engagement. Maria believes events like BDW made designers 'believ[e] that we are a part of a culture and that is worth delving into', that adds something beyond the Western canon. She also praised how it allowed people to meet craftspeople and venture out of Beirut and into different areas and cities around Lebanon. Rayan believes the aim should be for smaller scale sustainable events that happen more frequently and impact the local community. Reflecting on a design event he organised a few years back in the UAE, he tells me:

I would have [conducted] more outreach to the general public. More than just [...] people who are interested in what design is. We had schools [and] universities that visited, which was nice, but I think I would like more of like, the '7ukooma' [public] schools, younger kids to come.

Rayan tells me how some of the people who volunteered at the event switched their majors to design 'because they saw the potential that design has and the conversation that it kind of started.'

Salim's work revolves around outreach and creating connections. He is passionate about pushing away from the Cairo bubble and speaking to designers across Egypt:

Egypt has huge talent [...] that would stun, astonish you, but they're in remote areas [Port Said, Nubia for example] and distant areas from Cairo, [distant] from that demographic that prefers to speak in English. [...] 'Fa' [so] they're out of the conversation.

He wants to break what he calls the psychological barrier mindset between university graduates, which he describes as heavily influenced by European thinking, and self-taught designers:

Of course, there's language barriers, cultural barriers, economic barriers, so they tried to cross it. There are a lot of mistakes that will happen and are happening of these worlds mixing together. But this is a healthy thing; these mistakes will help us even become better and produce something even more representative of what Egypt is and this diversity. [...] [W]e as education institutions need to push the privileged kids towards the non-privileged ones and make both learn from each other and it's very important for this cross pollination to happen.

One approach is through Arabising content. Salim encourages students who start design initiatives to prioritise launching them in Arabic to connect with multiple design communities. When content is Arabised, it automatically quadruples the audience, he tells me. Salim explains the importance of Arabic:

[T]hey don't understand that how, how much they're taking [...] speaking another language [for granted] and even preferring it over their local language [...] [I]t's just out of laziness oh I have to translate 'kol shi' [everything]. Just hire a very decent, a cheap translator bas [but] change the text 'oo 5ala9 5ele9na y3ni' [and be done with it].

Outreach becomes a tool to counter the absence of design exposure at secondary schooling for most youth in state institutions.

Possibilities: open studios, workshops and libraries

The studio is not the only place where learning occurs. Curriculum should be viewed in totality, encompassing the formal curriculum (the official and planned curriculum), the informal curriculum (informal and extracurricular activities that engage other sites of design beyond the classroom) and the hidden curriculum, defined by Giroux and Penna (1979, p. 22) as 'the unstated norms, values and beliefs that are transmitted to students through the underlying structure of meaning in both the formal content as well as the social relations of the school and classroom life'. Throughout this book, I have focused on the first, and touched on the latter two. Bureaucratic red tape and funding prevent access to resources that enhance student experience and experimentation such as facilities for making, studios and libraries. Activating the informal curriculum – through access to open studios, workshops and libraries at sites outside of the university – becomes crucial to providing an expanded possibility for design education.

Books and magazines on design in both Arabic and English are lacking, causing issues for research, self-learning and class readings. Library resources are poor, leading students to use the web as a resource, relying on websites such as Behance, Pinterest and Instagram, resulting in poor research. Students are eager for resources, the designer Athar tells me, but gaining access to design books and magazines in English and Arabic in Jordan is difficult; distribution and shipping can be expensive and a logistical nightmare, discouraging designers from seeking them. Athar and Adam's Amman-based studio caters to this need by being an open space for anyone interested in design to drop by for a chat, a working session or to browse their library. Similarly, designers Rami and Laith wanted to have a section dedicated to design magazines and books in their studio space, where students could browse and buy, but they faced countless hurdles when registering their business. Their lawyer advised against including a library and selling publications because they would go through another round of checks with publishing and the *mukhabarat*. The Jordanian government considers the sale of publications and a public access library a 'publishing house,' and publishing houses are constantly monitored by the government. The demand for alternative resources is evident. Rayan, whose UAE studio has an accessible library, recounts a story of how the resource is used:

We have these two local girls walk in; they look super young. And they walk to the library, they went to the interactive design section, and started reading books. So, I was just curious [...] Just wanted to have a conversation. So, I just approached them, "Hi, how are you guys? Do you need anything?" You know, "what are you guys doing?" They were like, "we're just doing research for class." I was like "oh, which university do you go to?" they were like "we're still in high school." I [asked] "What are you doing?' "We're doing an interactive design project. [...] We found [your] website and we went to the library, and we searched for books and found that you have a good collection of interactive design books and coding. We thought we'd pass by and just find some books here, because we're working on something with processing and Python."

Beirut-based Studio Safar takes access to publications further through publishing *Journal Safar*, an annual and bilingual design and visual culture journal. *Journal Safar* attempts 'to remedy the scarcity of critical writings on design in the global south, and [...] acknowledge designers as active agents of cultural production' (Studio Safar, 2023 no pagination). The magazine creates a dialogue with designers and cultural producers in the Global South rather than focusing solely on local or regional issues, demonstrating the desire to be part of a wider global network.

Documentation becomes a tool to create new resources, particularly amongst the visual landscape of Instagram and TikTok resources. 'We need writers [...] [W]e need people who can look at the archives...not just archives popping on our windows on websites,' Maria says. For example, eyen design's Arabic Letter Lab 2022 workshops culminated in a book published by Khatt. It features findings and outcomes from the workshops and interviews with designers based regionally and in the diaspora, creating additional resources and documentation (see Figures 12 and 13).

Figure 12: eyen design's Arabic Letter Lab 2022 publication, published by Khatt, photo by Baha Suleiman

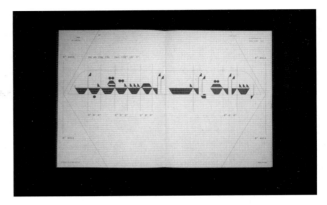

Figure 13: eyen design's Arabic Letter Lab 2022 publication, published by Khatt, photo by eyen design

Social media accounts showing archival design work as forms of alternative histories also play a role as vital educational resources. Amman-based Elharf, however, brings this archive to a physical space. Founded by designer Hussein Alazaat in 2017, Elharf is a space of art, culture and design, offering a range of workshops and courses in calligraphy, branding, typography, Islamic art, pottery and jewellery, lectures and a specialised library. It also sells designed products and artworks. The space includes a collection of old street signage, and a library with Arabic publications from the nineteenth century onwards, collected for their visual and cultural content, and targeting mostly students and researchers.

Designers are using their studios to address the gaps in design education. Rayan explains how his approach grew out of observing students' needs at the American university where he taught. While the faculty grew to include more Arabic-speaking faculty (and faculty familiar with both Latin and Arabic scripts), the American university still required them to teach entirely in English. 'But we always have to teach within the context in which we exist,' he says. Rayan's studio began to create its own programming to create new references and resources 'because most of the references that students were citing were Western and Eurocentric, and so we thought it'd be really interesting to start to [begin] a conversation [...] develop more research and try to create content that is relevant to us.'

Turbo, a studio located in downtown Amman based in a converted garage, doubles as a cultural event venue, hosting a biannual print sale, workshops, screenings and launch events, and was once a music recording studio. In Beirut, Waraq, a non-profit organisation, supports graphic design through education, research, production and publishing. The physical space includes a print production facility, an educational programme, a print celebration event and a research lab. Tashkeel, launched by Lateefa bint Maktoum (a member of the UAE royal family) in Dubai in 2008, aims to provide a nurturing environment to the country's art and design industries. Tashkeel encompasses workspaces and facilities, multidisciplinary studios and galleries, operating under an open membership model. It organises residencies, workshops, talks, exhibitions, trainings, international collaborations and produces publications.

The last 15 years has seen no shortage in alternative spaces, institutes and incubators focused on making up for specialisations absent from university design education, particularly in fashion design and furniture/product design. The Creative Space Beirut, the Starch Foundation, Design Institute Amman, Exil Collective, Qasimi Rising, House of Today and others attempt to tackle the lack in the formal curriculum or government support for the creative industries. Each of these has a different approach to design – ranging from socially focused to luxury – and many are funded by foreign grants which dictate their survival, putting the sustainability of such initiatives into the hands of organisations with specific agendas.

Possibilities: design advocates

Composed of organisations that range from professional associations to unions and councils, the goal of design advocates is to represent designers, to promote design, to systematise and to safeguard its practice. Organisations such as the Design Council, ICOGRADA and AIGA provide design with a voice, with measures and standards that the design industry should abide by, and they attribute value to the field. The absence of design advocacy regionally – aside from a trickle of mostly interior design associations, and the Lebanese Graphic Design Syndicate (est. 1976) – means designers lack representation, measures and standards for the profession and education, benefits and resources (such as help with clients and contracts). Throughout this book, I have demonstrated the challenges faced by the design disciplines – including students largely uninformed about design, a lack of awareness amongst the public, designers and ministries of education, and the absence of a body representing designers and their interests – have fuelled these challenges. Students, educators and designers alike were in agreement about establishing a design association representing designers, because it would create a sense of value, credibility, standards and regulation within industry and education. 'Art and architecture have more importance and weight largely because they have associations representing them,' Karma tells me. The benefits for education include setting standards for design programmes, admissions and more frequent revalidation processes, and in industry to introduce regulations, competitive salaries and standards for production.

The creation of a body representing designers is not straightforward due to Arab bureaucracy. The fate of the Jordanian Design Centre (JDC) serves as a case study to designers in Jordan looking for a form of representation. In my interview with educator Yazan, he detailed the process of establishing the JDC from 1999 until 2009, and an independent design lab located at the German Jordanian University. Inaugurated in 2007 by King Abdullah II, Yazan reported how people from Germany, Jordan and other countries worked on preparing documentation, policy and production for the JDC. The JDC possessed machinery, tools and technicians and funding from the university and other international funding bodies. Shortly after the King's visit, however, 'conflicts and egos prevented it from moving forward,' Yazan tells me. In other words, the neopatriarchal bureaucratic system based on patriarchal social relations prevented it from moving forward. Yazan explained how the centre was shut shortly after:

I had a conflict with the new president. [...] He wanted me to do something and I refused, and he took the stand that no more JDC. I said to myself to take my sabbatical leave. [...] Beginning of September nothing happened, waiting for the new director [of JDC]. [...] I find no chance that the new director will come and take place. [...] So, I left.

Despite having secured three international contracts for production, Yazan was excluded from further JDC activities. Although the JDC was an independent organisation, its placement at a university – and Yazan's insistence of involving the university President and Vice President in the dealings – institutionalised it. The placement of the JDC at a university is both positive and negative: machinery that is accessible to students provides the necessary access to resources for making. However, connecting it directly to the President and Vice President meant involvement from people who have their own agendas that conflict with the JDC's mission. Successful design associations cannot be tied to an institution but must be independent to it; they must work to actively advocate for design locally, regionally and internationally, develop connections between industry and with craftspeople, present new opportunities for design, conduct research and provide relevant resources and funding opportunities for designers. The funding used to produce large events could be rerouted to more sustainable and long-term opportunities such as establishing a design association, one that understands the local context and design education's role within it.

Establishing new forms of practice: who is design for?

Aggressive neoliberal agendas focus on employability, with an emphasis on the knowledge economy and building human capital (Keirl, 2015), thus, it is no surprise that design schools are driven towards professionalisation. Executive Director of L'École de design Nantes Atlantique Christian Guellerin (2012) states two reasons for this: the awareness that design is an engine for growth and increases business competitiveness and the diminishing influence of the graduation project as the judge of institutional quality. Quality is now based on the job opportunities acquired for students. In Jordan, the development of design programmes has been largely financial, confirmed by the mission and vision statements of universities teaching design where the purpose is to train a labour force, in line with Jordan priding itself in training labour for export (Zughloul, 2000). The same analysis can be applied regionally. Even with the disconnect between industry and education and high rates of unemployment amongst university graduates, educators emphasised employability, where preparation for the industry is a necessary ingredient. Does design education adequately prepare students for working in design? Are opportunities for designers too narrow, and forcing students to seek opportunities elsewhere? Is the sole purpose of the university to train future employees, or to train students for export to external markets and encourage brain drain?

Conflicting responses emerged in the interviews and focus groups. Some claimed the content of the curriculum and educators prepared students for industry, others experienced confusion about what to do with what you are learning, while others acknowledged that working in industry expands the skills you learn in university and bring the role of learner and designer as critical thinker into perspective. The critique of employability is that it is usually at the expense of critical thinking, where teaching focuses on transmitting skills and facts. By avoiding any questioning of the learning process or the subject, the curriculum restricts student 'potential for critical thought and action' (Shor, 1992, p. 12). With employability, educators focus on implementing what is useful for future employment and economic growth while disregarding other important aspects of learning. It transforms the classroom into 'new pedagogies', where the classroom becomes a space to acquire competencies for employability and a place for specific results, the 'return on investment' (Simons and Masschelein, 2012). Student Rashad reflects on the return on investment when he tells me that design programmes taught him the necessary competencies, but he is not necessarily seeing the return because he is not taught how to *explicitly* use them. His classmate Jenna replied that the first two years prepared her for industry and changed her thinking, but she remained confused on what they did, demonstrating the disconnect between what students learn and their experience. How can students begin to see how their learning is applied in practice? If denied the ability to question knowledge, how can they question the nature of the industry itself? Despite the focus on employability, discussion on industry preparation showed a disconnect between clients and designers, and industry and education. Addressing this disconnect could enable design to be valued and seen more strategically. I outline the moments of possibility to begin addressing this.

Possibilities: dialogue

The absence of dialogue between universities and the design industry is an opportunity for educators to teach students theory that is applicable within practice, to enable them to value design and to see how they can carve alternative career paths in an expanded design field. Dialogue between industry and universities is a way of dispelling common views the design industry has about the academy and vice versa. Dialogue between universities presents an opportunity for exchange and to build a design community that influences design culture and design education locally and regionally. The importance of local and regional dialogue between universities themselves was cited as highly valuable to 'discuss what we should focus on collectively,' educator and designer Zainab says. Indeed, any regional agreement between countries in the Arab League has been a failure, and even more so since 2011. Design programmes provide a grassroots moment of possibility to build connections between educators, without relying on official channels.

Short-term solutions to begin bridging the divide are proposed by participants: a programme of visiting lecturers/workshops and public talks, mentorship schemes, live briefs, student competitions organised by industry, design events and the implementation of a critical work placement/internship, particularly in the form of an internship module.

Placements, internships, and educators with ties to industry

The Precarious Workers Brigade (PWB), a UK-based group committed to developing practical, relevant research and actions in culture and education, outline important points in embedding placements and internships to avoid normalising unpaid or low paid work and countering uncertainty in job opportunities. They argue that framing work experience, placements, and/or internships as more than just a way into a profession would '[s]upport and empower students to have more autonomy' in the work place (Precarious Workers Brigade, 2017, p. 19). Placement modules should adequately prepare students by providing a critical outlook on work placements and internships; an overview of labour rights; contracts; the role of unions and bargaining; and on asking for a wage/fee. Paying attention to the working conditions of the industry and the students' experience encourages students to think critically of their placement and/or internship. PWB suggest offering students the opportunity to critique and share their experience with others. Their next suggestion, to '[d]iscuss different models of survival and subsistence and conceptions of success that artists and cultural workers use and the relationship their art practice has to earning a living' (Precarious Workers Brigade, 2017, p. 20) is an example of how visiting lecturers can introduce students to alternative models of making a living as designers. Placements and internships are excellent opportunities to expand the reach of design into different sectors and to build a stronger relationship between craftspeople and designers beyond visits to workshops and fetishising crafts-based practices.

These suggestions conclude that a critical work placement/ internship module allows students to reflect critically on their experience, working with employers who provide students with varying opportunities, mentorship and who instil confidence in students. The module should be in collaboration with industry to enable the employers offering these placements/internships to be self-reflective of their role in it.

Educators who are practitioners use their ties to industry to keep abreast with what is happening and maintain valuable connections, such as inviting industry professionals to sit on juries, give lectures and share their experience, which, some educators tell me, does not happen as often as it should. UAE-based educator Zainab tells me how she maintains her studio despite her Dean's objections, because it is crucial to her students:

It didn't make sense for me to abandon my practice because I hate this idea that I preach design but I don't practice it. The field is constantly changing, and I need to keep in [touch] with the industry, because I see how it benefits my students; they see themselves through me. They want this touch with the industry that I didn't have as a student.

As a female educator running a design studio, she provides a much-needed role model for her predominantly female student body.

Students are excited by industry-led live briefs because it motivates and assists them in relating to the environment and expectations, educator Hind tells me. Designers Rami and Laith valued the opportunities to share their experience with students to help them understand that there are different career trajectories available to them. Inviting designers from the industry allows learning for both students and educators by offering different points of view and topics not covered extensively in the formal curriculum. Moreover, design events contribute to creating connection. Salim expresses the importance of events like Cairo Design Week for introducing communication/graphic designers to Cairo's design culture:

The local industry, it's mostly architecture, interior and product design so 'e7na b3ad 3anhum bas' [we're far away from them but] we shouldn't be [...] and everybody will benefit to mingle, to see how they think, see how they operate, learn from them and they could make use of our fresh take on things and our professions.

The disconnect between industry and universities is also a cause of brain drain. Educator Khaled argued that a mutual non-recognition

– where industry does not recognise universities or their graduates and the other way around – is the cause. He suggested the establishment of a stakeholder who builds connections between universities and the design industry to clarify the design needs of the country and the type of designer required for the future. Otherwise, he argued, curricula will remain copy and pasted from outside models, where universities offer majors such as industrial design without assessing them, and the needs of the country will remain unknown.

Local and regional connections

Ties with local, regional and international universities, while still weak, are in development.[45] To build partnerships and encourage a stronger design community, Khaled organises online exchange workshops with universities in the UK, with over 200 students from five different universities enrolled, he tells me. In addition, he organises design lectures where attendance is open to students from across Jordan, and through his network of Arab educators he has generated dialogue between tutors countrywide. Khaled is optimistic about this collaboration as he feels it will lead to policy change in the future.

Karma, who has since moved away from education and into full-time practice, pushed for collaboration between universities, particularly in areas like curriculum design and publications. She argued that universities should focus their energies on establishing design as a serious profession in the industry and the MoHESR, and to provide youth with role models. As a strategy to improve the connections between universities, participants proposed collaboration and competitions between universities, suggesting exhibitions, talks and seminars at other campuses to encourage exchange.

Promoting collaboration and exchange can lead to dialogue between industry and universities and among universities and ministries of education. It also enables universities to capitalise on existing resources and share them with other universities, through opening up attendance to guest lectures to design students across the country or enabling access to labs, for example. The latter provides students with the opportunity to use materials they did not have access to and to create prototypes for their work. The same strategy is applies to increasing dialogue between industry and universities where universities could offer industry designers access to university resources. Anas, who teaches at a well-resourced American university, attempts to connect with state universities to use

---

45 For example, the Middle East Design Educators Association (MEDEA) was established in 2008, but their web presence is inactive.

their workshops and invite them to their events to make up for the lack of resources. Finally, collaboration could also begin to form a stronger design culture and introduce new role models for aspiring designers.

Possibilities: defining design

How design is defined within a local and regional context is a concern for designers and educators. Whereas design education (under many different names) dates back decades, only recently has a fully-fledged professionalisation of the field and a design culture started to develop regionally. I have discussed the interest in expanding the field of design, pushing both educators and designers towards multi- and interdisciplinary practices. The newness presents possibilities for defining design relevant to locality, rather than a definition produced in a different context during a different time. This is by no means a simple task, but it is underway, educator Masa tells me:

We're trying to establish this voice, a school of thought of what we're aiming to teach our students, but we always fail to come up with that school of thought. Only because we're just trying to define what design could be in this part of the world. [...] [L]et's try to understand who we are and how we design and what's our aesthetics or what is not.

The designer Rayan is tackling the same questions:

But I feel like in the Arab world, we need to really think about how would design be relevant to us, not only from a technological perspective, but also how is it going to be beneficial from a social perspective, from a political, from a cultural [one]. I think design does that in and of itself, but the way that it's taught needs to be more tailored to this part of the world, and it needs [to be] a lot more flexible and organic.

The designer Paul on the other hand is not so optimistic:

The issue with design in Lebanon, is that it started off very tradition-ally, which is I think, normal, that was everywhere. And it never developed into the understanding of design as we know it today.

There was however a window of opportunity to begin defining a new area through social design on a global level. Paul explains:

There is an opportunity for Lebanese designers to have their mark and say 'we've been through whatever enough, or we have enough experience to have a say in this, to contribute to the discussions of social design'. The opportunity is there, but I don't think we're taking it yet. Or I don't think we are equipped to take it yet. Because when we talk about social design it's imperative that you understand your own context before you go and practice it in different contexts.

Paul, who consults on social design, believes the area requires much more practice locally to develop further. The economic crisis in Lebanon means the opportunity is lost as people divert back to traditional disciplines that guarantee a job and are easy to understand:

There's so much going on that design does not exist, like what is design. People don't even want to have that conversation. What is really design? Maybe five years ago, we had a window to do that. But then with everything that's happening, it's not a priority [...] people have zero bandwidth to engage in anything that's not related to their daily lives, or to what kind of money they're making, what kind of jobs, what's the price of the dollar today, can we buy bread, you know, these things.

Defining design becomes more urgent within this context, to understand what relevance it has on people's everyday lives. Thinking of design and design education *otherwise* calls for a redirective practice. A redirective practice requires designers to acknowledge the material and immaterial consequences of their practice and the implications on the world (and the worlds within that world) (Fry, 2017). Doing this enables them to rethink their role as designers and their responsibility towards their audience, thereby shifting design's role as service provider. Viewing design as only a service provider does not acknowledge its ontological condition where, through design and designing, we are in turn designed by that which we have designed (what design scholar Anne-Marie Willis (2006)] terms ontological designing):

We design [...] we deliberate, plan and scheme in ways which pre-figure our actions and makings – in turn we are designed by our designing and by that which we have designed (i.e., through our interactions with the structural and material specificities of our environments); that this adds up to a double movement – we design our world, while our world acts back on us and designs us (Willis, 2006, p. 80).

Ontological design is best described by design scholar Mahmoud Keshavarz (2016, p. 87) through the example of the chair:

Once a chair is designed, it might be [...] an artefact providing a particular service to its users and consumers. However, it is always more than that. The designed chair has already performed some sort of designation because it has manipulated the environment by the resources it has used, the skills that were used, the labour that was invested in it, and so on. And because of this, the designed chair cannot exist only in interaction with its intended environment or end-users.

Defining design takes many forms, but most importantly it requires acknowledging the role designers play in making this world unsustainable and redirecting their practice.

Possibilities: generalist and graduate studies

Earlier, I discussed how educators described their programmes as non-discipline specific due to the context they work in and in order to navigate the bureaucratic requirements imposed on them by ministries of education. Their focus was centred on the process. But rather than an additive approach, there is an opportunity for eroding specialisations to shape philosophies and theories behind general and interdisciplinary design education, reshaping the programmes to be more locally and regionally centric.

Shaped by defining what design is, drawing on skills required to aid the future of digital transformation, capitalising on skills and knowledges required to equip future designers (writing, histories, design thinking, research, Arabic typography, and business and communication), and finding the right balance between process and outcome-based, Arab educators can work collaboratively and with different sectors (locally and regionally), and take advantage of their placement in a wider university network (drawing on other disciplines), to shape an iterative programme that meets the needs of its locale, convincing ministries of education and others of its necessity.

The other urgency to begin developing these skills is through the establishment of a graduate studies in design. General design graduate programmes have existed previously (MA Global Design at Academie Libanaise des Beaux-Arts [ALBA]) or were once considered but then abandoned (MA Design also at ALBA). Their failures were due to marketability. A programme is not marketable without a solid definition of what design means in a local context, however. The focus, then, should be on a specialised Masters offering in Arabic typography, and UX-UI/Digital Design (Arabic focus). These should blend research and practice tracks (not favouring one over the other) to enable knowledge to be generated and written about. Most of all, the creation of graduate programmes reduces brain drain and enables students to study the Arabic script in its situated context (rather than in Europe or the UK).

Work on developing an MA in Typography started six years ago as part of the Arabic Type Unit at the American University of Beirut, educator Maria tells me. 'The whole idea was to eventually start a master's program in type design. So how will it happen? When will it happen? Since [it launched], we've had an economic crisis, an explosion, and I don't know what's coming next,' she says. It has moved down on the priority list, and perhaps the opportunity can be taken on by the GCC states who have more funding to undertake the work, she tells me. Educators are frustrated by the lack of knowledge on Arabic type produced by Arab designers and researchers. Maria expresses frustration at books produced by non-native speakers on Arabic typography that disregard the works that came before:

> There's a book on Arabic typography [by Titus Nemeth], and it's called 'Arabic Typography'. This exact same title as Huda Abifarès's first book called 'Arabic Typography'. [...] [N]ot Arabs writing about Arabic typography.

The increase in Arabic web-content, the development of resources on typography, software accommodating different scripts (although it remains bound by Latin type rules), and designers specialising in Arabic typography are excellent starting points for establishing a graduate programme. Wherever it may be regionally, it is a priority.

Possibilities: design vocabularies

The creation of a design vocabulary or vocabularies is a daunting task, one that is not the sole responsibility of designers, students and educators. Participants provided a pathway to achieving its development: collaborating with language experts to begin developing terms, where the goal should be to develop new terms in Arabic rather than finding direct translations. The strategy is to start with basic terms to form a user-generated open library and begin using them in the studio from the foundation year.

The growing interest from designers, students and educators points to this direction as more projects are tackling knowledge of the Arabic language and developing an Arabic design vocabulary. 'We're thinking of developing a programme at [our studio] that teaches design completely in [the] Arabic language,' Rayan tells me. The idea for the programme started when he found himself writing about a project in English and decided to write in Arabic where 'the way that you think about things becomes so different, because of the language...the [nuances] of the language.' Talking about design in Arabic requires a different approach 'because the way that people think about it, they build connections to other things within the language that is non-existent in English,' he tells me. He uses the word 'system' as an example of translation differences:

[If] you want to communicate 'ne'9am mathalan' [system for example] a system. [...] There are so many other things that you think about in the Arab world that you can't think about in 'system.' 'Y3ni mathalan ne'9am, political ne'9am' [I mean for example system, political system] or like, you know, there's so many of these things that is so interesting.

Similarly, the designer and cultural organiser Dalal expresses her frustration over the loss of nuance:

The vocabulary doesn't exist. [...] [T]he concept of space, masa7a [space] doesn't fully elaborate that, nor is there an actual [term]. Frustratingly there are terms that are missing. Then you go over Beirut where they're using French alternatives rather than English. So, it's actually, there's no one set of words that then substitute. There's also the problem that the Arabs who use the English actually aren't strong English speakers.

Arabic is a language filled with nuance. We have already seen how terms are lost in translation, and where design students did not have the vocabulary to articulate their ideas in their mother tongue. Establishing design vocabularies would further Arab design culture by uniting the disparate worlds of the university-educated and the self-taught design world. It could instil educators with the confidence to teach content in Arabic and provide students with the ability to learn and speak about design in Arabic alongside English. With an emphasis and pride on Arabic spearheaded by the GCC countries, the idea of an Arabic design vocabulary becomes more urgent than ever.

TOWARDS DESIGN OTHERWISE:

178—Student-centred pedagogy: process and praxis
179—Valuing and representing design
180—Toppling inefficient bureaucracies
181—Resisting neopatriarchy, redefining design: curricular elements
    182 –The Arab story of design and design advocacy
    183 –Tackling brain drain
    184 –Connections
    184 –Admissions and recruitment
    185 –Encouraging research
    186 –Onwards
186—What is design and design education for?

AN ACTIONABLE ROADMAP

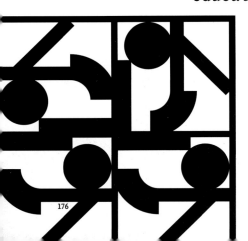

Chapter 6

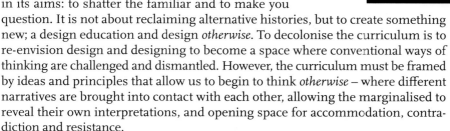

I opened this book with a quote from the late community organiser Saul Alinsky (1989) who stated that to begin changing the world, we begin from where it is now. I have attempted to carve one possibility towards changing it; one that draws on critical pedagogy and decolonial theory. The gravity of decoloniality lies in its aims: to shatter the familiar and to make you question. It is not about reclaiming alternative histories, but to create something new; a design education and design *otherwise*. To decolonise the curriculum is to re-envision design and designing to become a space where conventional ways of thinking are challenged and dismantled. However, the curriculum must be framed by ideas and principles that allow us to begin to think *otherwise* – where different narratives are brought into contact with each other, allowing the marginalised to reveal their own interpretations, and opening space for accommodation, contradiction and resistance.

This book has attempted to provide an understanding of design in higher education in the Arab region and a glimpse into it's design culture. In this chapter, I outline an actionable framework for developing a more contextually-based design education in the Arab region. The question I set out in the introduction was how design education curricula in the Arab region can be more relevant to place and to its communities, to imagine a design education and design *otherwise*. To achieve this, I examined different philosophies, theories, practices and models of pedagogy and curriculum; the perceived shifts in perceptions on design this requires; and possibilities for shifting these perceptions. Reports from international NGOs and agencies call for reforms in higher education and in research policy and planning, but reforms cannot take place without understanding the structure of the neopatriarchal state and its institutions and how education mirrors these structures. It calls for the revelation of the causes of issues, rather than focusing on the now and neglecting the past and the future. For example, academic freedom is a requirement, yet it is simple to say this is a point of reform without addressing *why* academic freedom does not exist. To break down the structures of a neopatriarchal society is not, as Sharabi (1988) warns, an all-at-once process. This book presents one possibility to challenge these through decolonial discourse. To address reform, it is vital to re-evaluate the pedagogic and curricular models in place by looking at the philosophies, theories, practices and models that define the types of people and the type of society education wants to build, where dismantling these is a possibility. It questions the Westernised university model, and focuses on design education, a field that warrants little to no scholarly attention in the Arab region, in the hopes of suggesting the area is taken more seriously in the region's ambitions to build a knowledge society. As design's interest in social practices grows, designers must redirect their practices and shift into a space that opens up possibilities grounded in reality.

Student-centred pedagogy: process and praxis

Education mirrors the structure of the neopatriarchal state because the curriculum is teacher-centred and based on the product/transmission model. The curriculum, however, must move into a process and praxis model and pedagogy should be student-centred. Educators emphasised the need to view students as individuals, critical thinkers and change agents (Shor, 1992) rather than a homogenous whole. They also demonstrated a focus on collective learning with a desire to build the classroom as a community, through listening, encouraging students to learn from each other, challenging students and their own convictions through respectful exchange, and recognising that learning reaches beyond the classroom by inviting other sites of design and acknowledging the professional aspect that informs learning. This is a direct challenge to the current banking model of education, one that rewards the obedient student and centres on the authority of the educator. The emphasis on students learning from each other inspires a meaningful form of participation that encourages students to question the subjects taught and the learning process, and to reflect and make meaning, in opposition to the curriculum as product/transmission based on technical expertise, where the central component is content and controlling student learning and behaviour. This enhances their potential for action and for critical thought.

The theories and practices introduced link to enabling student agency – challenging students to engage outside the traditional boundaries of design and presenting them with opportunities for *committed* action, as in the curriculum as praxis model. Despite the curriculum's focus on Western design theory and practice, participants challenged this reliance through engaging and developing their own design histories and narratives, questioning the position of dependency Arab universities have on Western models. Students are then able to create spaces for their own histories and narratives, challenging the design history canon by arguing for the inclusion of an Arab narrative, and address taboo issues through experimental forms. Although not necessarily a break from the disciplinary boundaries, this invites participants to travel between disciplines and experiment.

Defining what design is in the Arab region and presenting opportunities to explore design, beyond the traditional service-provider definition, and design's role in society are all challenges for the Arab design community. Moving beyond the idea of designer as service provider and introducing design in other sites beyond the agency or studio, as well as moving towards a student-centred pedagogy, requires a radical teaching practice: the teacher as researcher and critical-professional. Educators expressed interest in engaging critical thought and action rather than restricting it, questioning their role as the authority figure. These require a redirective practice.

Making Arabic the *lingua franca* of design education, while providing attention to English to engage internationally, calls for decolonising design education and breaking from the Westernised university model. This demonstrates an emphasis on the local language without closing the doors to a global engagement and a strategy for introducing new voices to represent the design culture(s). Arabising design education requires an official policy, one no Arab country currently has. Additionally, work on translating terms is an essential project as it can help design progress locally, regionally and internationally, and provide a comfort of speaking about one's work in their mother tongue. It also enables the design community to engage with designers working exclusively in Arabic and begins to break down class barriers between designers. However, the Arabic language itself is not accommodating to design. Work on both translation to and from Arabic, and generating content in Arabic, are imperative to the success of design in Jordan and the Arab region.

Work on mechanising Arabic type is a necessity to grow Arabic language content, but design education remains behind in the teaching of typography. The calls to decolonise design education begins with abolishing the hierarchy that exists between Arabic and Latin typography courses. However, decolonising education in general requires imagining teaching Arabic *otherwise* – by breaking away from the banking model.

Valuing and representing design

Transforming design pedagogy rests on how design is viewed and understood by the design community and the public, which plays a role in the success of the philosophies, theories, practices, models of curriculum and pedagogy. Otherwise, design will be inconsequential, and pedagogy will remain disconnected from its milieu and context. Public engagement through design weeks, exhibitions and events, for example, were considered irrelevant if they failed to engage the public. The development and credibility of the profession are crucial in allowing designers more decision-making power in the public and private sector and other organisations. Moreover, through public engagement, and exposure to design in secondary schools, design could integrate with national life. But awareness requires action. One possibility is through a form of design advocacy, whether a professional association or a union to represent designers, providing them with a voice in society, and building links between universities and industry and with universities locally and regionally. Design advocacy can begin to organise design professionally, to represent designer's interests to governments, the press, industry and the public, and contribute to how designers view themselves (Heskett, 2002).

The limited opportunities available to designers and the absence of experimentation within design practice reveals a need for design to move into other spaces to create more opportunities. The emphasis on value, society and new areas for design practice requires designers to redirect their practice, and stresses the necessity of representation for designers. Investing in strengthening design education and the design industry, by allowing room for experimentation and highlighting the work of designers following alternative paths, could offer a solution to brain drain, providing designers with an incentive to stay as it introduces them to role models they can relate to as well as new opportunities.

Design activities like design weeks act as incentives and give students, designers and educators alike learning opportunities within the informal curriculum. These activities, however, should be relevant to the context and not perceived as elitist or about luxury. In this way, they become valuable in the development of a local and regional design culture that also connects with the global design community.

Toppling inefficient bureaucracies

Shifts in perceptions on design should precede changes in design education. Reports and studies on higher education in the Arab region call for an overhaul of university governance, where bureaucracy must move away from *wasta* and towards providing services to its citizens. Bureaucratic red tape stands in the way of growth and change. For example, lack of resources such as materials, labs and studio space prevent students from accessing spaces for learning and collaboration, where they can experiment with making and can share ideas with their peers. Early closures and paperwork disrupt student learning, and an absence of spaces denies a university atmosphere, a culture of interaction and learning experiences.

Overwhelmingly, design admission criteria revealed a carelessness on the part of ministries of education, forcing the same requirements on design as other disciplines, which are detrimental to the recruitment of students and faculty and to the production of research. Placing little criteria on acceptance through current admission requirements denies design the capacity to train organisers and leaders that can redirect their practice and acquire new knowledge. Furthermore, it leads to a high number of students enrolling solely to obtain a degree, high dropout rates, confusion over what design means and poor quality of work. Moreover, the complicated requirements placed on faculty recruitment and the conducting of research needs rethinking. The criteria for recruiting faculty should be adjusted to align with design's needs. Moreover, the research requirements imposed on educators should balance teaching time and administrative duties to enable faculty to conduct research and practice design. The lack of qualified faculty – those that view themselves as the authority figure – led to an absence of the qualities of classroom dialogue (Shor, 1992). 'Dialogue,' as Paulo Freire says, 'is a moment where humans meet to reflect on their reality as they make and remake' (Shor and Freire, 1987, p. 13). Dialogue relates to clear aims and values, and educators and designers transmit their perceptions and values of design onto students. Universities could capitalise on the design expertise of their faculty and on the uniqueness of their surroundings (i.e. milieu). Value becomes of essence as educators and students engage in community projects. Perceived as elitist and an inconsequential activity of the middle classes, design should be more relevant to daily life and designers could better integrate themselves in society, in line with changes in design practice and pedagogy taking place globally.

Resisting neopatriarchy, redefining design: curricular elements

In this book, I have argued for a locally-centric design education and design *otherwise*. In this section, I outline the possible curricular elements that spread across the formal, informal and hidden curriculum that emerged to create space for this possibility. A curriculum should move from its current product model to a process and praxis model. It should be reflexive and transformative, dedicated to empowerment, experimentation and emancipation (committed and informed action). It should encourage critical thinking and asking *why*, where students can engage critically with their experiences, surroundings and reality. Necessary to this is viewing the educator as a researcher, who sets out to critically test her/his ideas into practice. Pedagogy should be student-centred and focus on how students learn, centering ideas of the collective where the classroom becomes a community, and everyone feels responsible to contribute. Educators should be interested in the growth of students as human beings, rather than seeing them as 'receptacles to be "filled"' (Freire, 2000, p. 72). Educators should encourage enquiry and discovery, supporting students to become active learners who engage with the world around them, in order to equip students with the tools they need for the changing nature of the roles and responsibilities of a designer. By breaking out of the disciplinary boundaries, a curriculum should challenge the status quo and the dominant educational structures in place.

In rejecting the neopatriarchal structures within education, design education should seek to equip students with creative and critical thinking skills that encourage curiosity and questioning in order to empower them as critical thinkers, as communicators and as citizens – to become 'change agents and social critics' (Shor, 1992, p. 16). Making design relevant to people and society requires an education system that values the field. For this to take shape, designers must be aware of design's value; to understand that design matters profoundly because it is part of being human and it affects everything (Heskett, 2002). This is to be cognisant of the ontological nature of design and designing and how design contributes to an unsustainable world.

The Arab story of design and design advocacy

The move to integrate an Arab story of design is a direct challenge to design history's narrow focus but it can only be genuine if it challenges the methodologies and Eurocentric historiography of design history. This action calls for a delinking from Eurocentric epistemologies. Furthermore, this book was critical of adopting a design-as-luxury and elitist approach. This provides an interesting example for the direction of design-related events and initiatives and the development of a form of design advocacy, imperative in shifting perceptions on the discipline and beginning to produce change. Design becomes increasingly important as states capitalise on it to brand cities like Amman. The reality is that design weeks are soft-power initiatives. In the case of ADW, it highlights Amman as a knowledge economy, and the initiative is part of the neoliberal reforms Jordan has aggressively undertaken to attract tourism and investment. Although I do not contest the presence of design weeks nor government funding to design, I question intentions and purpose. To be locally-centric, design events and initiatives should rid themselves of their fetishised consciousness. The first step is by acknowledging that design should serve and speak to the public, not the elites, and 'to connect views and theories with the concrete realities at hand' (Kassab, 2010, p. 338).

Tackling brain drain

Change requires an overhaul of the bureaucracy that stifles higher education and design. Government expenditure on higher education is insufficient and it is necessary to devote efforts to increase funding for public institutions, finding alternative forms of income other than tuition fees for private institutions, and abolishing unequal measures of access. Since the Arab region is a high exporter of brains, rather than educate scholars abroad scholarships should be created for students in Arab universities, and provide opportunities for students to stay. Moreover, preventing brain drain would consist of giving students, designers and educators a sense of hope – through role models they can look up to for example. Educators are predominantly male, whereas design students are overwhelmingly female, and women represent only a small percentage of the workforce in Jordan, Egypt and Lebanon. Empowering them with the presence of critical female educators could encourage them to join the workforce. But this is not possible if they constantly find themselves in male-dominated environments. The literature on higher education regionally from global governance organisations calls for the emancipation of women, but only through reforming laws. This is not enough for emancipation that requires a fundamental and radical shift in relations between genders.

Preventing brain drain requires expanding the design industry. The narrow outlook and stifling environment of design education and industry forces designers to migrate. But for experimentation to occur, it needs a shift in the culture and in society at large. Students, educators and designers are cognisant to not cross any lines, but to challenge the neopatriarchal society is questioning its discourse – the *impensé* (unthought) and the *non-dit* (unsaid) (Sharabi, 1988). A radical shift is a step in beginning to avoid the implications of the hidden curriculum where social and gender roles, and attitudes towards how one lives more generally, are learned accidentally. To make design and design education locally-centric means finding experimental and effective ways of speaking to the public that relate to their experiences and habits.

One reason curriculum is disconnected from the milieu and the lives of society is because university departments operate in silos. Grounding education in reality enables engagement with meaningful community work and to challenge the neopatriarchal society. Research should be meaningful to the lives of the people, and dialogue with different disciplines and approaches is key.

Connections

The learning environment makes up the formal, the informal and the hidden curriculum, and universities should provide a suitable one to students. Acknowledging that the classroom is not the only place where learning occurs is necessary. Bureaucratic red tape prevents access to resources that enhance student experience and experimentation such as facilities, studios and books, but there are possibilities to countering this. For example, developing connections with workshop spaces, studios and companies who are in possession of equipment and suitable workshops to support students. Furthermore, interest in community engagement projects and inviting in autodidactic and Arabic-speaking design cultures could benefit from engaging the city as an informal learning space, for example, by making the city a part of the formal and informal curriculum. Designer engagement with Amman, Beirut, Cairo and Dubai could help further research on how citizens engage with the city, define themselves through it and imagine possibilities of how citizens connect with their city.

Admissions and recruitment

Within the planning aspects of the formal curriculum, student recruitment requires a review of the admission requirements to better fit design's needs and ensure a better student/faculty ratio. Furthermore, faculty recruitment and the aims and values of institutions should be rethought, and the latter clarified. This is to ensure that degrees offered are relevant to the country's needs and based on the faculty's expertise. This could help educators review the curriculum structure to integrate disciplines better, to encourage inter- and multidisciplinary approaches to design, and inject research and business and management courses, plus critical placements and internships. These can be accomplished through dialogue with industry and departments across the university.

Changing faculty recruitment is challenging university and faculty requirements imposed by ministries of education. Part-time teaching options should be available for lecturers interested in maintaining a practice and supplementing it with teaching. Encouraging regional recruitment could help keep up with demand, diversify expertise, and attract educators with design backgrounds and those who approach design differently.

Encouraging research

The marginalisation of research region wide, and its absence in design departments, calls for a review of the requirements imposed on design faculty for research, and a serious consideration for graduate studies. Conducting research should be curiosity-driven rather than about economic and strategic objectives. It should have the aim of building a design research community, including publications, conferences and seminars. In addition, the establishment of design advocacy could supplement these activities and contribute to the informal curriculum by enabling other collaborations and translating this research to the public. Conducting research that is relevant to both the academy and social reality could decrease reliance on foreign sources of funding, encourage universities to support research and put design research on the agenda, and allow the establishment of research centres and research by private enterprises. Recognising research in design and building a tolerant and autonomous environment for it are necessary for its success in linking the different worlds that make up Amman, Jordan and the Arab region.

The question of language is an important one, and calls for a decolonial approach. Arabising the curriculum is not only about rewriting textbooks, but a *break* in the way Arabic is taught. Arabising education must not follow the same steps as Arab nationalism that undermined minority communities and their languages through the imposition of a monolingual policy favouring Arabic over any other language. A truly decolonial approach to education is pluriversal, an understanding of the many worlds that make up the region.

Onwards

The roadmap outlined is not a prototype, but an opening to study teaching and learning methods in the classroom, paying close attention to interrelations – such as interaction between students and educators, teamwork and peer-to-peer experiences of students from different backgrounds and across different universities. The process of changing education involves the public and policymakers, in order to understand how they perceive and value design and make it more relevant to citizens.

Beginning to decolonise education is a long-term process as it requires a societal shift – a spirit of openness and tolerance – however, considering the curriculum elements outlined is one step in thinking *otherwise*. Applying such a curriculum in the Arab region would require the cooperation of educators who consider the elements outlined in their teaching practice and begin to test them in their respective universities. Many of these elements could be implemented within the studio, such as integrating teaching practices that encourage reflection, experimentation, critical thinking and questioning, and making the studio a community by not homogenising students but viewing them as individuals and considering their experiences. They also involve educators being critical of their own convictions and practices and shifting away from a classroom centred on the authority of the educator. In addition, they require committed action from designers, students and educators to work collaboratively on strategies that they bring forward to decision makers.

What is design and design education for?

Throughout this book, I have tried to challenge the simplistic solutions proposed for reforms in Arab higher education. I have also challenged how efforts at writing histories and developing design cultures fails to acknowledge whose history is being written and in what language, and the apolitical and universalist rhetoric of design that does not consider context and milieu in the act of designing. This work considers alternative possibilities for imagining contextually situated education. It suggests that design is a field that should be valued and taken seriously by providing a framework in which to understand how different disciplines are taught and practiced depending on context. The implications suggest that while reforms are vital towards radical change, they do not eradicate systems of domination. What is required is a transformation of consciousness, or – in the short and medium term – considering *what* reforms are brought forward.

I have tried to demonstrate how the 'locally centric' refers less to the development of a national identity or an emphasis on difference such as East/West or modern/non-modern, but as an understanding of place, context and milieu. Defining it by geography or national culture is static, binary and unrepresentative of reality; defining it by a contingent reality gives it a tactile immediacy that is dynamic. The definition draws on the work of Syrian playwright Saadallah Wannous, whose plays were highly critical of abuses of power in the Arab world, calling for the empowerment and liberation of the Arabs, which could only be overcome through critique. Wannous spoke of a local theatre but did not define local exclusively in a geographical sense. While Wannous speaks of theatre, we can easily replace theatre with design. For Wannous, effectiveness is engaging the public: what counts is the relevance of the story to the lives of the audience (the common people, not the elite) and authenticity is found in the real problems and issues one attempts to address (Wannous, 1991).

The answers to questions such as: Who is the public that design is addressing? What does design want to convey to the public? How does it want to convey this? are contextual; they change with the historical situation and are to be sought constantly. The purpose of this relationship between design and the public provides both with an opportunity to contemplate their environments, to be critically aware of the issues, and to mobilise them to work towards changing these realities. 'Authenticity' comes 'from the authenticity of the issues it addresses and the effectiveness of the forms it uses in engaging its public' (Kassab, 2010, p. 55). Therefore, design and design education must always be relevant to its context and milieu, and be experimental in the sense that their purpose involves a 'constant search for means of effective interaction with the public, which can often be found in the habits of the people themselves' (Kassab, 2010, p. 56).

There is a new generation of Arab educators – who graduated prior or around the 2008 global recession and were in their formative years during the Arab Spring – who are trying to change the landscape of design and design education regionally. Unlike their predecessors, whose interests were in establishing design programmes, often with the help and support of faculty who taught them during their studies in North America or Europe, the new generation is focused on finding an identity relevant to its local context. They are less about a traditional approach and are more reflective practitioners.

The Arab region is a space where design is still being defined. Shedding itself of the matrix of measure can provide it with the confidence to establish its own narrative of imagining design relevant to its context and milieus, to imagine design *otherwise*. I hope that educators, designers and students find inspiration in the ideas presented in this book to mobilise and put them into practice.

I write this conclusion as Israel continues to bomb Gaza in Palestine indiscriminately and conduct arrests and deadly raids around the Occupied West Bank, all live streamed to the world. Al Jazeera's live tracker stands at 18,484 in 68 days, and the death toll climbs with every keyboard tap. But despite the collective helplessness we are drowning in and the faded euphoria around the Arab revolutions, I assert Sharabi's (1988, pp.151–152) caution that

waiting for the revolution to change the status quo is not a revolutionary stance. Truly radical action will undertake the difficult task of addressing feasible possibilities: possibilities to be found in the structures and institutions of the status quo, not in a utopian vision.

Therefore, we must not succumb to the fatalism of the current state of affairs, but to utilise criticism to transform consciousness and imagine an Arab world *otherwise*.

References

- Abbas, M.K. (2012) 'Educational Developments in Jordan from the 1950s until today', in S. Alayan, A. Rohde, and S. Dhouib (eds) *The Politics of Education Reform in the Middle East: Self and Other in Textbook and Curricula.* New York: Berghahn Books, pp. 61–79.
- Abdulla, D. (2021) 'Disciplinary Disobedience: a border-thinking approach to design', in C. Mareis and N. Paim (eds) *Design Struggles.* Amsterdam, The Netherlands: Valiz (PLURAL), pp. 227–241. Available at: https://www.valiz.nl/images/DesignStruggles-DEF_978-94-92095-88-6single-4March21-VALIZ-def.pdf.
- Abdulla, D. (2023) 'The "Myth" of Global Design History'. *BIPOC Design Histories: Design Histories in SWANA,* Online, 30 May. Available at: https://bipocdesignhistory.com/products/the-myth-of-global-design-history/ (Accessed: 30 May 2023).
- Abdulla, D. and de Oliveira, P.J.S.V., 2023. The Case for Minor Gestures. Diseña, (22), pp.1–14. https://doi.org/10.7764/disena.22.Article.6.
- AbiFarès, H. (2017) *The Modern Arabic Book: Design as Agent of Cultural Progress.* PhD. Leiden University.
- Abi-Mershed, O. (2010) *Trajectories of Education in the Arab World: Legacies and Challenges.* Abingdon, Oxon: Routledge.
- Abu Al Haija, A. (2011) 'Jordan: Tourism and conflict with local communities', *Habitat International,* 35(4), pp. 93–100. Available at: https://doi.org/10.1016/j.habitatint.2010.04.002.
- Abu al-Sheikh, M. and al-Khalailah, Y. (2012) 'The Philosophical Foundations of Education and the Range of its Implications for the Content of Civic Education Textbooks in Jordan', in S. Alayan, A. Rohde, and S. Dhouib (eds) *The Politics of Education Reform in the Middle East: Self and Other in Textbook and Curricula.* New York: Berghahn Books, pp. 154–173.
- Abu Awad, E. (2012) *Identification of competencies for sign designers in Jordan.* PhD. Coventry University.
- Abu-Lughod, I. (2011) *The Arab Rediscovery of Europe: A Study in Cultural Encounters.* Chatham: Saqi Books.
- Adonis (2006) 'Syrian Poet Adonis: The Arabs Are Extinct, Like the Sumerians, Greeks, and Pharaohs. If the Arabs Are So Inept They Cannot Be Democratic, External Intervention Will Not Make Them Democratic'. Available at: https://www.memri.org/tv/syrian-poet-adonis-arabs-are-extinct-sumerians-greeks-and-pharoahs-if-arabs-are-so-inept-they/transcript (Accessed: 17 March 2017).
- Al Nawas, B.A.D. (2016) 'Sector insiders say 3D printing holds great

potential for Jordan', *The Jordan Times*, 8 September. Available at: http://www.jordantimes.com/news/local/sector-insiders-say-3d-printing-holds-great-potential-jordan (Accessed: 14 March 2017).

- Al-Adwan, M. (2013) 'The Higher Education Situation in the Arab World: Jordan as an Example', in *LINKING-MED-GULF Erasmus Mundus Action 3 Project*. Barcelona, pp. 1–25.
- Al-Ali, N. and Pratt, N. (2009) *Women and War in the Middle East*. London: Zed Books.
- Aldersey-Williams, H. (1992) *World Design: Nationalism and Globalism in Design*. New York: Rizzoli.
- ALESCO (2008) *A Plan for the Development of Education in the Arab Countries*. Tunis: ALECSO Department of Education, League of Arab States, p. 234.
- Alinsky, S.D. (1989) *Rules for Radicals: A Pragmatic Primer for Realistic Radicals*. New York: Vintage Books.
- Alissa, S. (2007) 'The Economics of an Independent Palestine', in J. Hilal (ed.) *Where Now For Palestine?: The Demise of The Two-State Solution*. Atlantic Highlands, NJ: Zed Books, pp. 123–143.
- Allaq, A.J. (1997) 'The Dialogue of Ink, Blood, and Water: Modernity and Higher Education in Iraq', in K.E. Shaw (ed.) *Higher Education in the Gulf: Problems and Prospects*. Exeter, UK: University of Exeter Press, pp. 87–100.
- Al-Newashi, Q. (2012) 'Images of Europeans in Jordanian textbooks', in S. Alayan, A. Rohde, and S. Dhouib (eds) *The Politics of Education Reform in the Middle East: Self and Other in Textbook and Curricula*. New York: Berghahn Books, pp. 194–208.
- Al-Rashdan, A.-F. (2009) 'Higher Education in the Arab World: Hopes and Challenges', *Arab Insight*, 2(6), pp. 77–90.
- Altbach, P.G. (2006) 'Globalization and the University: realities in an unequal world', in J.J.F. Forest and P. Altbach (eds) *International Handbook of Higher education: Part One: Global Themes and Contemporary challenges*. Dordrecht: Springer, pp. 121–139.
- Amman Design Week (2017a) *2017: Design Moves Life Moves Design, Amman Design Week*. Available at: http://www.ammandesignweek.com/media/news/theme-write-up (Accessed: 25 March 2017).
- Amman Design Week (2017b) *About us, Amman Design Week*. Available at: http://www.ammandesignweek.com/#home (Accessed: 30 March 2017).
- Anderson, B. (2001) 'Writing the Nation: Textbooks of the Hashemite Kingdom', *Comparative Studies of South Asia, Africa and the Middle East*, 21(1 & 2), pp. 5–14.
- Badran, A. (2014) *Development and advancement of higher education in Jordan*.

Singapore: QS Showcase-Asia, Middle East and Africa, pp. 137–141. Available at: http://www.qsshowcase.com/ebook/2014/.

- Badran, A., Baydoun, E. and Hillman, J.R. (2019) 'Introduction', in *Major Challenges Facing Higher Education in the Arab World: Quality Assurance and Relevance.* Switzerland: Springer, pp. 1–11.
- Bannayan, H. *et al.* (2012) *The Jordan Education Initiative: A Multi-Stakeholder Partnership Model to Support Education Reform.* World Bank Human Development Network, pp. 1–18.
- Bierut, M. (2007) *79 Short Essays on Design.* New York: Princeton Architectural Press.
- Boissiere, M. (2011) *Project Performance Assessment Report: Hashemite Kingdom of Jordan.* World Bank, pp. 1–52.
- Booker, M.K. and Daraiseh, I. (2019) *Consumerist Orientalism.* London: I.B. Tauris.
- Bringhurst, R. (2015) *The Elements of Typographic Style.* 4th edn. Seattle, WA; Vancouver, BC: Hartley and Marks.
- Burdick, A. (1993) 'What has writing got to do with design?', *Eye*, pp. 4–5.
- Burke, D. and Al-Waked, A. (1997) 'On the threshold: Private universities in Jordan', *International Higher Education*, (9), pp. 2–4.
- Collins, P. (2000) *Black Feminist Thought: Knowledge, Consciousness, and the Politics of Empowerment.* New York: Routledge.
- Cornbleth, C. (1988) 'Curriculum in and out of context', *Journal of Curriculum and Supervision*, 3(2), pp. 85–96.
- Daher, R. (2009) 'Urban Agents, Actors and Activists: An appeal to the creative class', in R. Daher, P. Misselwitz and C. Altay (eds) *Amman/Neoliberal Urban Management* (Diwan Series). Rotterdam: IABR, p. 8. Available at: https://www.academia.edu/9225898/AMMAN_NEOLIBERAL_URBAN_MANAGEMENT_Edited_by_Rami_Farouk_Daher._DIWAN_Series_Edited_by_Philipp_Misselwitz_and_Can_Altay._IABR_2009.
- Daher, R. (2013) 'Neoliberal Urban Transformation in the Arab City: Meta-narratives, urban disparities and the emergence of consumerist utopias and geographies of inequalities in Amman', *Environement Urbain Urban Environment*, 7, pp. 99–115.
- Dawisha, A. (2003) *Arab Nationalism in the twentieth century: From triumph to despair.* Princeton, NJ: Princeton University Press.
- DeTurk, S. (2020) 'Dubai's Alserkal Avenue: Cultural District or Cultural Diaspora?', in S. Wakefield (ed.) *Museums of the Arabian Peninsula: Historical Developments and Contemporary Discourses.* Abingdon, Oxon: Routledge, pp. 160–172. Available at: https://doi.org/10.4324/9780429053597.

- Dilnot, C. (2005) 'Ethics? Design?', in S. Tigerman (ed.) *The Archeworks Papers, Volume 1, Number Two.* Chicago: Archeworks.
- Dilnot, C. (2016) 'A lexicon of concepts? How do we convert the insights of practice into politically actionable strategies that draw on the capabilities of designing?' *Intersectional Perspectives on Design, Politics and Power*, Malmö, Sweden, 14 November.
- Docherty, B. (2005) Reading between the "Red Lines": *The Repression of Academic Freedom in Egyptian Universities.* 6. New York: Human Rights Watch. Available at: https://www.hrw.org/reports/2005/egypt0605/egypt0605.pdf.
- Dormer, P. (1990) *The Meanings of Modern Design: Towards the Twenty-First Century.* London: Thames & Hudson.
- Dubai Culture (2023) *Who We Are, Dubai Culture.* Available at: https://dubaiculture.gov.ae/en/about-us/who-we-are (Accessed: 30 May 2023).
- Dubai Design and Fashion Council and Monitor Deloitte (2016) *MENA Design Education Outlook.* Dubai: Dubai Design and Fashion Council and Monitor Deloitte.
- Dunne, A. and Raby, F. (2007) *Critical Design FAQ, Dunne & Raby.* Available at: http://www.dunneandraby.co.uk/content/bydandr/13/0.
- El-Batraoui, M. (ed.) (2016) *The Traditional Crafts of Egypt.* Translated by N. Shawkat. Cairo and New York: The American University in Cairo Press.
- El-Said, M. et al. (2012) *Jordan: Selected Issues.* Washington, DC: International Monetary Fund, pp. 1–31.
- Elsheshtawy, Y. (2004) 'Redrawing Boundaries: Dubai, The emergence of a Global City', in Y. Elsheshtawy (ed.) *Planning Middle Eastern Cities: An Urban Kaleidoscope.* London: Routledge, pp. 169–199.
- Elsheshtawy, Y. (ed.) (2008) *The Evolving Arab City Tradition, Modernity and Urban Development.* Oxfordshire; New York: Routledge.
- Elzenbaumer, B. (2013) *Designing Economic Cultures: Cultivating socially and politically engaged design practices against procedures of precarisation.* PhD. Goldsmiths, University of London.
- Farajalla, N. (2013) 'Impact of Climate Change on the Arab World'. São Paulo. Available at: https://www.youtube.com/watch?v=ltnnO-oURDY (Accessed: 8 July 2017).
- Fergany, N. (2009) 'Education Reform Can Empower Youth in Arab Countries and Help Build Human Development', in. Barcelona: IEMed, pp. 43–50.
- Freire, P. (2000) *Pedagogy of the oppressed.* Translated by M. Berman Ramos. New York: Continuum.

- Freire, P. (2004) *Pedagogy of hope: reliving Pedagogy of the oppressed*. Translated by R.R. Barr. London and New York: Continuum.
- Fry, T. (1989) 'A Geography of Power: Design History and Marginality', *Design Issues*, 6(1), pp. 15–30.
- Fry, T. (2007) 'Redirective Practice: An Elaboration', *Design Philosophy Papers*, 5(1), pp. 5–20.
- Fry, T. (2017) 'Design for/by "The Global South"', Design Philosophy Papers, 15(1), pp. 3–37. Available at: https://doi.org/10.1080/14487136.2017.1303242.
- Galal, A. (2008) *The Road Not Traveled: Education Reform in the Middle East and Africa*. Washington, DC: World Bank.
- Gimeno-Martinez, J. (2016) *Design and National Identity*. London and New York: Bloomsbury.
- Giroux, H.A. (2005) *Border Crossings*. 2nd edn. New York: Routledge.
- Giroux, H.A. and Penna, A.N. (1979) 'Social Education in the Classroom: The Dynamics of the Hidden Curriculum', *Theory & Research in Social Education*, 7(1), pp. 21–42. Available at: https://doi.org/10.1080/0093310 4.1979.10506048.
- Gretzinger, K. (2012) 'The substance of design: a conversation with Helmut Draxler with Katja Gretzinger', in K. Gretzinger (ed.) *In a Manner of Reading Design*. Utrecht and Berlin: Casco-Office for Art, Design and Theory and Sternberg, pp. 53–87.
- Grosfoguel, R. (2013) 'The Structure of Knowledge in Westernized Universities: Epistemic Racism/Sexism and the Four Genocides/ Epistemicides of the Long 16th Century', *Human Architecture: Journal of the Sociology of Self- Knowledge*, 11(1), pp. 73–90.
- Grundy, S. (1987) *Curriculum: Product or Praxis*. Barcombe: The Falmer Press.
- Guellerin, C. (2012) 'Design schools: from creation to management, from management to a new entrepreneurship', in E.M. Formia (ed.) *Innovation in Design Education: Proceedings of the Third International Forum of Design as a Process. Innovation in Design Education: Theory, research and processes to and from a Latin perspective*, Turin: Umberto Allemandi & C, pp. 49–53.
- Guest, D. (1991) 'The hunt is on for the Renaissance Man of computing', *The Independent*, 17 September.
- Haddad, Y. (1992) 'Arab universities: goals and problems', *Journal of Arab Affairs*, 11, pp. 91–105.
- Hammond, A. (2007) *Popular Culture in the Arab World: Arts, Politics, and the Media*. Cairo: American University in Cairo Press.
- Hanafi, S. and Arvanitis, R. (2016) *Knowledge Production in the Arab World:*

The impossible promise. Abingdon, Oxon: Routledge.

- Hanieh, A. (2013) *Lineages of Revolt: Issues of Contemporary Capitalism in the Middle East.* Chicago: Haymarket Books.
- Hansen, M.T. (2010) 'IDEO CEO Tim Brown: T-Shaped Stars: The Backbone of IDEO's Collaborative Culture', *Chief Executive,* 21 January. Available at: http://chiefexecutive.net/ideo-ceo-tim-brown-t-shaped-stars-the-backbone-of-ideoaeTMs-collaborative-culture/ (Accessed: 20 February 2017).
- *#Hashtag* (2014). Available at: https://vimeo.com/user5013818.
- Herrera, L. (2006) 'Higher education in the Arab World', in J.J.F. Forest and P.G. Altbach (eds) *International Handbook for Higher Education.* Netherlands: Springer, pp. 409–421.
- Herrera, L. and Torres, C. (2006) *Cultures of Arab Schooling: Critical Ethnographies from Egypt.* New York: State University of New York Press.
- Herring, E. (2016) *Street furniture design: contesting modernism in post-war Britain.* London, England: Bloomsbury Academic.
- Heskett, J. (2002) *Toothpicks and Logos: Design in Everyday Life.* Edited by S. Boztepe and C. Dilnot. Oxford, England: Oxford University Press.
- Hillman, J.R. and Baydoun, E. (2019) 'Quality Assurance and Relevance in Academia: A Review', in A. Badran, E. Baydoun, and J.R. Hillman (eds) *Major Challenges Facing Higher Education in the Arab World: Quality Assurance and Relevance.* Switzerland: Springer, pp. 13–68.
- Hinchcliffe, P. and Milton-Edwards, B. (2009) *Jordan: A Hashemite Legacy Contemporary Middle East.* 2nd edn. Abingdon, Oxon: Routledge.
- Hirano, T. (1991) 'The Development of Modern Japanese Design: A Personal Account', *Design Issues,* 7(2), pp. 54–62. Available at: https://doi.org/10.2307/1511407.
- hooks, bell (1994) Teaching to Transgress: Education as the Practice to Freedom. Abingdon, Oxon: Routledge.
- hooks, bell (2000) *Feminism is for everybody: passionate politics.* London: Pluto Press.
- Hourani, A. (1983) *Arabic Thought in the Liberal Age 1789–1939.* 2nd edn. Cambridge, UK: Cambridge University Press.
- Hourani, N. (2014) 'Urbanism and Neoliberal Order: The Development and Redevelopment of Amman', *Journal of Urban Affairs,* 36(S2), pp. 634–649. Available at: https://doi.org/10.111/juaf.12092.
- Innab, S. (2016) 'Reading the Modern Narrative of Amman', in *The Arab City: Architecture and Representation.* New York: Columbia University Press, pp. 118–135.
- Jacobs, J. (2010) 'Re-branding the Levant: contested heritage and colonial

modernities in Amman and Damascus', *Journal of Tourism and Cultural Change*, 8(4), pp. 316–326. Available at: https://doi.org/10.1080/147668 25.2010.521251.

- Jaramillo, A. *et al.* (2011) *Internationalization of Higher Education in MENA: Policy Issues Associated with Skills Formation and Mobility*. World Bank, pp. 1–30. Available at: http://siteresources.worldbank.org/EDUCATION/ Resources/278200-1099079877269/547664-1099079956815/SELM2_ ReportMENA_EN.pdf.
- Johnson, C.G. (2011) 'The Urban Precariat, Neoliberalization, and the Soft Power of Humanitarian Design', 27(3–4), pp. 445–475. Available at: https:// doi.org/10.1177/0169796X1102700409.
- Jreisat, J. (2009) 'Bureaucracy and Reform in the Arab World', in A. Faramand (ed.) *Public Administration and Public Policy*. CRC Press, pp. 583–595. Available at: https://doi.org/10.1201/NOE0824723699-c34.
- Julier, G. (2014) *The Culture of Design*. 3rd edn. London: Sage.
- Kabbani, N. (2019) *Youth Employment in the Middle East and North Africa: Revisiting and Reframing the Challenge*. Doha, Qatar: Brookings Doha Center, pp. 1–15.
- Kanaan, T., Al-Salamat, M. and Hanania, M. (2009) *'Financing Higher Education in Jordan'*. Amman.
- Kandiyoti, D. (1988) 'Bargaining with Patriarchy', *Gender and Society*, 2(3), pp. 274–290.
- Karakhanyan, S. (2019) 'Quality Assurance in the Arab Region in the Era of Customizattion: Where Do We Stand in Terms of Relevance?', in J.R. Hillman and E. Baydoun (eds) *Major Challenges Facing Higher Education in the Arab World: Quality Assurance and Relevance*. Switzerland: Springer, pp. 211–223.
- Kassab, E. (2010) *Contemporary Arab Thought: Cultural Critique in Comparative Perspective*. New York: Columbia University Press.
- Kassir, S. (2006) *Being Arab*. London: Verso.
- Keirl, S. (2015) 'Against Neoliberalism; for Sustainable-Democratic Curriculum; Through Design and Technology Education', in K. Stables and S. Keirl (eds) *Environment, Ethics and Cultures: Design and Technology's Contribution to Sustainable Global Futures*. Rotterdam: Sense Publishers, pp. 153–174.
- Kelly, A.V. (2004) *The Curriculum Theory and Practice*. 5th edn. London: Sage Publications.
- Kelly, A.V. (2009) *The Curriculum: Theory and Practice*. 6th edn. London: Sage.

- Keshavarz, M. (2016) *Design-Politics*. PhD. Malmö University.
- Keshavarz, M. (2020) 'Violent Compassions: Humanitarian Design and the Politics of Borders', *Design Issues*, 36(4), pp. 20–32. Available at: https://doi.org/10.1162/desi_a_00611.
- Khader, F. (2009) 'Strategies and Roadmap for Effective Higher Education in Reform in Jordan', in *International Council on Education for Teaching Conference*. Muscat, pp. 1–15.
- Khan, Y. (2013) 'Amman's West Side Story Is soft power helping or hindering the state of the arts in Jordan?', *Ibraaz*. Available at: http://www.ibraaz.org/essays/65 (Accessed: 3 June 2014).
- Laabas, B. (ed.) (2002) *Arab Development Challenges of the New Millennium*. Aldershot: Ashgate.
- Lamine, B. (ed.) (2010) 'A Decade of Higher Education in the Arab States (1998–2009): Achievements & Challenges (Regional Report)', in *Towards an Arab Higher Education Space: International Challenges and Societal Responsibilities. Arab Regional Conference on Higher Education* (Cairo), Beirut: UNESCO Regional Bureau for Education in the Arab States, pp. 11–57. Available at: http://unesdoc.unesco.org/images/0018/001892/189272m.pdf (Accessed: 24 May 2014).
- Lavia, J. (2006) 'The practice of postcoloniality: a pedagogy of hope', *Pedagogy, Culture & Society*, 14(3), pp. 279–293. Available at: https://doi.org/10.1080/14681360600891787.
- Lichtman, S.A. (2009) 'Reconsidering the History of Design Survey', *Journal of Design History*, 22(4), pp. 341–350. Available at: https://doi.org/10.1093/jdh/epp043.
- Maasri, Z. (2013) 'I'm Still Here: Some thoughts on design education and the "real world"', in L. Musfy (ed.) *Revolution/Evolution: Two Decades and Four Hundred Designers Later*. Beirut: AUB Press, pp. 118–121.
- Maki, R. and Schneider, B. (2023) *Fashion in the Middle East: Optimism and Transformation, The Business of Fashion*. Available at: https://www.businessoffashion.com/reports/global-markets/fashion-in-the-middle-east-optimism-transformation-report/ (Accessed: 31 March 2023).
- Masalha, N. (2012) *The Palestine Nakba: Decolonising History, Narrating the Subaltern, Reclaiming Memory*. London: Zed Books.
- Masri, M. (2009) 'Policy Process and Education reform in the Arab World', *Mediterranean Journal of Educational Studies*, 14(1), pp. 129–144.
- Massad, J. (2001) *Colonial Effects: The Making of National Identity in Jordan*. New York: Columbia University Press.
- Maudet, N. (2021) 'Le designer-touriste, ou quelques limites des

collaborations en design', *Raddar no. 3: Politiques du Design/Design Politics*, (3), pp. 103–115.

- Mazawi, A.E. (2005) 'Contrasting Perspectives on Higher Education Governance in the Arab States', in J.C. Smart (ed.) *Higher Education: Handbook of theory and research Volume XX*. 20th edn. Dordrecht: Springer, pp. 133–189.
- Mazawi, A.E. (2010) 'Naming the imaginary "Building an Arab knowledge society" and the contest terrain of educational reforms for development', in O. Abi-Mershed (ed.) *Trajectories of Education in the Arab World: Legacies and Challenges*. New York: Routledge, pp. 201–225.
- Meggs, P.B. and Purvis, A.W. (2016) *Meggs' history of graphic design*. 6th edition. Hoboken, New Jersey: Wiley. Available at: http://lib.myilibrary.com/browse/open.asp?id=915535&entityid=https://idp.brunel.ac.uk/entity.
- Millman, D. (2013) *Brand Thinking and Other Noble Pursuits*. New York: Allworth Press.
- Mulderig, M.C. (2011) 'Adulthood Denied: Youth Dissatisfaction and the Arab Spring', *The Frederick S. Pardee Center for the Study of the Longer Range Future*, pp. 1–8.
- Mulderig, M.C. (2013) *An Uncertain Future: Youth Frustration and the Arab Spring*. 16. Boston, MA, USA: The Frederick S. Pardee Center for the Study of the Longer-Range Future Boston University. Available at: https://www.bu.edu/pardee/files/2013/04/Pardee-Paper-16.pdf.
- Najmabadi, A. (1998) 'Crafting an Educated Housewife in Iran', in L. Abu-Lughod (ed.) *Remaking Women: Feminism and Modernity in the Middle East*. Princeton, NJ: Princeton University Press, pp. 91–125.
- Nasser Eddin, N. (2011) *The Intersectionality of Class and Gender: Women's Economic Activities in East and West Amman*. PhD. University of Warwick. Available at: http://go.warwick.ac.uk/wrap/54468.
- Nortcliff, S. et al. (2009) '"Ever-growing Amman", Jordan: Urban expansion, social polarisation and contemporary urban planning issues', *Habitat International*, 33(1), pp. 81–92.
- Nye, J.S. (2004) *Soft power: the means to success in world politics*. New York: Public Affairs.
- OECD (2022) *Youth at the Centre of Government Action: A Review of the Middle East and North Africa*. OECD (OECD Public Governance Reviews). Available at: https://doi.org/10.1787/bcc2ddo8-en.
- Prado de O. Martins, L. and Vieira de Oliveira, P.J.S. (2014) 'Questioning the "critical" in Speculative & Critical Design: A rant on the blind privilege that permeates most Speculative Design projects', *Luiza Prado*, 4 February.

Available at: https://medium.com/a-parede/questioning-the-critical-in-speculative-critical-design-5a355cac2ca4#.76gskoqoo (Accessed: 20 March 2017).

- Precarious Workers Brigade (2017) *Training for Exploitation? Politicising Employability and Reclaiming Education*. London, Leipzig and Los Angeles: Journal of Aesthetics and Protest Press. Available at: http://joaap.org/press/pwb/PWB_TrainingForExploitation_smaller.pdf.
- Rawsthorn, A. (2015) 'The shifting influence of Milan's Salone del Mobile', *Frieze*, April, pp. 39–41.
- Reiter, Y. (2002) 'Higher Education and Sociopolitical Transformation in Jordan', *British Journal of Middle Eastern Studies*, 29(2), pp. 137–164.
- Ripley, A. (2017) 'Boys Are Not Defective', *The Atlantic*, 21 September. Available at: https://www.theatlantic.com/education/archive/2017/09/boys-are-not-defective/540204/?utm_source=fbb(Accessed22September2017).
- Rogan, E. (1996) 'The Making of a Capital: Amman 1918–1928', in J. Hannoyer and S. Shami (eds) *Amman: The City and its Society*. Beirut: CERMOC, pp. 89–107.
- Rojas, C. (2007) 'International Political Economy/Development Otherwise', *Globalizations*, 4(4), pp. 573–587. Available at: https://doi.org/10.1080/14747730701695836.
- Romani, V. (2009) 'The Politics of Higher Education in the Middle East: Problems and Prospects', *Middle East Brief*, (36), pp. 1–8.
- Sabry, M. (2009) 'Funding Policy and Higher Education in Arab Countries', *Comparative & International Higher Education*, (1), pp. 11–12.
- Sebaaly, M. (2019) 'Digital Transformation and Quality, Efficiency, and Flexibility in Arab Universities', in A. Badran, E. Baydoun and J.R. Hillman (eds) *Major Challenges Facing Higher Education in the Arab World: Quality Assurance and Relevance*. Switzerland: Springer, pp. 167–177.
- Selim, A. (2021) *The Challenges Behind Youth Leadership in the Arab World*. Washington, DC: Washington Institute. Available at: https://www.washingtoninstitute.org/policy-analysis/challenges-behind-youth-leadership-arab-world.
- Shami, S. (2007) '"Amman is not a City"': Middle Eastern Cities in Question', in A. Cinar and T. Bender (eds) *Urban Imaginaries: Locating the Modern City*. Minneapolis: University of Minnesota Press, pp. 208–235.
- Sharabi, H. (1988) *Neopatriarchy: A Theory of Distorted Change in Arab Society*. Oxford: Oxford University Press.
- Sharif, Y. (2017) *Architecture of Resistance: Cultivating Moments of Possibility within the Palestinian/Israeli Conflict*. London: Routledge.

- Shehab, B. and Nawar, H. (2020) *A history of Arab graphic design.* Cairo and New York: The American University in Cairo Press.
- Shor, I. (1992) *Empowering Education: Critical Teaching for Social Change.* Chicago and London: The University of Chicago Press.
- Shor, I. and Freire, P. (1987) 'What is the "Dialogical Method" of Education?', Journal of Education, 169(3), pp. 11–31.
- Simons, M. and Masschelein, J. (2012) 'School – A Matter of Form', in P. Gielen and P. De Bruyne (eds) *Teaching Art in the Neoliberal Realm Realism versus Cynicism.* Amsterdam, pp. 69–83.
- Smith, M.K. (1996) *Curriculum theory and practice: the encyclopaedia of informal education, infed.* Available at: http://infed.org/mobi/curriculum-theory-and-practice/ (Accessed: 18 February 2015).
- Spade, D. (2020) *Mutual aid: building solidarity during this crisis (and the next).* London: Verso.
- Sparke, P. (2013) *An Introduction to Design and Culture: 1900 to the Present.* 3rd edn. London: Routledge.
- Stenhouse, L. (1975) *An Introduction to Curriculum Research and Development.* London: Heinemann Educational Books.
- Studio Safar (2023) *Journal Safar, Journal Safar.* Available at: https://www.journalsafar.com/ (Accessed: 27 March 2023).
- Sultana, R. (1997) 'Conference Report Higher Education in the Mediterranean: Managing Change and Ensuring Quality', *Mediterranean Journal of Educational Studies*, 2(2), pp. 131–148.
- *The State of Fashion 2023* (2023). London, UK: Business of Fashion and McKinsey & Company. Available at: https://cdn.businessoffashion.com/reports/The_State_of_Fashion_2023.pdf.
- Tonkiss, F. (2014) 'Ridding Design of its Saviour Complex', *CityScapes.* Available at: https://www.cityscapesdigital.net/2014/07/14/ridding-design-saviour-complex/ (Accessed: 1 June 2017).
- United Nations Development Programme (2009) *Arab Human Development Report 2009: Challenges to Human Security in the Arab Countries.* New York: United Nations Development Programme. Available at: http://www.undp.org/content/undp/en/home/librarypage/hdr/arab_human_developmentreport2009.html.
- United Nations Development Programme (ed.) (2022) *Arab Human Development Report 2022: Expanding opportunities for an inclusive and resilient recovery in the post-Covid era.* New York, NY: United Nations Development Programme, Regional Bureau for Arab States.
- United Nations Development Programme and Mohammed bin Rashid

Al Maktoum Foundation (2014) *Arab Knowledge Report 2014 Youth and Localisation of Knowledge.* Dubai: United Nations Development Programme and Mohammed bin Rashid Al Maktoum Foundation. Available at: http://www.arabstates.undp.org/content/rbas/en/home/library/huma_development/arab-knowledge-report-20140/.

- Wannous, S. (1991) 'Al-Thaqafa al-Wataniyya wa al-Wa'y al-Tarikhi (National Culture and Historical Awareness)', *Qadaya wa Shahadat*, (4), pp. 5–39.
- Waterbury, J. (2020) *Missions impossible: higher education and policymaking in the Arab world.* Cairo and New York: The American University in Cairo Press.
- Wilkens, K. (2011) 'Higher Education Reform in the Arab World', in *2011 U.S.-Islamic World Forum Papers.* Washington, DC: Saban Center at Brookings. Available at: https://www.brookings.edu/wp-content/uploads/2016/06/08_education_reform_wilkins.pdf.
- Willis, A.-M. (2006) 'Ontological Designing — laying the ground', *Design Philosophy Papers*, 4(2), pp. 69–92.
- World Economic Forum (2020) *The Future of Jobs.* Geneva, Switzerland: World Economic Forum. Available at: https://www3.weforum.org/docs/WEF_Future_of_Jobs_2020.pdf.
- Yom, S.L. (2009) 'Jordan: Ten More Years of Autocracy', *Journal of Democracy*, 20(4), pp. 151–166.
- Zughloul, M. (2000) 'Private and Privatised higher educational institutions in Jordan', *Mediterranean Journal of Educational Studies*, 5(1), pp. 95–117.

Index

2008
Financial Crash, 66, 87
Global Recession, 187

A
Abedini, Reza, 140
Abifarès, Huda, 127, 173. *See also* Khatt
Abu Awad, Essam, 109
Abu Dhabi, 23, 40, 93
Academie Libanaise des Beaux-Arts (ALBA), 172
Adonis (poet), 60, 67
Advertising, 28, 41, 49, 50, 52, 66, 111
Alazaat, Hussein, 162. *See also* Elharf
Aleppo, 89
Alinsky, Saul, 177
Al Jazeera, 16, 188
Al-Naksah, 24
Al-Tuni, Hilmi, 138
Amman, 18, 21, 22, 23–28, 31, 43, 44, 48, 49, 50, 51, 68, 71, 87, 89, 90, 91, 92, 95, 98, 99, 100, 102, 103, 105, 106, 109, 110, 113, 114, 122, 135, 149, 157, 160,162,163,183,184,185
An-Najah University, 16, 17, 18. *See also* Nablus
Arab Countries, 21, 22, 39, 40, 65, 66, 72, 90, 147
Arab Governments, 31, 38, 47, 48, 63, 65
Arab League, 167
Arab Nationalism, 20, 185
Arab Region, 16, 18, 19, 20, 21, 22, 23, 24, 27, 28, 29, 31, 32, 33, 34, 38, 39, 40, 41, 44, 45, 47, 48, 52, 53, 58, 64, 65, 67, 68, 69, 70, 72, 73, 74, 75, 76, 83, 84, 87, 88, 90, 91, 92, 93, 95, 99, 104, 108, 109, 111, 113, 114, 117, 126, 127, 128, 129, 130, 131, 133, 134, 135, 136, 138, 139, 140, 141, 142, 145, 146, 147, 149, 150, 151, 155, 157, 158, 161, 163, 165, 167, 169, 170, 172, 173, 177, 178, 179, 180, 183, 185, 186, 187, 188
Arab Spring, 16, 187, 188
Arab Uprisings, 32, 188
Arab World, 16, 18, 21, 23, 31, 61, 63, 72, 91, 94, 113, 118, 136, 139, 140, 151, 170, 174, 187, 188
Arabising, 33, 117, 159, 179, 185
Architecture, 46, 49, 51, 63, 73, 74, 87, 95, 107, 109, 110, 138, 141, 164, 168
Arnaout, Abdulkader, 141
Art Dubai, 87, 90, 94
Arvanitis, Rigas, 64, 127
Atrissi, Tarek, 138

B
Banking Model of Education, 59, 60, 61, 120, 124, 126, 150, 178, 179, 182
Bauhaus, 45, 137
Baydoun, Elias, 48
Beirut, 18, 21–22, 24, 25, 28, 42, 50, 64, 75, 77, 78, 80,

87, 89, 90, 92, 95, 97, 108, 109, 112, 113, 122, 126, 129, 138, 141, 145, 150, 159, 161, 163, 174, 184
American University of Beirut (AUB), 40, 103, 139, 172
Port Explosion, 21, 173
Ben Ayed, Naïma, 150
Bloom's taxonomy pyramid, 134
Bouazizi, Mohamed, 18. *See also* Arab Spring, and Arab Uprisings
Brain Drain, 33, 38, 52, 57, 63–67, 72, 106, 108, 148, 166, 168, 172, 180, 183–184
Branding, 41, 44, 50, 87, 110, 111, 112, 142, 146, 148, 162
Bringhurst, Robert, 146
Burdick, Anne, 135
Bureaucracy, 33, 37, 50, 51, 64, 69, 84, 99, 164, 180, 183. *See also* Bureaucratic
Bureaucratic, 30, 66, 69, 71, 72, 84, 151, 160, 164, 172, 180, 184. *See also* Bureaucracy

C

Cairo, 16, 18, 21, 22, 25, 28, 66, 75, 76, 87, 89, 90, 95, 101, 109, 111, 113, 122, 129, 130, 134, 135, 146, 159, 168, 184
American University of Cairo (AUC), 40
Canon, 136, 138, 139, 141, 142, 146, 158, 178
Captan, Lara, 147, 149

Chahine, Nadine, 138
Community Engagement, 28, 31, 33, 37, 39, 57, 59, 70, 81, 94, 96, 97, 98, 99–104, 111, 125, 129, 138, 140, 143, 153–160, 179, 180, 181, 182, 184. *See also* Public Engagement
Conscientização, 119, 124
Context/Contextual/ Contextually-based, 18, 19, 20, 31, 32, 33, 34, 45, 46, 59, 75, 83, 90, 91, 94, 95, 96, 99, 100, 102, 104, 105, 108, 113, 115, 117, 121, 122–128, 129, 130–131, 133, 134, 136, 138–142, 143, 145, 147, 155, 156, 157, 162, 165, 170, 171, 172, 177, 179, 180, 186–188
COVID-19, 21, 22, 47, 89
Crafts/Craftsmanship, 22, 89, 90, 91, 95, 100, 134, 168. *See also* Craftspeople/ Craftsperson
Craftspeople/Craftsperson, 46, 52, 82, 89, 103, 120, 144, 158, 165, 168. *See also* Crafts/Craftsmanship
Creative Industries, 48, 50, 55, 90, 94, 97, 136, 163
Critical Design, 132, 133
Cultural Capital, 79
Cultural Producers, 18, 113, 161
Curriculum
Curricula/Curricular, 17, 19, 20, 31, 32, 33, 37, 38, 40, 46, 50, 55, 57, 58, 59,

61, 62, 63, 66, 68, 69, 70, 74, 81, 84, 93, 108, 110, 111, 113, 117, 122, 123, 124, 133, 134, 136, 137, 138, 139, 142, 143, 144, 146, 147, 156, 157, 160, 163, 166, 168, 169, 177, 178, 179, 180, 181, 182, 184, 185, 186

as praxis model, 33, 119, 124–125, 134, 178, 182

as process model, 33, 81, 117, 123–124, 134, 178–179, 182

as product/transmission model, 20, 31, 57, 58–63, 81, 84, 111, 117, 122, 178, 182

D

Daher, Rami, 28

Damascus, 25, 89

Dawaween, 42

Decolonisation, 88, 116, 122, 130, 142, 147, 177–179, 185, 186

Delvaray, Homa, 140

Design
Art, 73, 90, 91, 92, 94
Culture(s), 18, 19, 28, 32, 33, 42, 51, 70, 84, 87, 88–89, 90, 93, 94, 112, 113, 114, 127, 128, 130, 135, 136, 139, 155, 167, 168, 170, 174, 177, 179, 180, 184, 186
Education, 17, 18, 28, 29, 31, 32, 33, 34, 37, 38–39, 41, 42, 45–46, 47, 61, 65, 66, 79, 83, 84, 88, 89, 96,

104, 109, 110, 117, 122, 126, 128, 129, 130, 131, 135, 139, 150, 152, 156, 157, 160, 162, 163, 165, 167, 170, 171, 172, 177, 179, 180, 181, 182, 183, 184, 186–188
High Design, 73, 90, 91, 94
History, 31, 33, 44, 46, 93, 117, 135–142, 146, 162, 172, 177, 178, 182, 186
Industry, 28, 29, 33, 41, 46, 47, 48, 49, 50, 51–52, 55, 63, 65, 71, 74, 92, 93, 106, 107, 119, 120, 121, 125, 130, 143, 145, 153, 155, 156, 163, 164, 165–169, 180, 183, 185
as Luxury, 28, 78, 93, 95, 97, 98, 110, 113, 146, 163, 180, 182
Otherwise, 32, 33, 34, 117, 128, 155, 171, 177, 179, 181, 186, 188
Public Engagement, 32, 87, 98, 110, 155, 157, 158, 159, 179, 180, 187
Studio/Agency, 48, 49, 50, 52, 55, 66, 71, 73, 87, 89, 109, 114, 126, 133, 143, 145, 148, 152, 156, 160, 161, 162, 163, 168, 178, 179
Writing, 134–136, 141, 142, 148, 152, 153, 161, 172, 173
Design Institute Amman, 83, 163
Design Weeks, 85, 97, 99, 102, 143, 176, 181

Amman Design Week (ADW), 51, 66, 69, 70, 83, 89, 91, 97, 98, 99, 100, 105, 143, 149, 183

Beirut Design Week (BDW), 97, 98, 102, 105, 107, 158, 159

Cairo Design Week (CDW), 103, 166

Dubai Design Week (DDW), 90, 91, 94, 97, 105, 145

Draxler, Helmut, 95

Dubai, 18, 21, 22–23, 28, 50, 75, 76, 82, 83, 87, 89, 90, 91, 92, 93, 95, 108, 109, 113, 114, 122, 126, 130, 135, 147, 148, 163, 184

Dubai Institute of Design and Innovation (DIDI), 47, 93, 108, 146

E

Egypt, 16, 17, 19, 21, 22, 24, 38, 40, 41, 44, 49, 53, 55, 58, 62, 66, 68, 70, 71, 75, 79, 90, 101, 104, 114, 136, 142, 148, 151, 159, 183

Elharf, 162. *See also* Hussein Alazaat

El-Khairy, Muhammad, 26

Ellabbad, Mohieddin, 138, 140

Elsheshtawy, Yasser, 92

Émigré designer, 93

Eurocentric, 40, 93, 97, 141, 163, 178, 182

Exil Collective, 163

Eyen Collective, 149, 150, 161, 162

F

Fashion Design, 28, 47, 49, 52, 91, 92, 114, 130, 134, 163

Fetishised Consciousness, 33, 88, 96, 106, 108, 139, 183. *See also* Sharabi, Hisham

Fez, 25

FF Amman, 89, 92

Freire, Paulo, 61, 120, 123, 181. *See also* Banking Model of Education

Furniture/Product Design, 22, 28, 47, 83, 87, 88, 90, 91, 94, 97, 106, 107, 109, 113, 114, 132, 145, 153, 162, 163

G

Gaza, 16, 17, 19, 188

Islamic University of Gaza, 19. *See also* Tayeh, Sufian

General Assembly, 48

German Jordanian University, 66, 74, 102, 164

Giroux, Henry, 160

Global North, 31, 33, 46, 74, 130

Global South, 40, 97, 161

Graphic Design, 17, 28, 41, 43, 45–49, 51, 52, 71, 75, 81, 103, 135–136, 138, 141, 145–150, 163, 168

Greater Amman Municipality (GAM), 89, 98

Grosfoguel, Ramon, 37, 40. *See also* Westernised University

Guellerin, Christian, 165
Gulf Cooperation Council (GCC), 20–21, 22, 26, 27, 28, 40, 65, 77, 89, 90, 92, 148, 152, 173, 174
GCC/Gulf capital, 27, 89–93, 148, 152, 173

H

Hanafi, Sari, 64, 127
Hanieh, Adam, 27
Hawa, Kameel, 141
Herring, Eleanor, 113
Heskett, John, 17
Hillman, John, 48
Hirano, Takuo, 153
House of Today, 163
Human Capital, 21, 39, 58, 59, 64, 87, 90, 165

I

Industrial Design, 50, 70, 82, 90, 141, 169
Informal/Hidden Curriculum, 32, 73, 83, 111, 160, 180, 181, 184, 185
Interdisciplinary, 121, 144, 145, 146, 152, 170, 172, 185
Interior Design, 28, 41, 45, 47, 49, 61, 138, 164, 168
International Monetary Fund (IMF), 25, 37
Iraq, 19, 21, 24, 114
Israel, 19, 20, 24, 26, 188
Israeli Occupation, 16, 17, 19, 21, 24

J

Jeddah, 157
Jo Bedu, 114
Jordan, 18, 19, 21, 23–28, 29–31, 32, 37, 40, 41, 44–46, 48, 49, 50, 51, 53, 54, 55, 58, 62, 65, 66, 67, 68, 69, 70, 72, 73, 74, 76, 77, 79, 81, 83, 89, 90, 92, 95, 96, 99, 104, 106, 107, 108, 110, 111, 114, 121, 128, 129, 134, 138, 139, 142, 143, 146, 147, 148, 150, 157, 160, 164, 165, 169, 179, 183, 185
Ministry of Higher Education and Scientific Research (MoHESR), 41, 44, 45, 69, 71, 72, 81, 169
University of Jordan, 44, 74, 138, 146
Jordanian Design Centre (JDC), 164–165
Jreisat, Jamil, 84

K

Kabbani, Nader, 21, 75. *See also* Waithood
Kalimat Magazine, 18, 134
Keshavarz, Mahmoud, 171
Khatt, 139, 140, 141, 161, 162. *See also* Abifarès, Huda
King Abdullah II, 23, 26, 164
Knowledge Economy/Society, 29, 39, 58, 59, 99, 104, 165, 177, 183

L

Lebanon, 16, 19, 21, 24, 40, 41, 44, 49, 53, 55, 58, 64, 66, 68, 70, 73, 74, 76, 90, 91, 92, 100, 104, 105, 114, 121, 122, 142, 145, 148, 159, 170, 171, 183

Libya, 21

Lichtman, Sarah, 137

Locality, 18, 170

Locally-Centric, 32, 181, 183, 184, 187

M

Maasri, Zeina, 103

Madaba, 89

Maktoum, Lateefa bint, 163

Matriculation Exam, 17. *See also* Tawjihi, and Thanawiyyah Ammah

Middle East and North Africa (MENA), 21, 22, 28, 87, 92, 93, 99, 100, 105, 113, 136, 138

Middle East Design Educators Association (MEDEA), 169

Migration, 24, 52, 57, 64, 65, 99, 108. *See also* Brain Drain

Milieu, 20, 28, 31, 32, 59, 103, 104, 109–113, 114, 117, 124, 125, 130–131, 133, 138, 150, 156, 179, 181, 184, 186, 187, 188

Minor Gestures, 130

Mlabbas, 114

Mukhabarat (secret service), 22, 23, 25, 30, 63, 160

N

Nablus, 16. *See also* An-Najah University

Najmabadi, Afsaneh, 55

Nakba, 24

National Association of Schools of Art and Design (NASAD), 45, 71, 108, 145

Nawwar, Haytham, 136

Neopatriarchy, 29–31, 52, 53, 55, 58, 60, 61, 62, 67, 69, 88, 117, 122, 123, 124, 127, 164, 177, 178, 181, 182, 184. *See also* Sharabi, Hisham

Notre Dame University, 108, 151

Nye, Joseph, 106. *See also* Soft Power

O

Ontological Design, 171, 182. *See also* Anne-Marie Willis

Outdated, 31, 38, 62, 63, 69, 70, 72, 73, 156

P

Palestine, 16, 19, 21, 24, 188. *See also* Israeli Occupation

Palestine Liberation Organisation (PLO), 24

Pedagogy, 18, 31, 32, 33, 37, 55, 57, 58, 68, 117, 124–126, 137, 144, 150, 177–180, 181, 182

Penna, Anthony, 160

Precarious Workers Brigade, 167

Princess Wijdan Ali, 138

Private Universities, 21, 28, 40, 44, 45, 72, 74, 77, 110, 134, 183

Public Universities, 23, 40, 44, 45, 74, 77, 81, 183

Q

Qasimi Rising, 163

Queen Rania Al-Abdullah, 97, 99, 101, 103

S

Sarkis, Kristyan, 149

Saudi Arabia, 23, 47, 58, 157

Shami, Seteney, 24, 25, 28

Sharabi, Hisham, 29, 30, 151, 177, 188. *See also* Fetishised Consciousness, and Neopatriarchy

Sharif, Yara, 155

Sharjah, 75

Shehab, Bahia, 136

Shillington Education, 48

Shor, Ira, 121, 125, 141

Sisi, Abdel-Fatah, 16

Social Design, 96, 97, 98, 100, 170, 171

Soft Power, 87, 88, 104–106, 183. *See also* Nye, Joseph

Starch Foundation, 163

Stenhouse, Lawrence, 123, 124

Studio Kargah, 140

Studio Safar, 161

Studio Turbo, 163

Sudan, 19, 21

Syntax, 89, 109

Syria, 19, 21, 24, 67, 70, 114, 131, 187

T

Tashkeel, 83, 94, 163

Tawjihi, 79, 81. *See also* Matriculation Exam, and Thanawiyyah Ammah

Tayeh, Sufian, 19. *See also* Islamic University of Gaza

Teaching Philosophy, 33, 118–122, 132

Thanawiyyah Ammah, 75, 79, 81. *See also* Tawjihi, and Matriculation Exam

The Creative Space, 163

Transjordan, 23. *See also* Jordan

Tunisia, 18, 19, 150

Typography, 45, 127, 130, 140, 146–150, 162, 172, 179 Arabic Typography, 40, 44, 125, 132, 145, 146, 147, 149, 160, 170, 171, 176

U

United Arab Emirates (UAE), 19, 22, 23, 29, 33, 40, 41, 44, 47, 48, 49, 50, 53, 55, 58, 66, 68, 70, 74, 77, 83, 93, 94, 95, 129, 133, 142, 146, 147, 159, 161, 163, 168

UX/UI, 146, 172

V

Visual Communication, 18, 43, 45, 70, 87

W

Waithood, 21, 75, 158. *See also* Kabbani, Nader

Wannous, Saadallah, 131, 187

Waraq, 163
Wasta, 77, 112, 180
Westernised University, 31,
    33, 37, 40, 177, 179. *See
    also* Grosfoguel, Ramon
Willis, Anne-Marie, 171. *See
    also* Ontological Design
World Bank, 25, 31, 37

Y

Yarmouk University, 45, 79,
    108, 111
Yemen, 19, 21
Youth, 21, 31, 44, 47, 50, 64,
    75, 99, 113, 127, 138, 158,
    160, 169

Z

Zoghbi, Pascal, 138